Communications in Computer and Information Science 2903

Rationale
The CCIS series is devoted to the publication of proceedings of computer science conferences. Its aim is to efficiently disseminate original research results in informatics in printed and electronic form. While the focus is on publication of peer-reviewed full papers presenting mature work, inclusion of reviewed short papers reporting on work in progress is welcome, too. Besides globally relevant meetings with internationally representative program committees guaranteeing a strict peer-reviewing and paper selection process, conferences run by societies or of high regional or national relevance are also considered for publication.

Topics
The topical scope of CCIS spans the entire spectrum of informatics ranging from foundational topics in the theory of computing to information and communications science and technology and a broad variety of interdisciplinary application fields.

Information for Volume Editors and Authors
Publication in CCIS is free of charge. No royalties are paid, however, we offer registered conference participants temporary free access to the online version of the conference proceedings on SpringerLink (http://link.springer.com) by means of an http referrer from the conference website and/or a number of complimentary printed copies, as specified in the official acceptance email of the event.

CCIS proceedings can be published in time for distribution at conferences or as post-proceedings, and delivered in the form of printed books and/or electronically as USBs and/or e-content licenses for accessing proceedings at SpringerLink. Furthermore, CCIS proceedings are included in the CCIS electronic book series hosted in the SpringerLink digital library at http://link.springer.com/bookseries/7899. Conferences publishing in CCIS are allowed to use our online conference service (Meteor) for managing the whole proceedings lifecycle (from submission and reviewing to preparing for publication) free of charge.

Publication process
The language of publication is exclusively English. Authors publishing in CCIS have to sign the Springer CCIS copyright transfer form, however, they are free to use their material published in CCIS for substantially changed, more elaborate subsequent publications elsewhere. For the preparation of the camera-ready papers/files, authors have to strictly adhere to the Springer CCIS Authors' Instructions and are strongly encouraged to use the CCIS LaTeX style files or templates.

Abstracting/Indexing
CCIS is abstracted/indexed in DBLP, Google Scholar, EI-Compendex, Mathematical Reviews, SCImago, Scopus. CCIS volumes are also submitted for the inclusion in ISI Proceedings.

How to start
To start the evaluation of your proposal for inclusion in the CCIS series, please send an e-mail to ccis@springer.com

Weizhi Meng · Qingni Shen · Tao Zhang · Jing Yu
Editors

Advanced Security on Software and Systems

International Conference, ASSS 2025
Guilin, China, December 3–5, 2025
Proceedings

Editors
Weizhi Meng
Lancaster University
Lancaster, UK

Qingni Shen
Peking University
Beijing, China

Tao Zhang
Macau University of Science and Technology
Macau, China

Jing Yu
Minzu University of China
Beijing, China

ISSN 1865-0929 ISSN 1865-0937 (electronic)
Communications in Computer and Information Science
ISBN 978-3-032-21599-4 ISBN 978-3-032-21600-7 (eBook)
https://doi.org/10.1007/978-3-032-21600-7

This Springer imprint is published by the registered company Springer Nature Switzerland AG
The registered company address is: Gewerbestrasse 11, 6330 Cham, Switzerland

Preface

The 4th International Conference on Advanced Security on Software and Systems (ASSS 2025) was held on 3–5 December 2025, in Guilin, China.

With the development of new software technologies and Application Programming Interfaces (APIs), software and system development becomes more complicated and requires a more advanced skill set. Such complexity may result in unwanted and unintended bugs during the development phase, which can be utilized by cyber-attackers. The rapid evolution of technology (e.g., AI, quantum computing) and increasingly sophisticated cyber threats are driving major advancements in software and system security. As software is a crucial part of existing infrastructures, e.g., smart grid systems, how to secure software and system security is a big challenge. This conference aims to provide a platform for professionals from academia and industry to share advanced techniques, experiences and lessons learned for securing software and systems.

This year, ASSS received 35 submissions, and each submission was reviewed by at least three reviewers in a single-blind process. Based on the novelty and quality, 10 regular papers were accepted, giving an acceptance rate of 28.6%. For the conference program, we had two keynote speakers: Guangdong Bai (City University of Hong Kong, China), and Zhi Zhang (University of Western Australia, Australia).

For the success of ASSS 2025, we would like to thank the authors of all submissions and all the PC members for their great efforts in selecting the papers. We would like to thank our General Chairs: Keke Gai, Xiapu Luo and Guangdong Bai; Publicity Chairs: Jiachi Chen and Jiale Zhang; Publication Chairs: Wei-Yang Chiu and Yao Li; and Local Chair: Chunhai Li. We also thank all the external reviewers for participating in the reviewing process.

December 2025

Weizhi Meng
Qingni Shen
Tao Zhang
Jing Yu

Preface

Organization

General Co-chairs

Keke Gai	Beijing Institute of Technology, China
Xiapu Luo	Hong Kong Polytechnic University, China
Guangdong Bai	University of Queensland, Australia

Program Co-chairs

Weizhi Meng	Lancaster University, UK
Qingni Shen	Peking University, China
Tao Zhang	Macau University of Science and Technology, China
Jing Yu	Minzu University of China, China

Publicity Chairs

Jiachi Chen	Zhejiang University, China
Jiale Zhang	Yangzhou University, China

Publication Chairs

Wei-Yang Chiu	Technical University of Denmark, Denmark
Yao Li	Macau University of Science and Technology, China

Local Chair

Chunhai Li	Guilin University of Electronic Technology, China

Technical Program Committee

Nuno Antunes	University of Coimbra, Portugal
Arcangelo Castiglione	University of Salerno, Italy
Wei-Yang Chiu	Technical University of Denmark, Denmark
Ludovic Claudepierre	INRIA, France
Michel Cukier	University of Maryland, College Park, USA
Cuiyun Gao	Chinese University of Hong Kong, China
Xing Hu	Zhejiang University, China
Wenjuan Li	Education University of Hong Kong, China
Yao Li	Macau University of Science and Technology, China
Wu Luo	Peking University, China
Yang Luo	Peking University, China
Weizhi Meng	Lancaster University, UK
Roberto Natella	University of Naples Federico II, Italy
Xiaolei Ren	Macau University of Science and Technology, China
Guanping Xiao	Nanjing University of Aeronautics and Astronautics, China
Haofan Zheng	University of California, Santa Cruz, USA
Cong Zuo	Beijing Institute of Technology, China
Wun-She Yap	Universiti Tunku Abdul Rahman, Malaysia
Shoichi Hirose	University of Fukui, Japan
Yicheng Zhang	University of California, Riverside, USA
Mingjun Wang	Xidian University, China
Albert Levi	Sabanci University, Turkey
Jun Shao	Zhejiang Gongshang University, China
Xiong Li	Hunan University of Science and Technology, China
Beibei Li	Sichuan University, China
Giovanni Livraga	University of Milan, Italy
Xue Yang	Tsinghua University, China
Gao Liu	Chongqing University, China
Qianhong Wu	Beihang University, China
Yunhe Feng	University of North Texas, USA
Xin Jin	Ohio State University, USA
Reza Malekian	Malmö University, Sweden
Ahmed Sherif	University of Southern Mississippi, USA
Chunhua Su	University of Aizu, Japan
Stefanos Gritzalis	University of Piraeus, Greece
Alessandro Brighente	University of Padua, Italy

Additional Reviewer

Cong Li

Steering Committee

Qingni Shen	Peking University, China
Tao Zhang	Macau University of Science and Technology, China
Weizhi Meng (Chair)	Lancaster University, UK

Contents

Privacy-Preserving Federated Learning with Knowledge Distillation for Heterogeneous IoT Nodes

Keyu Fang[1,2], Shilong Li[2], Chengyu Tan[1], Wei Luo[1], Xiangyang Wang[1], Mingrui Zhang[2], Lin Xu[2], and Lei Zhang[1,2](✉)

[1] State Key Laboratory of Intelligent Vehicle Safety Technology, Chongqing 401133, China
{tancy2,luowei2,wangxy4}@changan.com.cn, leizhang@sei.ecnu.edu.cn

[2] East China Normal University, Shanghai 200062, China
{zhangmingrui,linxu}@stu.ecnu.edu.cn

Abstract. Federated learning (FL) faces significant challenges when applied to Internet of Things (IoT) environments, including node heterogeneity, high communication overhead, and data privacy concerns. To address the above challenges, we first propose a Federated Learning with Knowledge Distillation (FLwKD) architecture that enables collaborative training among heterogeneous IoT nodes. Building on this architecture, we develop a concrete privacy-preserving FLwKD scheme. Our scheme supports node heterogeneity by allowing each IoT node to adopt a model tailored to its resource capacity. Communication overhead is significantly reduced by exchanging soft label predictions instead of full model parameters/model updates. Data privacy is ensured through threshold homomorphic encryption, which protects soft label predictions during aggregation without revealing individual outputs—even in the presence of partially colluding nodes. Extensive experiments demonstrate that our scheme achieves high model accuracy with significantly reduced communication overhead, making it well-suited for IoT deployments.

Keywords: Federated learning · Knowledge Distillation · Heterogeneous Node Support · Data Privacy

1 Introduction

The Internet of Things (IoT) has experienced explosive growth, creating demand for collaborative yet privacy-preserving machine learning [1–3]. Federated Learning (FL) [4,5] enables multiple nodes to train a shared model collaboratively

(Keyu Fang, Shilong Li, Chengyu Tan, Wei Luo, Xiangyang Wang, Mingrui Zhang, and Lin Xu), identifying Lei Zhang as the corresponding author, and acknowledging funding from the NSF of China (Grant No. 62372177) and the State Key Laboratory of Intelligent Vehicle Safety Technology (No. IVSTSKL-202407).

W. Meng et al. (Eds.): ASSS 2025, CCIS 2903, pp. 1–16, 2026.
https://doi.org/10.1007/978-3-032-21600-7_1

without exchanging raw data, keeping data locally while only transmitting model updates for aggregation.

However, traditional FL faces critical challenges in IoT environments. First, **communication overhead** from transmitting model updates is prohibitive—transmitting ResNet-18 (11M parameters) requires 44MB per round [1]. Second, **privacy risks** exist through gradient inversion attacks that can reconstruct training data [6,7]. Third, IoT networks are inherently **heterogeneous**—nodes differ significantly in computational capacity, making uniform model architectures impractical [8].

FL with Knowledge Distillation (FLwKD) addresses communication overhead by exchanging compact soft label predictions (kilobytes versus megabytes per round). However, existing FLwKD schemes either lack robust privacy protection (relying on differential privacy with accuracy loss) or fail to support heterogeneous nodes. Most works assume uniform computing resources, unrealistic for IoT where devices range from powerful edge servers to resource-constrained sensors.

1.1 Related Work

Federated Learning with Knowledge Distillation. FLwKD has emerged as a promising alternative to conventional FL by reducing communication overhead. Early FLwKD methods replace model parameter transfers with soft label predictions, exemplified by FedMD [9], where nodes exchange only soft logits, and the work by Jeong *et al* [10], which transmits class-wise aggregated soft labels. To enhance scalability, several studies leverage shared public datasets [11], with further optimizations achieved through server-side logit caching and gradient compression [12]. However, these approaches either assume all participants use identical model architectures or provide limited support for heterogeneous devices.

Privacy-Preserving Federated Learning. Privacy protection [13] in FL is primarily achieved through differential privacy (DP) [14,15] and secure multi-party computation (SMC), including homomorphic encryption (HE) [16]. DP-based methods add calibrated noise to model updates or aggregated results, providing provable privacy guarantees. However, they often degrade model utility under strong privacy constraints. HE-based approaches enable secure aggregation without revealing individual updates but suffer from high computational overhead, making them challenging for resource-constrained IoT devices [17]. Recent works [18–20] explore lightweight privacy-preserving techniques, but they focus primarily on traditional FL rather than knowledge distillation.

Privacy-Preserving FLwKD. While privacy-preserving FLwKD remains underexplored, a few recent works have made initial attempts. Most existing approaches [21,22] rely solely on differential privacy, which degrades accuracy. Importantly, none of the existing privacy-preserving FLwKD methods adequately address node heterogeneity in IoT environments, where devices vary significantly in computational capacity and cannot all participate equally in the training process. Our work fills this gap by proposing a threshold homomorphic encryption-based FLwKD scheme that supports heterogeneous IoT nodes while maintaining high model accuracy.

1.2 Our Contribution

To make federated learning with knowledge distillation (FLwKD) practical in IoT settings characterized by device heterogeneity, privacy risks, and limited bandwidth, we design an architecture and a concrete privacy-preserving protocol tailored to heterogeneous IoT nodes. Our main contributions are summarized as follows.

FLwKD Architecture for Heterogeneous IoT Nodes. We design an FLwKD architecture that enables collaborative training among heterogeneous IoT devices via knowledge distillation. Devices are partitioned into strong and weak nodes according to their resource capacities. Strong nodes run inference on a shared public dataset and send threshold-homomorphically encrypted soft labels to a cloud server, which aggregates them without decryption and returns global soft labels. Strong nodes refine their local models using these labels, while weak nodes update lightweight models by distilling from the strong nodes. This architecture explicitly supports model heterogeneity and reduces communication overhead compared with parameter-level aggregation.

Privacy-Preserving FLwKD Scheme. Building on this architecture, we instantiate a concrete FLwKD scheme that preserves privacy while supporting heterogeneous models. The scheme exchanges only soft label predictions instead of full model parameters, substantially reducing communication cost. A threshold homomorphic encryption mechanism enables secure aggregation even in the presence of partially colluding nodes, preventing recovery of individual predictions. Experiments on representative IoT workloads show that the scheme achieves competitive accuracy with strong privacy protection and communication efficiency, making it suitable for real-world IoT deployments.

2 Background

2.1 System Architecture

Figure 1 illustrates the system architecture, which consists of the following entities:

(1) Certificate Authority (CA): The CA is responsible for initializing the system parameters and issuing digital certificates for all entities in the system. It selects appropriate cryptographic schemes (key agreement, threshold homomorphic encryption, and symmetric encryption) and generates corresponding public parameters. Each entity registers with the CA to obtain a certificate that binds its public key to its identity, enabling authentication during communication.

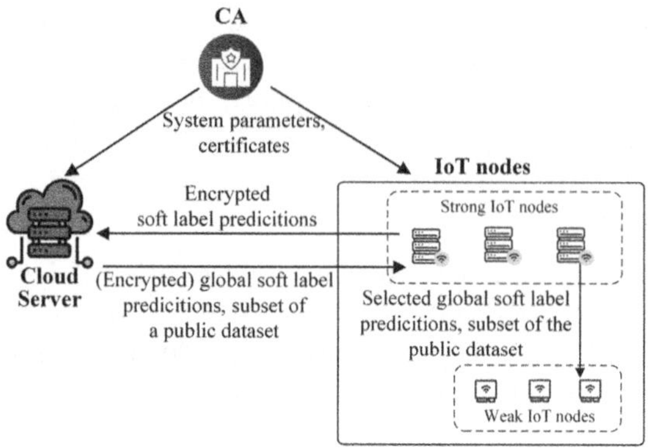

Fig. 1. System Architecture

(2) Cloud Server: The cloud server plays a coordinating role in FLwKD. It initiates the training process by selecting and distributing a public dataset (or subsets thereof) to participating strong IoT nodes. In each training round, it collects encrypted soft label predictions generated by strong IoT nodes, aggregates them without decryption using the additive homomorphic property, and coordinates threshold decryption to obtain global soft label predictions. The server then distributes the decrypted global predictions back to all participating strong IoT nodes.

(3) IoT Nodes: Based on computational capacity, IoT nodes are categorized as follows:

- *Strong IoT nodes:* These nodes possess sufficient resources to directly participate in FLwKD. They train local models (e.g., ResNet-18) on private data, encrypt soft label predictions using threshold homomorphic encryption, upload ciphertexts to the server, jointly perform threshold decryption, and refine models through knowledge distillation using global predictions.
- *Weak IoT nodes:* These nodes adopt lightweight models (e.g., MobileNet) due to limited resources. They receive public data and global predictions from associated strong nodes via encrypted channels, then update models through knowledge distillation.

2.2 Threat Model and Design Goals

Threat Model: We consider honest-but-curious adversaries who follow the protocol but attempt to infer private information. Up to $t-1$ strong IoT nodes may collude with the cloud server. External adversaries may eavesdrop on communications.

Design Goals: (1) *Heterogeneous Node Support*: The scheme accommodates IoT nodes with diverse computational capabilities, enabling each node to adopt a model architecture suited to its resource constraints. (2) *Communication Efficiency*: The scheme minimizes communication overhead by exchanging compact soft label predictions rather than full model parameters. (3) *Data Privacy*: The scheme protects soft label predictions from any uncompromised node, ensuring confidentiality even when up to $t-1$ strong nodes collude with the server. Note that weak nodes receive knowledge from associated strong nodes via encrypted channels and do not directly participate in threshold cryptography. (4) *High Model Accuracy*: The scheme maintains model accuracy comparable to non-privacy-preserving FLwKD while providing strong cryptographic privacy guarantees without accuracy degradation.

2.3 Federated Learning with Knowledge Distillation

FLwKD enables participants to exchange soft label predictions over a shared public dataset D^{pub}, rather than transmitting model parameters. Each training round iterates: (1) participants train local models $\mathcal{M}$ on private data D_i, (2) generate soft predictions on D^{pub} and send to server, (3) server aggregates to obtain global predictions P_{agg}, (4) participants refine models using composite loss.

The composite loss integrates cross-entropy loss L_{CE} and distillation loss L_{DL} as follows: $L = L_{CE} + \eta L_{DL}$, where $\eta > 0$ is a weighting factor balancing local supervision and global knowledge. For a participant with model $\mathcal{M}$ and local dataset D_i, given input sample x with ground-truth label y, the cross-entropy loss is defined as:

$$L_{CE} = \sum_{(x,y)\in D_i} CE(\mathcal{M}(x), y) = -\sum_{(x,y)\in D_i} \mathbf{1}_y \cdot \log(\mathcal{M}(x)),$$

where $\mathbf{1}_y$ is a one-hot indicator vector with value 1 at the y-th position and 0 elsewhere. The distillation loss measures the divergence between global predictions and local predictions using KL divergence. For each sample $x \in D^{pub}$, let $p_1 = P_{agg}(x) = \{v_1^1, v_1^2, \ldots, v_1^M\}$ and $p_2 = \mathcal{M}(x) = \{v_2^1, v_2^2, \ldots, v_2^M\}$ denote two distributions over M classes. The distillation loss is:

$$L_{DL} = KL(p_1, p_2) = \sum_{m=1}^{M} v_1^m \log\left(\frac{v_1^m}{v_2^m}\right).$$

By minimizing this composite loss, participants align their local models with both local ground-truth labels and aggregated knowledge from the collaborative training process.

2.4 Cryptographic Primitives

Our scheme leverages three standard cryptographic primitives to ensure secure and efficient communication. We formally define each primitive along with its security properties.

Key Agreement (KA). A key agreement protocol enables two parties to establish a shared secret key over an insecure channel. We denote $KA = (KA.setup, KA.gen, KA.agree)$, where:

- $KA.setup(\lambda) \rightarrow params$: Takes security parameter λ and outputs public parameters $params$.
- $KA.gen(params, p_i) \rightarrow (sk_i, pk_i)$: Generates a key pair for participant p_i.
- $KA.agree(params, p_i, p_j) \rightarrow sk_{ij}$: Two parties p_i and p_j execute the protocol to derive a shared session key sk_{ij}.

The KA protocol must satisfy security under the Decisional Diffie-Hellman (DDH) assumption, ensuring that an adversary cannot distinguish the shared key from a random value.

Symmetric Encryption (SE). A symmetric encryption scheme provides efficient confidential communication. We denote $SE = (\mathcal{E}, \mathcal{D})$, where:

- $\mathcal{E}(k, M) \rightarrow C$: Encrypts plaintext message M using secret key k to produce ciphertext C.
- $\mathcal{D}(k, C) \rightarrow M$: Decrypts ciphertext C using secret key k to recover plaintext M.

The SE scheme must achieve IND-CPA (indistinguishability under chosen-plaintext attack) security. Common instantiations include AES-GCM or ChaCha20-Poly1305.

Threshold Additive Homomorphic Encryption (THE). This is the core cryptographic primitive enabling privacy-preserving aggregation. We adopt threshold Paillier encryption [23], which supports distributed key generation, additive homomorphism, and threshold decryption. Formally,

$$THE = \{TSetup, TSGen, TEnc, TDec, TComd, TAdd\}:$$

- $TSetup(\lambda) \rightarrow pp$: Takes security parameter λ and generates public parameters pp, including group descriptions and generators.
- $TSGen(pp, n, t, \mathcal{P}) \rightarrow (pk, vk, \{sk_i\}_{i=1}^n)$: Performs distributed key generation for n participants $\mathcal{P} = \{p_1, \ldots, p_n\}$ with threshold t. Outputs a public encryption key pk, a public verification key vk, and private key shares $\{sk_i\}_{i=1}^n$, where each participant p_i receives sk_i. The threshold t satisfies $1 \leq t \leq n$, meaning at least t participants must collaborate for decryption.
- $TEnc(pp, M, pk) \rightarrow C$: Encrypts plaintext message M under public key pk to produce ciphertext C.
- $TDec(pp, C, sk_i, vk) \rightarrow (\rho_i, V_i)$: Participant p_i uses its private key share sk_i to compute a partial decryption ρ_i of ciphertext C, along with a verification value V_i that can be publicly verified using vk.

- $TComd(pp, \mathcal{V}, \rho, t) \rightarrow M$: Given at least t partial decryption results $\rho = \{\rho_1, \ldots, \rho_t\}$ with corresponding verification values $\mathcal{V} = \{V_1, \ldots, V_t\}$, this algorithm first verifies the correctness of each partial decryption using vk. If all verifications pass, it combines the partial results to recover the original plaintext M. Otherwise, it outputs $\perp$ to indicate failure.
- $TAdd(pp, C_1, C_2) \rightarrow C_{sum}$: Given two ciphertexts $C_1 = TEnc(pp, M_1, pk)$ and $C_2 = TEnc(pp, M_2, pk)$, this operation computes a new ciphertext C_{sum} such that decrypting C_{sum} yields $M_1 + M_2$. This additive homomorphism is crucial for aggregating soft label predictions without revealing individual values.

The threshold property ensures that even if up to $t-1$ participants collude (possibly with an external adversary), they cannot decrypt any ciphertext or learn anything about the plaintext beyond what is revealed by the final aggregated result.

3 Our FLwKD Scheme

3.1 High-Level Description

Our scheme operates in four phases: (1) *System Setup*: CA generates parameters and entities obtain certificates; (2) *Group Establishment*: cloud server distributes public dataset, strong nodes generate threshold encryption keys and establish secure channels; (3) *FL Initialization*: IoT nodes prepare models (large for strong, lightweight for weak); (4) *Training*: IoT nodes train locally, perform secure aggregation via threshold encryption, and refine models through knowledge distillation.

3.2 System Setup

In this phase, the CA generates the system parameters. The CA performs the following operations:

1. Select
   a secure key agreement protocol $KA = (KA.setup, KA.gen, KA.agree)$, a threshold additive homomorphic encryption scheme
   $$THE = \{TSetup, TSGen, TEnc, TDec, TComd, TAdd\}$$
   , and a secure symmetric encryption scheme $SE = (\mathcal{E}, \mathcal{D})$.
2. Invoke $KA.setup(\lambda)$ to generate the public parameters $params$ for key agreement and $TSetup(\lambda)$ to generate the public parameters pp for threshold homomorphic encryption.
3. Set the system parameters to be $pub = (KA, THE, SE, params, pp)$ and publish them to all entities.

After the system parameters are generated, the IoT nodes and the cloud server proceed to registration. For a strong IoT node p_{s_i}, it executes the key generation algorithm $KA.gen(params, p_{s_i})$ to produce a public-private key pair $(d^{sk}_{p_{s_i}}, d^{pk}_{p_{s_i}})$ and submits the public key to the CA for certification. Similarly, each weak IoT node p_{w_i} generates its key pair $(d^{sk}_{p_{w_i}}, d^{pk}_{p_{w_i}})$, and the cloud server p_c generates $(d^{sk}_{p_c}, d^{pk}_{p_c})$. The CA issues certificates binding each public key to its owner's identity, enabling mutual authentication in subsequent communications.

3.3 Group Establishment

In this phase, the cloud server p_c selects a public dataset D^{pub} and distributes it to strong IoT nodes $\mathcal{P}_s = \{p_{s_1}, \ldots, p_{s_a}\}$ whose data align with the training task. These nodes then collaboratively generate threshold encryption keys and establish secure channels with weak IoT nodes $\mathcal{P}_w = \{p_{w_1}, \ldots, p_{w_b}\}$. The procedure proceeds as follows:

1. p_c distributes the full public dataset D^{pub} to all strong nodes in $\mathcal{P}_s$. During training rounds, subsets are specified via sample indices to reduce communication overhead.
2. The strong IoT nodes in $\mathcal{P}_s$ jointly run $TSGen(pp, a, t, \mathcal{P}_s)$ to generate a public encryption key pk, a public verification key vk, and private key shares $\{sk_i\}_{i=1}^{a}$. The threshold $t \leq a$ ensures that at least t nodes are needed for decryption, protecting privacy even if up to $t-1$ nodes collude.
3. Each strong IoT node p_{s_i} establishes a session key sk_{ic} with the cloud server p_c via $KA.agree(params, p_{s_i}, p_c)$ for secure transmission of aggregated predictions.
4. Each strong IoT node establishes secure session keys with its associated weak IoT nodes. For a weak node p_{w_i} associated with strong node p_{s_j}, they execute $KA.agree(params, p_{w_i}, p_{s_j})$ to establish session key sk_{ij} for secure transmission of public data and global predictions.

3.4 FL Initialization

The cloud server sets a delay threshold ΔT defining the maximum upload time for strong nodes' predictions per round, balancing participant inclusion and training speed.

Strong nodes p_{s_i} employ large models $\mathcal{M}_{s_i}$ (e.g., ResNet-18/50) with strong representation capacity, while weak nodes p_{w_i} adopt lightweight models $\mathcal{M}_{w_i}$ (e.g., MobileNet/TinyCNN) based on resource constraints. Models require compatible output layers (same number of classes) for effective knowledge distillation. Both node types initialize parameters randomly or with pre-trained weights.

3.5 Training

This phase consists of multiple training rounds. Each round comprises three key steps: local training, secure aggregation, and distillation adjustment.

Step 1: Local Training. Each node independently trains its model on local data for E_{local} epochs. For strong node p_{s_i} with dataset D_{s_i}, the model $\mathcal{M}_{s_i}$ minimizes cross-entropy loss:

$$L_{CE}^{p_{s_i}} = \sum_{(x,y)\in D_{s_i}} CE(\mathcal{M}_{s_i}(x), y),$$

with parameter updates via SGD: $\theta_{s_i} \leftarrow \theta_{s_i} - \alpha\nabla_{\theta_{s_i}} L_{CE}^{p_{s_i}}$, where α is the learning rate. Weak nodes train similarly using lightweight models $\mathcal{M}_{w_i}$ on D_{w_i}.

Step 2: Secure Aggregation. The cloud server p_c coordinates secure aggregation of soft label predictions from strong IoT nodes:

1. Once the delay threshold ΔT is reached and at least t nodes are ready, p_c selects a subset $D_{sub}^{pub} \subseteq D^{pub}$ and broadcasts it to all participating strong IoT nodes in $\mathcal{P}_s$.
2. Each strong IoT node $p_{s_i} \in \mathcal{P}_s$ performs forward inference using $\mathcal{M}_{s_i}$ to generate soft label predictions $P_i \in \mathbb{R}^{|D_{sub}^{pub}|\times K}$ (where K is the number of classes), encrypts them as $c_i = TEnc(pp, P_i, pk)$, and sends c_i to p_c.
3. Let $\mathcal{P}'_s = \{p_{s_1}, \ldots, p_{s_a}\}$ denote nodes whose ciphertexts are received within ΔT (where $a \geq t$). The server computes the aggregated ciphertext using homomorphic addition: $c_{agg} = TAdd(pp, c_1, \ldots, c_a)$, which satisfies $Dec(c_{agg}) = \sum_{i=1}^{a} P_i$. The server forwards c_{agg} to nodes in $\mathcal{P}'_s$ for partial decryption.
4. Each $p_{s_i} \in \mathcal{P}'_s$ computes partial decryption $(\rho_i, V_i) = TDec(pp, c_{agg}, sk_i, vk)$ and sends it to p_c.
5. Once p_c receives at least t partial decryptions, suppose the partial decryption results received are $\rho = \{\rho_1, \ldots, \rho_l\}$ and the associated verification values are $\mathcal{V} = \{V_1, \ldots, V_l\}$, where $l \geq t$, it invokes $TComd(pp, \mathcal{V}, \rho, t)$ to verify and combine them, obtaining the averaged global predictions: $P_{agg} = \frac{1}{a}\sum_{i=1}^{a} P_i$. The server then encrypts P_{agg} using symmetric encryption $C_{agg}^{(i)} = \mathcal{E}(sk_{ic}, P_{agg})$ and sends to each $p_{s_i} \in \mathcal{P}'_s$.

Step 3: Distillation Adjustment. Both strong and weak IoT nodes refine their local models by distilling knowledge from the global soft label predictions P_{agg}.

For Strong IoT Nodes: Each strong node $p_{s_i} \in \mathcal{P}'_s$ performs the following:

1. Decrypt $C_{agg}^{(i)}$ to obtain $P_{agg} = \mathcal{D}(sk_{ic}, C_{agg}^{(i)})$.
2. Compute the cross-entropy loss and distillation loss on D_{sub}^{pub}:

$$L_{CE}^{p_{s_i}} = \sum_{(x,y)\in D_{sub}^{pub}} CE(\mathcal{M}_{s_i}(x), y), \quad L_{DL}^{p_{s_i}} = \sum_{(x,y)\in D_{sub}^{pub}} KL(P_{agg}(x)||\mathcal{M}_{s_i}(x)).$$

3. Compute the composite loss $L^{p_{s_i}} = L_{CE}^{p_{s_i}} + \eta \cdot L_{DL}^{p_{s_i}}$, where $\eta > 0$ balances local supervision and global knowledge.
4. Update model parameters: $\theta_{s_i} \leftarrow \theta_{s_i} - \alpha\nabla_{\theta_{s_i}} L^{p_{s_i}}$.

For Weak IoT Nodes: Each weak node p_{w_i} associated with strong node p_{s_j}:

1. Receives encrypted data $C_{weak} = \mathcal{E}(sk_{ij}, \hat{D}^{pub}_{sub}||\hat{P}_{agg})$ from p_{s_j}, where $\hat{D}^{pub}_{sub} \subseteq D^{pub}_{sub}$.
2. Decrypts to obtain $(\hat{D}^{pub}_{sub}, \hat{P}_{agg})$ and computes:

$$L^{p_{w_i}} = \sum_{(x,y)\in\hat{D}^{pub}_{sub}} CE(\mathcal{M}_{w_i}(x), y) + \eta \sum_{(x,y)\in\hat{D}^{pub}_{sub}} KL(\hat{P}_{agg}(x)||\mathcal{M}_{w_i}(x)).$$

3. Update parameters: $\theta_{w_i} \leftarrow \theta_{w_i} - \alpha\nabla_{\theta_{w_i}} L^{p_{w_i}}$.

The training process iterates through Steps 1–3 for R_{global} rounds or until convergence.

4 Security Analysis

Based on the threat model and design goals, the primary security concern arises from potential privacy breaches by the cloud server and IoT nodes during collaborative training. This section provides a formal proof demonstrating that our scheme achieves data privacy against colluding adversaries while maintaining efficient knowledge distillation.

Theorem (Security of the Proposed Scheme): Given a security parameter λ and the auxiliary information z of the system, even if up to $t-1$ strong IoT nodes collude with the cloud server, the proposed scheme achieves data privacy. Specifically, the ideal-world view and the real-world view remain computationally indistinguishable:

$$\{Ideal_{\mathcal{F},\mathcal{S}(z)}(\{P_i\}_{i=1}^{\mathcal{U}}, \lambda)\}_{\{P_i\}_{i=1}^{\mathcal{U}},\lambda,z} \stackrel{c}{\equiv} \{Real_{Step_{2,3},\mathcal{A}(z)}(\{P_i\}_{i=1}^{\mathcal{U}}, \lambda)\}_{\{P_i\}_{i=1}^{\mathcal{U}},\lambda,z},$$

where λ is the security parameter; z is the auxiliary input information; t is the threshold for decryption; $\mathcal{U}$ denotes the set of entities that adversary $\mathcal{A}$ can capture; $\{P_i\}_{i=1}^{\mathcal{U}}$ represents the soft label predictions; $\mathcal{F}$ is the ideal functionality; $\mathcal{S}$ is a PPT simulator; $\mathcal{A}$ is a PPT adversary; and $A \stackrel{c}{\equiv} B$ indicates computational indistinguishability.

The ideal functionality $\mathcal{F}$ receives soft label predictions from all participants and outputs only the aggregated result to authorized parties. Intuitively, the security provided by threshold additive homomorphic encryption scheme THE ensures data privacy between strong IoT nodes and the cloud server. Additionally, the security of symmetric encryption $\mathcal{SE}$ and key agreement protocol KA guarantees privacy in other communications.

Proof: We prove the theorem using the ideal-real paradigm. We employ the hybrid model to formally prove security under the specified threat model:

Hybrid 0 : In this hybrid, we begin the analysis in the real world. The adversary $\mathcal{A}$ corrupts up to $t-1$ strong nodes (denoted $\mathcal{P}_{corrupt}$) and the cloud server, obtaining their views. Let $\mathcal{P}_{honest}$ denote honest strong nodes. The adversary's view is $\mathcal{H}_0 = \{View_{\mathcal{A}}^{Real}\}$.

Hybrid 1 : Simulator $\mathcal{S}$ interacts with ideal functionality $\mathcal{F}$. For each honest node $p_{s,i} \in \mathcal{P}_{honest}$, $\mathcal{S}$ replaces real predictions P_i with random values $P'_i \xleftarrow{\$} \mathbb{R}^{|D_{sub}^{pub}| \times K}$ and encrypts: $c'_i = TEnc(pp, P'_i, pk)$. By THE semantic security, $\{c'_i\}_{i \in \mathcal{P}_{honest}}$ are indistinguishable from real ciphertexts. Thus $\mathcal{H}_1 \stackrel{c}{\equiv} \mathcal{H}_0$.

Hybrid 2 : Simulator computes aggregated ciphertext: $c'_{agg} = TAdd(pp, \{c'_i : i \in \mathcal{P}_{honest}\} \cup \{c_j : j \in \mathcal{P}_{corrupt}\})$. By the homomorphic property of THE, this aggregation produces a valid ciphertext of the sum, and the adversary's view remains indistinguishable. Hence $\mathcal{H}_2 \stackrel{c}{\equiv} \mathcal{H}_1$.

Hybrid 3 : Threshold decryption is simulated. Honest nodes compute $(\rho'_i, V'_i) = TDec(pp, c'_{agg}, sk_i, vk)$. Since $|\mathcal{P}_{corrupt}| \leq t-1$, the adversary cannot decrypt c'_{agg} alone. By threshold security of THE, adversary cannot distinguish whether underlying plaintext corresponds to $\{P_i\}$ or $\{P'_i\}$. Thus $\mathcal{H}_3 \stackrel{c}{\equiv} \mathcal{H}_2$.

Hybrid 4 : Cloud server encrypts P'_{agg} using symmetric encryption: $C_{agg}^{(i)} = \mathcal{E}(sk_{ic}, P'_{agg})$ with session key from KA. By IND-CPA security of SE and DDH security of KA, $\mathcal{H}_4 \stackrel{c}{\equiv} \mathcal{H}_3$.

Hybrid 5 : For weak nodes, strong nodes encrypt $C_{weak} = \mathcal{E}(sk_{ij}, \hat{D}_{sub'}^{pub} || \hat{P}'_{agg})$ using session keys. By security of SE and KA, $\mathcal{H}_5 \stackrel{c}{\equiv} \mathcal{H}_4$.

By transitivity: $\mathcal{H}_5 \stackrel{c}{\equiv} \mathcal{H}_4 \stackrel{c}{\equiv} \mathcal{H}_3 \stackrel{c}{\equiv} \mathcal{H}_2 \stackrel{c}{\equiv} \mathcal{H}_1 \stackrel{c}{\equiv} \mathcal{H}_0$. The simulator $\mathcal{S}$ successfully simulates the adversary's view without knowing real predictions of honest participants. The adversary cannot distinguish real-world from ideal-world execution in polynomial time, proving that soft label predictions of honest participants remain confidential even when up to $t-1$ strong nodes collude with the cloud server. □

5 Performance Evaluation

5.1 Experimental Setup

Experiments were conducted on MNIST and CIFAR-10 datasets (with EMNIST and STL-10 as public distillation datasets) using PyTorch 1.12.1 on an Intel i9-10850K/RTX 4090 system. Strong nodes employ ResNet-18 while weak nodes use MobileNet. We compare against four baselines: FedAvg [4], basic FLwKD (BFLwKD) [12], differential privacy-based FLwKD (DP-FLwKD) [21] with $\varepsilon = 6$, and homomorphic encryption-based FL (HE-FL) [24]. Training uses SGD with learning rate 0.01 (decayed by 0.1 at rounds 50 and 75), momentum 0.9, weight decay 5×10^{-4}, and distillation weight $\eta = 50$.

5.2 Model Accuracy

Strong IoT Nodes. We evaluate our scheme against non-privacy-preserving baselines (FedAvg [4], BFLwKD [12]) that establish accuracy upper bounds, and privacy-preserving alternatives (DP-FLwKD [21], HE-FL [24]). Figure 2 shows results across 10 strong nodes over 100 rounds. Our scheme achieves accuracy within 0.5% of BFLwKD despite using threshold encryption, outperforms DP-FLwKD by 5–7% (encryption vs noise addition), and maintains only 1–2% gap from FedAvg. Notably, our convergence (60–70 rounds) matches BFLwKD and surpasses FedAvg (80–90 rounds), demonstrating that threshold homomorphic encryption provides strong privacy with minimal accuracy degradation.

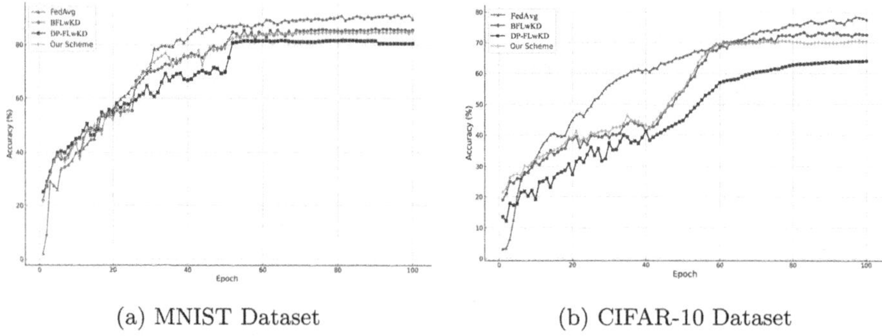

(a) MNIST Dataset (b) CIFAR-10 Dataset

Fig. 2. Comparison of Model Accuracy on Strong IoT Nodes. The x-axis represents communication rounds, and the y-axis represents test accuracy (%). The curves include two categories: *non-privacy-preserving schemes* (FedAvg and BFLwKD) that establish accuracy upper bounds, and *privacy-preserving schemes* (DP-FLwKD and Our Scheme) that provide data protection. This comparison demonstrates that our scheme achieves near-optimal accuracy while maintaining strong privacy guarantees.

Weak IoT Nodes. Figure 3 demonstrates the effectiveness of our heterogeneous architecture for resource-constrained devices. With limited resources (MobileNet, $\leq$500 samples, 30% labels), weak nodes achieve 20–30% accuracy improvement on MNIST and 25–35% on CIFAR-10 compared to independent training. This significant enhancement validates our design principle: weak nodes successfully leverage global knowledge from strong nodes via secure knowledge distillation without bearing cryptographic overhead, enabling practical deployment on heterogeneous IoT devices with varying computational capacities.

5.3 Communication Cost

Table 1 compares communication overhead per round (ResNet-18). Among non-privacy-preserving schemes, BFLwKD and DP-FLwKD (which provides

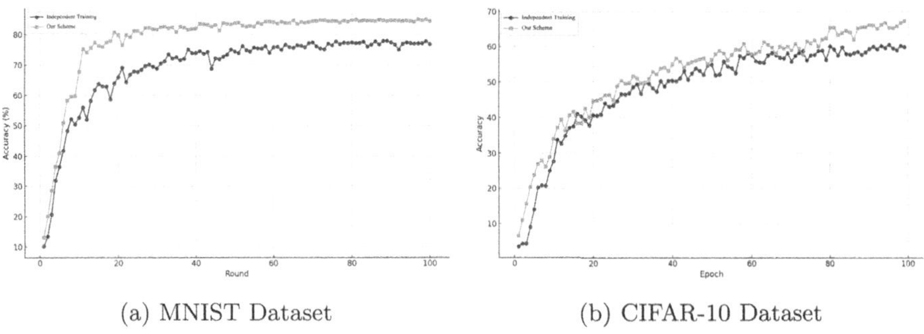

(a) MNIST Dataset (b) CIFAR-10 Dataset

Fig. 3. Comparison of Model Accuracy on Weak IoT Nodes. The x-axis represents communication rounds, and the y-axis represents test accuracy (%). The curves compare two training approaches: "Independent Training" (baseline where weak nodes train only on their limited local data) and "Our Scheme" (where weak nodes leverage knowledge from strong nodes via distillation).

Table 1. Comparison of Communication Overheads per Training Round

Method	Upload (KB)	Download (KB)	Total (KB)
Scheme in [12]	45	45	90
Scheme in [21]	48	48	96
Scheme in [24]	2925000	47872	2972872
Scheme in [4]	47872	47872	95744
Our Scheme	409	413	822

only weak privacy through noise addition) have the lowest costs (90-96KB) by exchanging only soft predictions, but BFLwKD lacks privacy protection while DP-FLwKD sacrifices significant accuracy (5–7% loss). Among privacy-preserving schemes with strong guarantees, our scheme maintains practical efficiency (822KB) with strong privacy via threshold encryption—demonstrating a favorable accuracy-communication-privacy trade-off. Compared to non-private baselines, we incur 8–9× overhead vs BFLwKD as the cost of cryptographic protection, but remain 116× more efficient than FedAvg (95.7MB) and 3600× more efficient than HE-FL (2.97GB), making our approach practical for IoT deployments where both privacy and efficiency are critical.

5.4 Property Comparison

In this section, we conduct a property-level comparison of the proposed FLwKD scheme against baseline methods, with results summarized in Table 2. The baselines are categorized as: (1) *Non-privacy-preserving schemes* (FedAvg and BFLwKD), which serve as benchmarks for achievable performance without privacy constraints, and (2) *Privacy-preserving schemes* (DP-FLwKD and HE-FL), which represent alternative cryptographic approaches. As illustrated,

Table 2. Property Comparison

Schemes	Heterogeneous Nodes Support	Communication Efficiency	Data Privacy Protection	High Model Accuracy
Scheme in [4]	✗	✗	✗	✓
Scheme in [12]	✓	✓	✗	✓
Scheme in [21]	✓	✓	✓	✗
Scheme in [24]	✗	✗	✓	✓
Our scheme	✓	✓	✓	✓

only our scheme satisfies all key design properties simultaneously. Compared to non-privacy-preserving schemes, our approach achieves comparable accuracy and communication efficiency while adding strong privacy guarantees—demonstrating that cryptographic protection need not severely compromise performance. Compared to alternative privacy-preserving schemes, FedAvg achieves high accuracy but fails in all other aspects, particularly lacking privacy protection. BFLwKD supports heterogeneity and communication efficiency but lacks privacy protection. DP-FLwKD provides privacy but sacrifices accuracy significantly (5–7% degradation). HE-FL offers privacy and accuracy but suffers from poor communication efficiency (3600× overhead) and lacks heterogeneous node support. Through this comparison, it is evident that the proposed FLwKD scheme offers a balanced and comprehensive solution that simultaneously meets the critical requirements of communication efficiency, data privacy, and model performance in heterogeneous IoT environments.

5.5 Discussion

Scalability and Security. Our scheme exhibits favorable scalability with constant per-node communication overhead and linear computational growth. The threshold parameter t provides a tunable trade-off between privacy guarantees and fault tolerance, with $t = \lceil n/2 \rceil + 1$ offering practical balance for most deployments.

Limitation and Future Work. The primary challenge in real-world heterogeneous IoT deployments is device connectivity instability. IoT nodes, particularly weak devices, may experience intermittent network connections, node failures, or dynamic join/leave patterns due to mobility or resource constraints. While our current design assumes relatively stable participation during training rounds, connection disruptions could affect both strong nodes (potentially failing to meet the threshold t for decryption) and weak nodes (missing knowledge distillation opportunities). Future work will focus on developing robust mechanisms for handling dynamic node participation, including adaptive threshold adjustment, asynchronous knowledge transfer protocols, and recovery strategies for partial round failures. These enhancements would significantly improve the practical applicability of our scheme in real-world IoT environments characterized by unstable connectivity.

6 Conclusion

We proposed a privacy-preserving federated learning scheme with knowledge distillation for heterogeneous IoT environments. By categorizing nodes into strong and weak groups based on computational capacity, our approach enables resource-constrained devices to benefit from collaborative learning without cryptographic overhead. Strong nodes employ threshold homomorphic encryption to protect soft label predictions during aggregation, ensuring privacy against up to $t-1$ colluding adversaries. Experimental results demonstrate that our scheme achieves accuracy within 0.5% of non-private baselines while outperforming differential privacy approaches by 5–7%, with communication overhead of only 822KB per round. Weak nodes achieve 20–35% accuracy improvement through secure knowledge distillation. Future work will address connectivity instability in dynamic IoT environments to further enhance practical deployability.

References

1. Zhang, T., et al.: Federated learning for the Internet of Things: applications, challenges, and opportunities. IEEE Internet Things Mag. **5**(1), 24–29 (2022)
2. Dong, Y., et al.: Multi-task federated split learning across multi-modal data with privacy preservation. Sensors **25**(1), 233 (2025)
3. Wang, L., et al.: Dual-server privacy-preserving collaborative deep learning: a round-efficient, dynamic and lossless approach. IEEE Trans. Dependable Secure Comput. **22**(6), 7759–7772 (2025)
4. McMahan, B., Moore, E., Ramage, D., Hampson, S., y Arcas, B.A.: Communication-efficient learning of deep networks from decentralized data. In: Proceedings of the 20th International Conference on Artificial Intelligence and Statistics, AISTATS 2017, 20-22 April 2017, Fort Lauderdale, FL, USA, vol. 54, pp. 1273–1282 (2017)
5. Dong, Y., Zhang, L., Xu, L.: Privacy-preserving and reliable distributed federated learning. In: Proceedings of International Conference on Algorithms and Architectures for Parallel Processing (ICA3PP), pp. 130–149 (2023)
6. Zhu, L., Liu, Z., Han, S.: Deep leakage from gradients. In: Advances in Neural Information Processing Systems 32: Annual Conference on Neural Information Processing Systems 2019, NeurIPS 2019, December 8-14, 2019, Vancouver, BC, Canada, pp. 14747–14756 (2019)
7. Nasr, M., Shokri, R., Houmansadr, A.: Comprehensive privacy analysis of deep learning: passive and active white-box inference attacks against centralized and federated learning. In: 2019 IEEE Symposium on Security and Privacy, SP 2019, San Francisco, CA, USA, May 19-23, 2019, pp. 739–753 (2019)
8. Diao, E., Ding, J., Tarokh, V.: HeteroFL: computation and communication efficient federated learning for heterogeneous clients. In: 9th International Conference on Learning Representations, ICLR 2021, Virtual Event, Austria, May 3-7, 2021 (2021)

9. Li, D., Wang, J.: FedMD: Heterogenous Federated Learning via Model Distillation. CoRR, vol. abs/1910.03581 (2019)
10. Jeong, E., Oh, S., Kim, H., Park, J., Bennis, M., Kim, S.-L.: Communication-Efficient On-Device Machine Learning: Federated Distillation and Augmentation under Non-IID Private Data, CoRR, vol. abs/1811.11479 (2018)
11. Itahara, S., Nishio, T., Koda, Y., Morikura, M., Yamamoto, K.: Distillation-based semi-supervised federated learning for communication-efficient collaborative training with Non-IID private data. IEEE Trans. Mob. Comput. **22**(1), 191–205 (2023)
12. Sattler, F., Marbán, A., Rischke, R., Samek, W.: CFD: communication-efficient federated distillation via soft-label quantization and delta coding. IEEE Trans. Netw. Sci. Eng. **9**(4), 2025–2038 (2022)
13. Zhong, L., et al.: Dual-server-based lightweight privacy-preserving federated learning. IEEE Trans. Netw. Serv. Manag. **21**(4), 4787–4800 (2024)
14. Zhao, L., Wang, Q., Zou, Q., Zhang, Y., Chen, Y.: Privacy-preserving collaborative deep learning with unreliable participants. IEEE Trans. Inf. Forensics Secur. **15**, 1486–1500 (2020)
15. Naseri, M., Hayes, J., Cristofaro, E.D.: Local and central differential privacy for robustness and privacy in federated learning. In: 29th Annual Network and Distributed System Security Symposium, NDSS 2022, San Diego, California, USA, April 24-28, 2022 (2022)
16. Hijazi, N.M., Aloqaily, M., Guizani, M., Ouni, B., Karray, F.: Secure federated learning with fully homomorphic encryption for IoT communications. IEEE Internet Things J. **11**(3), 4289–4300 (2024)
17. Doan, T.V.T., Messai, M.-L., Gavin, G., Darmont, J.: A survey on implementations of homomorphic encryption schemes. J. Supercomput. **79**(13), 15098–15139 (2023)
18. Wang, L., et al.: PriVeriFL: privacy-preserving and aggregation-verifiable federated learning. IEEE Trans. Serv. Comput. **18**(2), 998–1011 (2025)
19. Wu, C., Zhang, L., Xu, L., Choo, K.-K.R., Zhong, L.: Privacy-preserving serverless federated learning scheme for Internet of Things. IEEE Internet Things J. **11**(12), 22429–22438 (2024)
20. Gao, Y., Zhang, L., Wang, L., Choo, K.-K.R., Zhang, R.: Privacy-preserving and reliable decentralized federated learning. IEEE Trans. Serv. Comput. **16**(4), 2879–2891 (2023)
21. Gad, G., Fadlullah, Z.M., Fouda, M.M., Ibrahem, M.I., Nasser, N.: Joint knowledge distillation and local differential privacy for communication-efficient federated learning in heterogeneous systems. In: IEEE Global Communications Conference, GLOBECOM 2023, Kuala Lumpur, Malaysia, December 4-8, 2023, pp. 2051–2056 (2023)
22. Zhang, J., Shi, C.: Efficient privacy-preserving federated learning for IIoT using dual proxy re-encryption. IEEE Internet Things J. (2025)
23. Gennaro, R., Jarecki, S., Krawczyk, H., Rabin, T.: Secure distributed key generation for discrete-log based cryptosystems. J. Cryptol. **20**(1), 51–83 (2007)
24. Li, Y., Li, H., Xu, G., Huang, X., Lu, R.: Efficient privacy-preserving federated learning with unreliable users. IEEE Internet Things J. **9**(13), 11590–11603 (2022)

TraceBlock: Cyberattack Traceback System Based on Blockchain

Dagula, Lei Xu(✉), Keke Gai, and Liehuang Zhu

School of Cyberspace Science and Technology, Beijing Institute of Technology, Beijing, China
1329289632@qq.com, {6120180029,gaikeke,liehuangz}@bit.edu.cn

Abstract. With the continuous development of cyberattack techniques, attack provenance graph has become an important tool for network defense decision-making. Although existing research has made progress in the logical representation and automatic generation of provenance graphs, the provenance graphs constructed by single organization cannot support collaborative traceability. This paper proposes a blockchain-based cyberattack traceback system called TraceBlock to enable the sharing of graphs across multiple organizations. In TraceBlock system, alert records, which are raw data for contracting, are generated by hosts, securely transmitted by oracle, and filtered by CTI filter. The CTI filter uses a pre-trained model to identify critical threat intelligences (CTIs) and uploads CTIs to the blockchain network. Three smart contracts are deployed on the blockchain network, respectively responsible for CTI verification, provenance graph construction, and subgraph extraction. We conduct simulations using an open-source blockchain platform and the DARPA 1999 dataset. The results demonstrate the feasibility of the proposed system.

Keywords: Provenance graph · Blockchain · Smart Contract · Subgraph extraction

1 Introduction

With the continuous advancement of cyberattack techniques, researchers have increasingly focused on attack provenance graphs. Attack provenance graphs play an important role in network defense decision-making. The provenance graph treats all system entities as vertices and operations between these entities as edges [1]. As a result, attack provenance graph can build the entire attack process and enable the visualization of complex attack paths. How to achieve efficient generation and distributed parsing of provenance graphs has become a hot research topic in the filed of network security. Previous studies have successfully implemented the logical representation and automatic generation of attack graphs, significantly improving the handling of time and space complexity during the provenance process [2,3]. However, as attack methods become increasingly

W. Meng et al. (Eds.): ASSS 2025, CCIS 2903, pp. 17–34, 2026.
https://doi.org/10.1007/978-3-032-21600-7_2

sophisticated, traditional provenance graphs built upon attack records from single organization can no longer meet practical needs. While in practice, it is generally difficult to find a platform trusted by multiple organizations to share the information of provenance graphs.

As a decentralized distributed ledger technology [4], blockchain enables trusted data sharing among multiple organizations. It can ensure data immutability and transparency during the sharing process through a decentralized architecture and cryptographic mechanisms. In recent years, a few studies have applied blockchain technology to provenance graph sharing. The PROV-DM model proposed by Sun et al. [15] utilizes blockchain to store the provenance graph, so that the provenance graph can be protected from being corrupted and forged. The SEDNP proposed by Liu et al. [12] also leverages blockchain to store the provenance graph. They considered the limited storage capability of blockchain ledger, thereby they utilized constant-size digests to minimize the on-blockchain storage and computation overhead. However, blockchain can only ensure that the provenance graph recorded on the blockchain ledger is tamper-proof, but it cannot ensure the security of the raw data before being sent to blockchain network.

Previous studies have demonstrated that it is feasible to store provenance graphs on the blockchain and build a cyberattack traceback system shared provenance graphs among multiple organizations. Nevertheless, the following issues still need to be considered. Firstly, the raw data used to construct the provenance graph comes from different devices. When being transmitted from source devices to the blockchain network, the raw data may be tampered with. Therefore, the transmission channel of the raw data used to construct the provenance graph need to be secure. Secondly, due to the distributed nature of blockchain network, storing data on blockchain ledger is more costly than storing data in a centralized database. On the other hand, the raw data used to construct provenance graph generally includes low-risk alerts and false alerts. And the false alerts will hurt the accuracy of succeeding analysis based on provenance graphs. When utilizing the blockchain to store the provenance graph, it may lead to a waste of storage resources if directly uploading all the raw data to the blockchain network. Thirdly, the scale of the provenance graph can be quite large, while for a specific organization or host, it may only have interest in a small part of the provenance graph. Hence, it is necessary to provide a service to users to help them obtain the graph data in an efficient way.

In order to address the above issues, we propose a cyberattack traceback system based on blockchain. We refer to the proposed system as TraceBlock. TraceBlock uses alerts to construct provenance graphs and employs the k-hop algorithm to extract provenance subgraphs. TraceBlock includes blockchain network and three off-chain modules, namely hosts, Cyber Threat Intelligence filters (CTI filters), and oracles. The alert for constructing the provenance graph is generated by the hosts. The security of alerts transmitted from the hosts to the blockchain network is ensured by the oracle. Then the oracle passes the signed alert to the CTI filter. In order to reduce the number of on-chain data, the CTI filter utilizes a pre-trained classification model to distinguish between low-risk and high-risk alerts, namely CTIs, and uploads CTIs to blockchain network. The smart contract deployed on the blockchain network verifies the digital signatures and utilizes CTIs to construct the provenance graphs. The provenance graph which is represented by an adjacency matrix is stored in the blockchain ledger. When a host in the system queries the provenance subgraph related to itselif, the smart contract deployed on the blockchain network will use the host's IP as the center node to extract a k-hop provenance subgraph and send the subgraph to the host.

The remaining of this paper is organized is as follows. Section 2 introduces some related studies. Section 3 presents some basics about provenance graph, oracle and aggregate signature. Section 4 introduces the architecture, the basic workflow and the threat model of the proposed system. Section 5 describes in detail how the proposed system works. Simulation results are presented in Sect. 6. Finally, we summarize this paper in Sect. 7.

2 Related Work

With evolving cyber attacks, investigation based on provenance graph has become a research hotspot, as it intuitively reveals attack causality for easier root cause tracing. King et al. [5] were among the early researchers to use provenance graphs for attack investigation. Hossain et al. [6] proposed SLEUTH, a cross-platform real-time attack scenario reconstruction system based on in-memory dependency graphs and tag-based techniques, capable of efficiently detecting, analyzing, and visualizing attack steps. Milajerdi et al. proposed both the POIROT [7] and HOLMES [8] systems. POIROT leverages CTI correlations and kernel audit logs to model threat hunting as a graph pattern matching problem, enabling efficient search and precise identification of large-scale attack graphs across multiple operating systems. CTI is evidence-based knowledge that includes the context, mechanisms, indicators, impacts, and action-oriented recommendations related to existing or emerging threats [17]. HOLMES achieves high-precision real-time detection with low false alarms of advanced persistent threats (APTs) by correlating suspicious information flows arising from attacker activities. Alsaheel et al. [9] proposed the ATLAS framework which leverages causality analysis and machine learning to build attack behavior models from audit logs, enabling efficient and accurate identification and reconstruction of APT attack steps. Liu et al. [10] proposed the TRACEGADGET framework, which leverages provenance graphs to achieve efficient detection and complete path reconstruction of cross-host APT lateral movements, demonstrating high accuracy and robustness. To sum up, research on the construction of provenance graphs has become relatively mature. Nevertheless, above approaches require complete provenance graphs and excessive manual intervention, resulting in low efficiency and lack of timeliness. In addition, early studies rarely consider the issue of sharing provenance graphs among multiple parties.

Recently, a few previous studies have used blockchain technology for sharing provenance graphs. The ProvChain [11] proposed by Liang et al. introduces cloud computing into the provenance graph sharing system, using blockchain as the underlying storage structure. The SEDNP [12] proposed by Liu et al. also aims to construct a provenance graph using network logs and it uses blockchain to store the provenance graph. Blockchain technology can be applied not only in the field of sharing provenance graph, but also in other provenance scenarios. Blinker [13] proposed by Bose et al. is an extensible framework based on standard provenance models and blockchain technology, designed for capturing, storing, analyzing, and visualizing software provenance data with support for interactive presentation. The BSTProv system [14] proposed by Sun et al. leverages blockchain technology to achieve secure decentralized cross-domain data provenance sharing and tracing through encrypted subgraph partitioning and flexible authorization. The PROV-DM model [15] proposed by Sun et al. is an IoT data provenance model that also uses blockchain technology to ensure the security of provenance information. The BPDAC scheme [16] proposed by Sun et al. achieves decentralized, behavior-based dynamic access control by integrating blockchain and data provenance. In this paper, we also utilize blockchain technology to realize the sharing of provenance graph. While different from above studies, we use oracle to ensure the security of the provenance data recorded on the blockchain ledger.

3 Preliminaries

3.1 Provenance Graph

Provenance graph [5] is a directed heterogeneous graph that can be used to analyze various sequences of events, including attack alert records or CTIs. These sequence events are generated by the intrusion detection system (IDS) deployed on the devices. The provenance graph $G = (V, E)$ is constructed by a set of nodes V, where each node represents an IP in the system. Next, based on node set and attack events occurring within the system, we can construct the edge set E which represent operational relationships between two nodes. The direction of edges indicates causal relationships , reflecting dependencies and interactions among nodes. Finally, the node set V and edge set E are combined to form the complete provenance graph $G = (V, E)$. For any given node $node_i$, its provenance subgraph G_i refers to the set of all nodes and edges related to the node that have been filtered under specific conditions.

3.2 Oracle

Blockchain is a decentralized distributed ledger technology that ensures data security and immutability through cryptography. The blockchain network itself is closed, so accessing off-chain data requires the use of oracles. Oracles are responsible for guaranteeing the security and reliability of data uploaded to the chain. An oracle is a complete ecosystem that allows decentralized applications to collect, transmit, and insert external data [18]. The oracle ecosystem typically consists of three components, namely data sources, oracle nodes, and smart contracts. Data sources are the origins of the data collected by the oracle. Oracle nodes gather data from these sources and deliver them to smart contracts for execution. Sometimes, oracle nodes overlap with blockchain nodes, but this is not always the case [19]. Smart contracts are deployed on the blockchain network and contain the codes that manage the collected data. Usually, they predefine quality standards for accepting or rejecting data. They can perform computations to pass appropriate data to the contracts as well. The three components of the oracle are not always independent, as the same entity may sometimes fulfill two or all three roles.

3.3 Aggregate Signature

Aggregate Signature (AS) [20] is a cryptographic technique that allows multiple signatures from different signers on different messages to be combined into a single, compact signature. With aggregate signatures, a verifier only needs to verify this combined signature to simultaneously confirm the validity of all the original signatures, significantly reducing storage space and verification time. Boneh–Lynn–Shacham (BLS) Aggregate Signature is a short signature scheme proposed by Boneh et al. [21], based on the Computational Diffie–Hellman assumption. This short signature scheme is designed for systems that require manual input of signatures or signature propagation over low-bandwidth channels. For standard security parameters, the signature length is approximately half that of a digital signature algorithm with the same security level. It is well-suited for applications in blockchain networks.

The BLS signature scheme consists of the following components

$$AS = (\text{Setup}, \text{KeyGen}, \text{Sign}, \text{Verify}, \text{AggS}, \text{AggV}). \tag{1}$$

- **Setup**: Setup initializes the system parameters required for the signature scheme.
- **KeyGen**: KeyGen is an algorithm which is responsible for generating the public and private key pairs used in signing and verification.
- **Sign**: Sign is an algorithm which is responsible for using the private key to generate a signature on a given message.
- **Verify**: Verify is responsible for using the public key to check the validity of a given signature.
- **AggS**: AggS is the abbreviation for Aggregate Signature Generation Algorithm. The algorithm implements at least three sub-functions. The first sub-function is the standard signature function. The second sub-function aggregates three vectors, namely the message vector $(m_1, \ldots, m_n)$, the user vector $(u_1, \ldots, u_n)$, and the individual signature vector $(\sigma_1, \ldots, \sigma_n)$. The third sub-function generates the aggregated signature σ_{agg}.
- **AggV**: AggV is the abbreviation for Aggregate Signature Verification Algorithm. The algorithm is responsible for verifying the aggregated signature. Suppose each user $user_i$ has a private key sk_i and a public key pk_i. If AggV(pk_1, ..., pk_n, m_1,..., m_n, σ_{agg}) = 1, then the signature is valid. Otherwise, the signature is in valid.

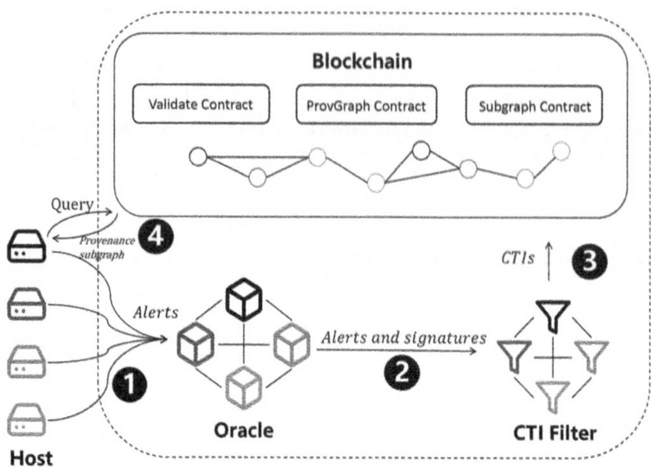

Fig. 1. A simple illustration of the architecture of the proposed TraceBlock system.

4 System Model

In this section, we first introduce the system architecture and then present the threat model.

4.1 System Architecture

The proposed attack traceability system TraceBlock performs attack traceability by analyzing alert records. It uses blockchain network to share provenance graph. As shown in Fig. 1, at the architecture level, the TraceBlock system mainly consists of a blockchain network and some off-chain modules, which include a number of hosts, oracle nodes and CTI filter nodes. The entire system is managed by a coalition of security-focused organizations, with each entity within the system belongs to one of these organizations. A detailed overview of the system architecture is provided below.

- **Host**: The host is responsible for collecting network patkets and generating alerts. Each host is equipped with an intrusion detection system that can identify abnormal packets. The host organizes abnormal packets into security alerts, which are then sent to the oracle. Additionally, the host can query and download provenance subgraph from the blockchain ledger.
- **Oracle**: The oracle is responsible for ensuring that the alert records provided by the hosts are complete. To prevent single point of failure, the oracle in the proposed system is consisted of several nodes. Each node is referred to as an oracle node. Each oracle node checks the alerts from hosts and generate signatures as its endorsements. Then the oracle node passes the signed alerts along with the signatures to the CTI filter.

- **CTI Filter**: The CTI filter is responsible for distinguishing between low-risk alerts and high-risk alerts. The CTI filter is consisted of multiple nodes each of which is referred to as a filter node. Each filter node belongs to one specific organization. The filter node utilizes the labeled alerts provided by hosts to train a machine learning model to identify high-risk alerts, namely CTIs. The identified CTIs are then sent the blockchain network.
- **Blockchain Network**: The blockchain network is responsible for constructing and storing the provenance graphs. At the network architecture level, the blockchain network consists of nodes that reach consensus through a Byzantine fault tolerance (BFT) algorithm. Each node maintains a copy of the blockchain ledger. And the provenance graph is essentially recorded on the ledger. Three smart contracts are deployed on the blockchain network. The first contract is responsible for verifying the CTIs. The second contract is responsible for constructing provenance graphs. And the third contract is responsible for generating provenance subgraphs according to the queries of hosts (Fig. 2).

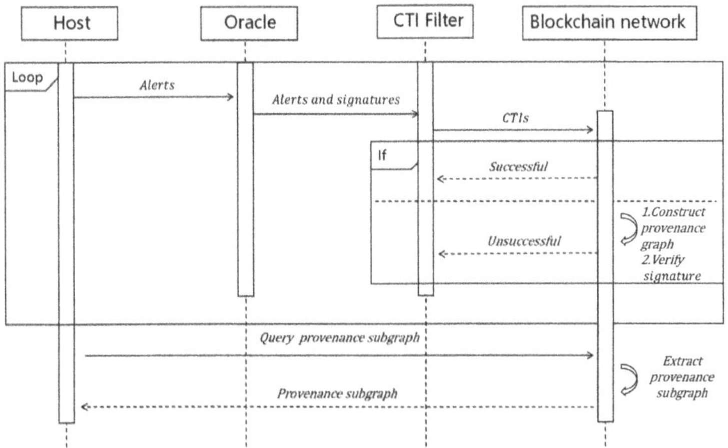

Fig. 2. The basic workflow of the proposed TraceBlock system.

4.2 Basic Workflow

The proposed TraceBlock system constructs provenance graphs utilizing the alert data generated by multiple hosts. Since the hosts generate alerts continuously, the provenance graph is updated accordingly. We divide time into multiple update epochs, (e.g. update the provenance graph every three days). As shown in Fig. 2, during each update epoch t, each host $host_i$ sends a number of labeled alerts to the oracle. Each oracle node verifies whether the content of alert is complete. If the content of alert is complete, the oracle node will sign the alert and send both alert and its signature to the CTI filter. The filter node utilizes alerts to train a machine learning model to generate CTIs. In this paper, CTI defined as the combination of a high-risk alert and the corresponding list of signatures generated by oracle nodes. And the filter node uploads CTIs to the blockchain network. Once the CTIs are sent to the blockchain network, the *Validate Contract* begins aggregating signatures of oracle nodes for the same CTI. Then the *Validate Contract* verifies the legality of the aggregated signature. If the aggregated signature passes verification, the CTI will be stored on the blockchain ledger. If not, the CTI will not be stored. The *Provgraph Contract* uses the CTIs stored on the ledger to construct a provenance graph. After the provenance graph is constructed and stored on the ledger, the host can invoke the *Subgraph Contract* to obtain the provenance subgraph related to itself.

4.3 Threat Model

For the proposed TraceBlock system to work, we make the following assumptions. First, we assume that transactions can be correctly processed by the blockchain network. Specifically, some blockchain nodes may intentionally fail to validate blocks, even tamper with blocks. We assume that the proportion of these corrupted nodes does not exceed the limit specified by the consensus mechanism. Second, we assume that the oracle and CTI filter can work properly. Some oracle nodes and filter nodes may attempt to alter the alert data. Let p denote the number of malicious oracle nodes and q denote the number of malicious filter nodes. It is assumed that the number of oracle nodes is more than $3p$, and the number of filter nodes is more than $3q$. Third, we assume that all hosts involved in the system are honest. That is, the hosts will not intentionally provide false alerts.

5 Design Details

5.1 Initialization

As described in previous section, the proposed TraceBlock system is maintained by a group of organizations. At the very beginning, the organizations prepare the oracle nodes, CTI filter nodes and blockchain nodes to build the oracle, the CTI filter and the blockchain network respectively. After the blockchain network is ready, each oracle node $oracle_j$ $(j = 1, 2, \ldots, m)$ generates a key pair (pk_j, sk_j), where pk_j denotes the public key and sk_j denotes the private key. Specifically, each oracle $oracle_j$ randomly selects a private key sk_j from the finite field $\mathbb{Z}_q$. And $\mathbb{Z}_q$ is a set of integers modulo q, where q is a large prime number. Then, using a group of elliptic curves G_1 of order q, the oracle node can calculate the generator g_1 of G_1. By using the generator g_1 and private key sk_j, the oracle node can calculate the public key pk_j as

$$pk_j = g_1^{sk_j}. \tag{2}$$

Then the public key is sent to the blockchain network and stored on the ledger. ïž£

5.2 Alert Upload

Alert Generation. After initializing, the system proceeds to the periodically update process of the provenance graph. During each epoch t, the IDS deployed on each host $host_i$ $(i = 1, 2, \ldots, n)$ monitors network activities to identify potential attack events. The IDS continuously analyzes incoming and outgoing traffic, and upon detecting suspicious behavior, it extracts and integrates key attributes of each attack event. Suppose that the host $host_i$ detects K events in epoch t. For the k-th $(k = 1, ..., K)$ attack event, the extracted attributes include the source IP address $IP\_s^{(t)}_{i,k}$, the destination IP address $IP\_t^{(t)}_{i,k}$, the type of alert triggered $T^{(t)}_{i,k}$, the exact timestamp of the event $Time^{(t)}_{i,k}$, and the associated threat label $Label^{(t)}_{i,k}$ that categorizes the severity or nature of the attack. The above attributes are consolidated into a structured alert record

$$alert^{(t)}_{i,k} = (IP\_s^{(t)}_{i,k}, IP\_t^{(t)}_{i,k}, T^{(t)}_{i,k}, Time^{(t)}_{i,k}, Label^{(t)}_{i,k}). \tag{3}$$

Subsequently, the host sends a set of K alert records to the oracle via a secure channel.

Alert Verification. Suppose that the oracle node $oracle_j$ first receives the alert record $alert^{(t)}_{i,k}$ $(k = 1, 2, \ldots, K)$ sent from the host $host_i$. Then the node broadcasts $alert^{(t)}_{i,k}$ to every other oracle node. Given the alert record $alert^{(t)}_{i,k}$, each oracle node $oracle_j$ verifies whether the attributes of $alert^{(t)}_{i,k}$ are complete. If $alert^{(t)}_{i,k}$ passes the verification, then the node $oracle_j$ will use its private key sk_j to sign the alert record. Signature is recorded as $\sigma^{(t)}_{i,k,j}$. The alert record $alert^{(t)}_{i,k}$ and the corresponding signature $\sigma^{(t)}_{i,k,j}$ are then sent to the CTI filter.

5.3 Alert Filtering

As defined in Eq. (5.2), each alert record $alert^{(t)}_{i,k}$ contains a threat label which is a variable measured in the range 0 to 100, indicating the severity or risk level of a threat. The CTI filter leverages this label information to identify high-risk alert and reorganizes high-risk alert into CTI.

The threat level of alert varies from one to another. Based on the distribution of the threat labels and business requirements, each CTI filter nodes sets a threshold τ. For each alert record $alert^{(t)}_{i,k}$, the filter node first assigns a binary label

$$y^{(t)}_{i,k} = \begin{cases} 1, \; Label^{(t)}_{i,k} \geq \tau, \\ 0, \; Label^{(t)}_{i,k} < \tau, \end{cases} \tag{4}$$

The label $y_{i,k}^{(t)}$ indicates whether the alert record is high-risk. Considering that the IDS deployed on the host does not have perfect accuracy and may generate false alert, in the proposed system we use the CTI filter to regenerate the threat label of each alert record. A machine learning model is trained by the CTI filter to predict the threat label.

During the initialization phase, namely epoch 0, each host uploads a certain amount of alert records. We require these alert records to be checked by professional analysts. Hence there is no false alert and the threat label of each alert record is accurate.

Each filter node collects these alert records and organizes them into a structured training dataset

$$\mathcal{D}' = \{[IP\_s_{i,k}^{(0)}, IP\_t_{i,k}^{(0)}, T_{i,k}^{(0)}.Time_{i,k}^{(0)}], y_{i,k}^{(0)}\}. \tag{5}$$

Given the training dataset, the filter node can select a classification algorithm (e.g. random forest) and a loss function (e.g. cross-entropy) to train the classification model $M(\cdot)$. During training, a validation set may be used to monitor performance and prevent overfitting.

In epoch t ($t > 0$), each filter node $filter_l(l = 1, 2, \ldots, L)$ receives labeled alert records $\{alert_{i,1}^{(t)},\ alert_{i,2}^{(t)}, \ldots, alert_{i,K}^{(t)}\}$ from the oracle. The filter node $filter_l$ first leverages the threat label $Label_{i,k}^{(t)}$ of each alert record $alert_{i,K}^{(t)}$ to calculate $y_{i,k}^{(t)}$ as Eq. (5.3). Then the filter node $filter_l$ uses the classification model $M(\cdot)$ to predict the label as

$$\hat{y}_{i,k}^{(t)} = M(alert_{i,k}^{(t)}). \tag{6}$$

Then the filter node $filter_l$ compares $\hat{y}_{i,k}^{(t)}$ and $y_{i,k}^{(t)}$. If they are consistent, the filter node $filter_l$ defines CTI as

$$CTI_{i,k,l}^{(t)} = (alert_{i,k}^{(t)}, \sigma_{i,k,1}^{(t)}, \ldots, \sigma_{i,k,m}^{(t)}). \tag{7}$$

The CTI $CTI_{i,k,l}^{(t)}$ will be uploaded to blockchain network. If the labels are inconsistent, the alert record $alert_{i,k}^{(t)}$ will be discarded. By this way, the filter node can effectively filter out low-risk alerts and reduce the probability of false alert records being stored on the blockchain ledger.

5.4 Provenance Graph Construction

Verification. For an alert record $alert_{i,k}^{(t)}$, if it is identified as high-risk alert by the CTI filter node $filter_l(l = 1, 2, \ldots, L)$, the corresponding CTI record $CTI_{i,k,l}^{(t)}$ will be sent to the blockchain network. Upon receiving the CTI, the *Validate Contract* deployed on the blockchain will be triggered. As shown in Algorithm 1, the *Validate Contract* first organizes CTIs corresponding to the same alert record

Algorithm 1: Validate Contract

```
Input: All CTIs in epoch tCTI = (CTI^{(t)}_{i,k,1}, ..., CTI^{(t)}_{i,k,L}), List of private keys
       pk = (pk_1, pk_2, ..., pk_m)
Function Validate(CTI, pk):
    CTI^{(t)}_{i,k} = [ ]
    for l ∈ range(1, L) do
        count = 0
        for x ∈ range(1, L) do
            CTI^{(t)}_{i,k} = CTI[l]
            if CTI^{(t)}_{i,k} = CTI[x] then
                count = count + 1
            end
            if count >= L/3 then
                break
            end
            if count < L/3 and l=L and x=L then
                return
            end
        end
    end
    pk_agg = ∏_{j=1}^{m} pk_j // Aggregate public keys
    σ^{(t)}_{i,k} = ∏_{j=1}^{m} σ^{(t)}_{i,k,j} // Aggregate signatures
    if e(g_1, σ^{(t)}_{i,k}) = e(pk_agg, H(alert^{(t)}_{i,k})) then
        store CTI^{(t)}_{i,k} in blockchain ledger
        Call ProvGraph(CTI^{(t)}_{i,k})
    end
```

If more than one-third of the nodes submit the same CTI, the CTI will be recorded on the blockchain ledger as $CTI^{(t)}_{i,k}$.

Then the *Validate Contract* aggregates the public keys of oracle nodes as

$$pk_{agg} = \prod_{j=1}^{m} pk_j. \tag{8}$$

Then, the contract aggregates multiple signatures into a single short signature

$$\sigma^{(t)}_{i,k} = \prod_{j=1}^{m} \sigma^{(t)}_{i,k,j}. \tag{9}$$

After that, the contract uses the bilinear pairing function $e(\cdot,\cdot)$ to verify the validity of the aggregated signature $\sigma^{(t)}_{i,k}$ as follows

$$e(g_1, \sigma^{(t)}_{i,k}) = e(pk_{agg}, H(alert^{(t)}_{i,k})), \tag{10}$$

Algorithm 2: Provgraph Contract

```
Input: All CTIs for epoch t
       CTI^(t) = (CTI^(t)_{1,1}, ..., CTI^(t)_{1,K}, ..., CTI^(t)_{n,1}, ..., CTI^(t)_{n,K})
Output: Provenance Graph ProvGraph
Function ProvGraph(CTI^(t)):
    for i ∈ range(1, n) do
        for k ∈ range(1, K) do
            if NodeList doesn't exist then
                NodeList = [ ] ;      // Initialize node list if not exists
            end
            if ProvGraph doesn't exist then
                ProvGraph = [ ][ ] ; // Initialize empty provenance graph
            end
            if IP_s^(t)_{i,k} ∉ NodeList then
                Append IP_s^(t)_{i,k} to NodeList ;      // Add source node if new
            end
            if IP_t^(t)_{i,k} ∉ NodeList then
                Append IP_t^(t)_{i,k} to NodeList ;      // Add target node if new
            end
            src ← NodeList[IP_s^(t)_{i,k}] ;             // Get index of source node
            dst ← NodeList[IP_t^(t)_{i,k}] ;             // Get index of target node
            ProvGraph[src][dst] ← (IP_s^(t)_{i,k}, IP_t^(t)_{i,k}, T^(t)_{i,k}, Time^(t)_{i,k}, Label^(t)_{i,k}) ;
             // Add edge with attributes to graph
        end
    end
    return ProvGraph[src][dst] ;    // Return the constructed provenance
     graph
```

where $H(\cdot)$ denotes a hash function If the verification passes, it indicates that the alert record in $CTI_{i,k}^{(t)}$ is untampered. And the *Provgraph Contract* will be invoked and $CTI_{i,k}^{(t)}$ will be used to upload provenance graph.

Construction. When the *Provgraph Contract* receives all CTIs in current epoch, namely epoch t, the contract will first check the node list to determines whether the source IP of each CTI $CTI_{i,k}^{(t)}$ already exists in the node list. As shown in Algorithm 2, the node list stores all source IPs and destination IPs of all CTIs in the previous $t-1$ epoches. Each IP corresponds to a node in the provenance graph. If source IP $IP\_s_{i,k}^{(t)}$ in $CTI_{i,k}^{(t)}$ already exists in the node list, there is no need to add it. If $IP\_s_{i,k}^{(t)}$ don't exist in the node list, the contract adds it as a new node. Similarly, the contract checks whether the target IP $IP\_t_{i,k}^{(t)}$ exists, and if not, the target IP will be added as a new node.

Based on the node list, the contract constructs the provenance graph $G^{(t)}$. It represents $G^{(t)}$ using the adjacency matrix. The adjacency matrix is a two-dimensional array

$$\mathbf{ProvGraph} = [p_{ij}]_{n \times n}, \tag{11}$$

where each row represents source IP, each column represents target IP, and each element p_{ij} represents there is an edge pointing from $i - th$ source IP to $j - th$ target IP. If an edge exists, the contract will store the the associated attributes in p_{ij} as

$$p_{ij} = [IP\_s_{i,k}^{(t)}, IP\_t_{i,k}^{(t)}, T_{i,k}^{(t)}, Time_{i,k}^{(t)}, Label_{i,k}^{(t)}], \tag{12}$$

Finally, the contract saves the adjacency matrix *ProvGraph* to the blockchain ledger.

5.5 Subgraph Query

After the provenance graph is saved to the blockchain ledger, each host $host_i$ can query it. But for the host, downloading the complete provenance graph is a waste of bandwidth and memory, and querying the provenance subgraph G_{sub}^i related to it is sufficient. The provenance subgraph G_{sub}^i is defined as the k-hop subgraph centered on IP of $host_i$, namely IP_i. The provenance subgraph G_{sub}^i includes all nodes and edges that are within k hops from IP_i in the full provenance graph G. The hop refers to one step along an edge connecting two nodes. To extract this k-hop subgraph, generally a breadth-first search (BFS) algorithm is applied to the complete graph. BFS starts from the node representing IP_i and explores all its neighboring nodes (1-hop neighbors), then the neighbors of those neighbors (2-hop neighbors), and so on, until nodes at distance k are reached. This method efficiently collects all relevant nodes and edges within k hops, capturing the local context and interactions related to IP_i without the overhead of downloading the entire graph.

Specifically, if $host_i$ wants to query the subgraph G_{sub}^i related to itself, it can invoke the query function of the *Subgraph Contract* by sending a request with its IP IP_i as the center node and specifying the hop count k. After receiving this request, the *Subgraph Contract* initializes three key variables. The first one is the adjacency matrix of the provenance subgraph *SubGraph*, which is initially empty. The second one is the node set $NodeSet$, which initially contains only the center node IP_i. And the third one is the $Frontier$, a working set of nodes to be explored at the current depth, initially set to $\{IP_i\}$. Then the contract enters the breadth first traversal loop that continues until the traversal depth reaches k. In each loop, it creates an empty set $NextFrontier$ to hold nodes discovered at the this hop. For every node in the current $Frontier$, the contract queries its neighbors by querying the related nodes in *ProvGraph*. For each neighbor found, if it has not been visited before, which means it is not in $NodeSet$, it is added to both $NodeSet$ and $NextFrontier$. After processing all nodes in $Frontier$, the contract updates $Frontier$ to $NextFrontier$ and increments *depth* by one. This iterative process effectively performs a BFS starting from IP_i,

Algorithm 3: Subgraph Contract

```
Input: Center node IP_i, Hop count k, Provenance graph ProvGraph
Output: Provenance subgraph SubGraph
Function QuerySubgraph(IP_i, k, ProvGraph):
    SubGraph = [ ][ ]
    NodeSet ← {IP_i}
    Frontier ← {IP_i}
    depth ← 0
    while depth < k do
        NextFrontier ← ∅ ; // Initialize next layer nodes as empty set
        for node ∈ Frontier do
            // Get neighbors of current node (both outgoing and
               incoming edges)
            neighbors ←
              ProvGraph[node][ ].IP_t_{i,k}^{(t)} ∪ ProvGraph[ ][node].IP_s_{i,k}^{(t)}
            // Add edges connected to current node into the subgraph
            SubGraph ← ProvGraph[node][ ] ∪ ProvGraph[ ][node]
            for neighbor ∈ neighbors do
                if neighbor ∉ NodeSet then
                    NodeSet ← {neighbor} ; // Add new neighbor to visited
                      nodes
                    NextFrontier ← {neighbor} ;    // Add new neighbor to
                      next layer frontier
                end
            end
        end
        Frontier ← NextFrontier ;                    // Move to next layer
        depth ← depth + 1 ;                    // Increment depth counter
    end
    return SubGraph ;                 // Return the constructed subgraph
```

expanding outward layer by layer until reaching the specified k hops. Throughout the traversal, all visited nodes and their connecting edges are collected, forming a comprehensive k-hop provenance subgraph centered on IP_i. Finally, the *Subgraph Contract* returns *SubGraph* back to the requesting caller $host_i$.

6 Implementation and Evaluation

To demonstrate the feasibility of the proposed system, we implement the system using an open-source platform and conduct a series of simulations.

6.1 Experimental Setup

Implementation. The simulations are conducted mostly in the environment of Windows 11. The parts involving on-chain operations of blockchain are implemented using the Ubuntu 20.04.6 LTS system. We use the open-source platform

FISCO BCOS[1] to construct the blockchain network and execute the smart contracts written in the Solidity. We control the number of CTIs to test the performance of the *Provgraph Contract* in constructing the provenance graph. We control the number of subgraph's edges to test the performance of the *Subgraph Contract* in extracting the provenance subgraph. As for the CTI filter, we use Random Forest (RF) to train the classification model.

Datasets. We use the DARPA 1999 dataset[2] to conduct simulations. The DARPA 1999 dataset, which was created by the Defense Advanced Research Projects Agency, covers 58 typical attack methods across 5 major categories. It is currently one of the most comprehensive attack testing datasets and widely used in research fields. The original dataset contains three weeks of attack alert generated in simulated network environments. Here we use data of one week to conduct simulations. There are 1048576 alert records in total. And each record mainly contains five attributes, namely source, target, protocol type, time, and info.

6.2 Simulation Results

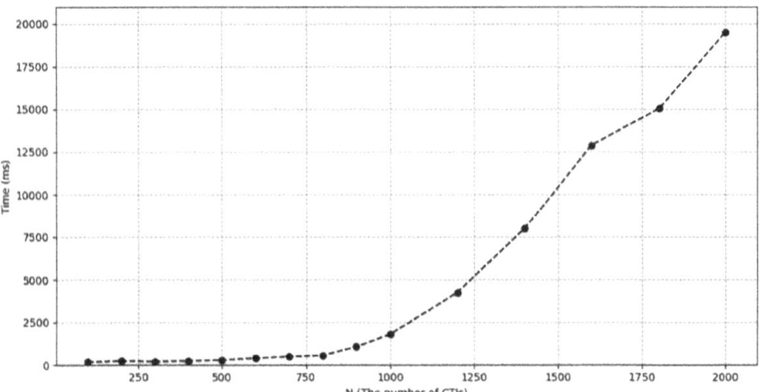

Fig. 3. The time for constructing the provenance graph as the number of CTIs varies.

The data processing speed of the smart contract is a key factor affecting the overall system efficiency. We conducted simulation experiments on constructing provenance graphs using CTIs. Since the *Provgraph Contract* uses adjacency matrices to store the provenance graphs, it consolidates all CTIs with the same source IP and destination IP into a single matrix variable, namely merging these CTIs as one edge. There are a total of 1048576 CTIs in the dataset. As shown in Table 1, the constructed provenance graph only has 754 nodes and 3352 edges.

[1] https://github.com/FISCO-BCOS/FISCO-BCOS.

[2] https://archive.ll.mit.edu/ideval/data/1999/training.

Let N denote the number of CTIs submitted to the *Provgraph Contract*. We vary the value of N and measure the corresponding time spent on constructing the provenance graph. As shown in Fig. 3, as the number of CTIs N increases, the time spent on constructing the provenance graph grows slowly. Specifically, when the number of CTIs increases from 100 to 800, the time increases linearly. And when the number of CTIs exceeds 800, the time grows exponentially.

Table 1. Subgraph size and extraction time statistics for random IPs under different settings of hop count k.

Center Node IP	Hop Count k	Number of Nodes	Number of Edges	Time (seconds)
	1	2	2	1.863
161.188.250.169	2	176	349	16.38
	3	204	1753	87.21
	1	2	2	1.827
151.193.131.5	2	176	349	15.93
	3	204	1753	86.78
	1	2	2	2.114
209.143.240.130	2	134	266	12.72
	3	156	1116	53.65
	1	3	4	2.424
129.63.122.196	2	258	572	28.17
	3	285	1779	88.51
	1	2	2	1.800
198.3.96.170	2	119	246	11.03
	3	144	1493	73.54

We else conducted simulations on extracting provenance subgraphs by using the *Subgraph Contract*. Let k denote the hop count of the provenance subgraph. We vary the value of k and measure the corresponding time spent on extracting provenance subgraphs of different center IPs. The central IP is randomly selected. As shown in Table 1, as the hop count k increases, the time spent on extracting the provenance subgraph grows exponentially. By selecting different central IPs, the size and structure of the provenance subgraph constructed are also different.

7 Conclusion

In this paper, we propose a cyberattack traceback system TraceBlock that leverages blockchain to overcome challenges in traditional cyberattack traceback systems. TraceBlock includes blockchain network and three off-chain modules, namely hosts, CTI filters, and oracles. Hosts generate alerts for constructing the provenance graph, and the oracle ensures their secure transmission to the blockchain network. The CTI filter uses a pre-trained model to identify CTIs. There are three smart contracts deployed on the blockchain. One of the smart contracts verifies the signature of CTI, the other uses CTIs to build provenance graphs and the last one extracts subgraphs. Simulation results show that the proposed smart contracts can finish the construction of provenance graph or the extraction of subgraph in a reasonable amount of time. In future study, we will optimize the underlying structure of system to improve efficiency.

Acknowledgements. This work was supported by National Defense Basic Scientific Research Program of China (No. JCKY2023602C026).

References

1. Lv, Y., Qin, S., Zhu, Z., Yu, Z., Li, S., Han, W.: A review of provenance graph based APT attack detection: applications and developments. In: 2022 7th IEEE International Conference on Data Science in Cyberspace (DSC), Guilin, China, pp. 498–505 (2022). https://doi.org/10.1109/DSC55868.2022.00075
2. Kaynar, K., Sivrikaya, F.: Distributed attack graph generation. IEEE Trans. Dependable Secure Comput. **13**(5), 519–532 (2015)
3. Ou, X., Boyer, W.F., McQueen, M.A.: A scalable approach to attack graph generation. In: Proceedings of the 13th ACM Conference on Computer and Communications Security (2006)
4. Nakamoto, S.: Bitcoin: a peer-to-peer electronic cash system. Satoshi Nakamoto (2008)
5. King, T., Chen, P.M.: Backtracking intrusions. In: Proceedings of the 19th ACM Symposium Operating System Principle, New York, NY, USA, pp. 223–236 (2003)
6. Hossain, M.N., Milajerdi, S.M., Wang, J.: SLEUTH: real-time attack scenario reconstruction from COTS audit data. In: Proceedings of USENIX Security, pp. 487–504 (2017)
7. Milajerdi, S.M., et al.: Poirot: aligning attack behavior with kernel audit records for cyber threat hunting. In: Proceedings of the 2019 ACM SIGSAC Conference on Computer and Communications Security (2019)
8. Milajerdi, S.M., et al.: Holmes: real-time apt detection through correlation of suspicious information flows. In: 2019 IEEE Symposium on Security and Privacy (SP). IEEE (2019)
9. Alsaheel, A., et al.: ATLAS: a sequence-based learning approach for attack investigation. In: 30th USENIX security symposium (USENIX security 21) (2021)
10. Liu, H., Wang, Y., Su, Z., Wang, Z., Pan, Y., Lit, R.: TRACEGADGET: detecting and tracing network level attack through federal provenance graph. In: ICC 2024 - IEEE International Conference on Communications, Denver, CO, USA, 2024, pp. 2713–2718 https://doi.org/10.1109/ICC51166.2024.10623080
11. Liang, X., Shetty, S., Tosh, D., Kamhoua, C., Kwiat, K., Njilla, L.: ProvChain: a blockchain-based data provenance architecture in cloud environment with enhanced privacy and availability. In: 17th IEEE/ACM International Symposium on Cluster, Cloud and Grid Computing (CCGRID). Madrid, Spain, vol. 2017, pp. 468–477 (2017). https://doi.org/10.1109/CCGRID.2017.8
12. Liu, D., et al.: Secure and efficient distributed network provenance for IoT: a blockchain-based approach. IEEE Internet Things J. **7**(8), 7564–7574 (2020)

13. Bose, R.J.C., et al.: Blinker: a blockchain-enabled framework for software provenance. In: 2019 26th Asia-Pacific Software Engineering Conference (APSEC). IEEE (2019)
14. Sun, L.-S., et al.: BSTProv: blockchain-based secure and trustworthy data provenance sharing. Electronics **11**(9), 1489 (2022)
15. Sun, S., Tang, H. and Du, R.: A novel blockchain-based IoT data provenance model. In: 2022 2nd International Conference on Computer Science and Blockchain (CCSB). IEEE (2022)
16. Sun, L., et al.: BPDAC: a blockchain based and provenance enabled dynamic access control scheme. IEEE Access **11**, 142552–142568 (2023)
17. Möller, D.P.F.: Threats and threat intelligence. Guide to cybersecurity in digital transformation: trends, methods, technologies, applications and best practices, pp. 71–129. Springer Nature Switzerland, Cham (2023). https://doi.org/10.1007/978-3-031-26845-8_1
18. Feig, E.: A framework for blockchain-based applications. arxiv preprint arxiv:1803.00892 (2018)
19. Damjan, M.: The interface between blockchain and the real world. Ragion Pratica **2**, 379–406 (2018)
20. Boneh, D., et al.: A survey of two signature aggregation techniques. RSA Cryptobytes **6**(2), 1–10 (2003)
21. Boneh, D., Lynn, B., Shacham, H.: Short signatures from the Weil pairing. In: International Conference on the Theory and Application of Cryptology and Information Security. Springer, Heidelberg (2001). https://doi.org/10.1007/3-540-45682-1_30
22. Boneh, D., Drijvers, M., Neven, G.: Bls multi-signatures with public-key aggregation (2018). https://crypto.stanford.edu/dabo/pubs/papers/BLSmultisig.html

CrossBuffer: Achieving Complete Atomicity for Cross-Chain Applications via Revocable State Buffering and Order-Preserving Conflict Resolution

Bohang Wei[1,2], Yang Yang[1], Fuyang Deng[1], Minghang Li[1], Qianhong Wu[1,2], and Bo Qin[3(✉)]

[1] School of Cyber Science and Technology, Beihang University, Beijing 100191, China
{bohang,y_yang,fuyang,liminghang,qianhong.wu}@buaa.edu.cn
[2] Hangzhou Innovation Institute, Beihang University, Zhejiang 310051, China
[3] School of Information, Renmin University of China, Beijing 100872, China
bo.qin@ruc.edu.cn

Abstract. Cross-chain interoperability has emerged as a critical requirement for blockchain ecosystems, enabling applications to coordinate operations across heterogeneous networks while requiring robust atomicity guarantees to prevent partial failures. Existing cross-chain protocols either impose expensive state rollback costs when transactions abort, or employ bilateral abortion strategies that cascade failures across chains, both degrading system performance under concurrent execution while lacking principled mechanisms for maintaining causal dependencies among related transactions. This paper presents CrossBuffer, a protocol achieving complete atomicity for cross-chain transactions through three synergistic mechanisms that collectively address these limitations. First, revocable state buffering introduces managed queues before on-chain persistence, maintaining cross-chain states as revocable until consensus to achieve atomicity without rollback overhead. Second, unilateral conflict reordering resolves cross-chain conflicts through age-based priority management, transforming bilateral abortion into optimistic single-sided adjustment to ensure system availability under high-conflict scenarios. Third, causal dependency preservation maintains dependency ordering through DAG-based modeling and constraint propagation, preventing descendant transactions from committing before predecessors regardless of conflict-induced reorderings. Implementation on Cosmos blockchain infrastructure and experimental evaluation CrossBuffer's operational viability, successfully coordinating concurrent conflicts and dependency chains while maintaining bounded abortion rates and resource consumption under varying workload intensities.

Keywords: Cross-chain · Interoperability · atomicity

W. Meng et al. (Eds.): ASSS 2025, CCIS 2903, pp. 35–53, 2026.
https://doi.org/10.1007/978-3-032-21600-7_3

1 Introduction

Blockchain interoperability has emerged as a fundamental enabler for decentralized ecosystems, facilitating seamless interactions across heterogeneous blockchain networks [1,2]. Cross-chain decentralized applications (dApps) have evolved from simple asset transfers [3] to sophisticated multi-party workflows involving complex state transitions across multiple blockchains [4,5]. This evolution extends the applicability of cross-chain systems to diverse domains including supply chain management [6], metaverse environments [7], and decentralized finance [8].

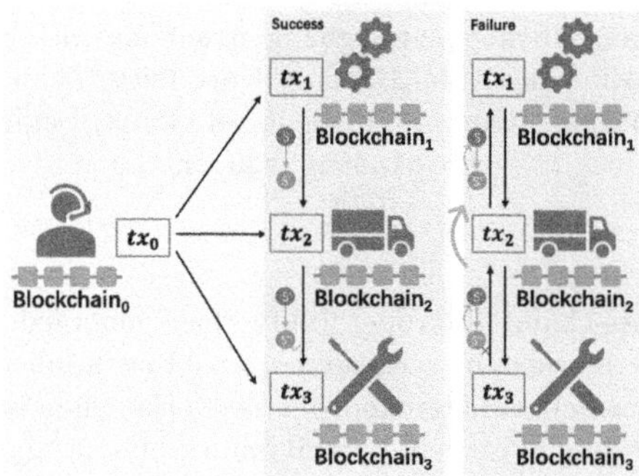

Fig. 1. Complete atomicity in cross-chain

Ensuring atomicity in cross-chain transaction execution is critical for maintaining application correctness. Consider a cross-chain supply chain dApp depicted in Fig. 1, where a manufacturing order issued by Party A requires the coordinated production of multiple components across different suppliers, each operating their own blockchain. The order is decomposed into dependent subtasks tx_1, tx_2, and tx_3, where tx_2 depends on the output of tx_1 (e.g., component specifications), and tx_3 requires results from tx_2 (e.g., assembly instructions). Each subtask execution triggers state transitions $S \rightarrow S'$ on its respective blockchain, recording production progress, resource allocation, and quality certificates. If subtask tx_3 fails due to resource unavailability or quality issues, the entire manufacturing order must be cancelled atomically. However, previous subtasks tx_1 and tx_2 have already modified persistent states on Blockchain$_1$ and Blockchain$_2$, creating inconsistent execution traces where partial work is recorded despite order cancellation. Traditional *financial atomicity* [3,4] addresses this by refunding transferred assets but cannot revert state modifications representing completed manufacturing steps, quality certifications, or resource commitments. In contrast, *complete atomicity* requires that either all state transitions ($S \rightarrow S'$) commit successfully across all participating blockchains, or the system maintains the initial state S everywhere as if no execution occurred, ensuring end-to-end correctness for complex cross-chain workflows.

Existing blockchain interoperability solutions fall short in three critical aspects. First, prior work achieves financial atomicity through compensatory refunds [3,4], which cannot undo complex state updates in smart contracts. Recent attempts at complete atomicity [9] employ checkpoint-based rollback mechanisms that incur additional consensus overhead and compromise correctness when concurrent transactions read intermediate states. Second, conflict resolution strategies adopt bilateral abortion [10] or pessimistic locking [9], severely limiting throughput in high-concurrency scenarios where multiple cross-chain executions contend for shared resources. Third, existing approaches lack explicit mechanisms to preserve causal dependencies in multi-step workflows, failing to guarantee execution ordering when parent transactions are delayed or reordered.

To address these limitations, we present CrossBuffer, a cross-chain transaction execution framework that achieves complete atomicity through three synergistic innovations. First, we introduce a queue-based state buffering mechanism that defers blockchain persistence until global consensus is reached, enabling efficient abort-by-removal without expensive rollback operations. Second, we propose a unilateral reordering strategy with age-based compensation that resolves concurrency conflicts by deprioritizing contending transactions rather than aborting them bilaterally, significantly improving system throughput. Third, we design a DAG-based dependency tracking mechanism that maintains causal consistency by enforcing parent-child ordering constraints and propagating reordering decisions throughout the dependency graph. Our main contributions are as follows:

- **Revocable State Buffering.** We design a queue-based state buffering commitment mechanism that caches tentative cross-chain state transitions and commits them to blockchain for persistent storage only when the cross-chain task is confirmed to execute successfully, achieving complete atomicity without incurring rollback overhead on committed states.
- **Unilateral Conflict Reordering.** We propose a unilateral reordering mechanism that resolves cross-chain concurrency conflicts through age compensation and priority adjustment instead of bilateral abortion, significantly improving transaction throughput while preserving serializability guarantees.
- **Causal Dependency Preservation.** We design a DAG-based dependency tracking mechanism that maintains causal consistency across complex multi-step cross-chain workflows by enforcing parent-child ordering constraints and propagating reordering effects throughout the dependency graph.

We implement CrossBuffer as smart contracts in the Cosmos ecosystem and conduct comprehensive evaluations under various workloads and conflict scenarios. The experimental results demonstrate that CrossBuffer achieves practical gas and latency while maintaining low abort rates, validating the effectiveness of our design.

2 Related Work

Cross-chain interoperability has been pursued through diverse architectural approaches. Academic solutions employ relay-based [2] or light client verification [6] mechanisms to enable authenticated state transmission between heterogeneous blockchains. Industrial systems like Cosmos [15] utilize the Inter-Blockchain Communication (IBC) protocol for cross-chain message passing, while Polkadot [11] employs a shared security model through parachains and a central relay chain. Hyperledger Cactus [12] provides a plugin-based architecture supporting multiple blockchain platforms. Despite architectural differences, ensuring atomicity remains fundamental to maintaining correctness in cross-chain transaction execution.

A recent systematic review [13] categorizes cross-chain atomicity guarantees into three levels: Financial Atomicity (FA), which prevents monetary loss; Semantic Atomicity (SA), which uses compensation logic; and Complete Atomicity (CA), which ensures either all state transitions commit or none occur. Early work focused on FA through Hashed Time-Lock Contracts (HTLCs) [3,14] and escrow-based mechanisms [8], effectively handling asset swaps but unable to revert arbitrary smart contract state modifications. HyperService [4] introduced programmable cross-chain workflows with FA via insurance contracts, yet still lacks state rollback capabilities. Recent attempts at CA include Avalon [10], which employs layered state commitment to defer persistence, and the checkpoint-based approach by Lu et al. [9], which triggers rollback through additional consensus rounds. However, existing CA solutions suffer from either high overhead in conflict scenarios or inability to handle high-concurrency workloads efficiently.

Concurrency control mechanisms in cross-chain systems largely adopt strategies from distributed databases. Optimistic Concurrency Control (OCC) [16] validates conflicts at commit time, minimized locking overhead. OmniLedger [17] applies OCC within blockchain sharding to handle intra-shard conflicts, while approaches using Two-Phase Commit (2PC) with pessimistic locking [18,19] coordinate cross-chain transactions but incur significant latency from lock acquisition. He-HTLC [20] addresses conflicts in pairwise token transfers through bilateral abortion upon detecting concurrent operations, a strategy that degrades throughput under contention.

Dependency management in distributed workflows has been explored through Saga patterns [21] for long-running transactions and Business Process Model and Notation (BPMN) [13] for workflow orchestration. Directed Acyclic Graphs (DAGs) model task dependencies in systems like Apache Airflow, but their application to cross-chain execution ordering remains limited. Existing cross-chain protocols either assume sequential execution [4] or lack explicit mechanisms to preserve causal consistency when parent transactions are reordered or aborted (Table 1).

These limitations reveal three critical gaps in existing cross-chain atomicity solutions. First, state management approaches either sacrifice completeness (FA-based refunds and insurance) or incur prohibitive overhead (checkpoint roll-

Table 1. Comparison of Cross-Chain Atomicity Approaches

Approach	Decentral	Atomicity Type	Rollback Method	Concurrency Control	Conflict Strategy	Ordering
HTLC [3]	Full	FA	Refund	N/A	N/A	No
HyperService [4]	Partial	FA	Insurance	Serial	N/A	Sequential
2PC+Lock [18]	Coordinator	CA	Undo Log	Pessimistic	Locking	No
He-HTLC [20]	Full	FA	Refund	Optimistic	Bilateral Abort	No
Lu et al. [9]	Coordinator	CA	Checkpoint	Pessimistic	Locking	No
Avalon [10]	Full	CA	Layer Removal	Optimistic	Bilateral Abort	No

back requiring additional consensus rounds, undo logs necessitating distributed coordination). Second, conflict resolution strategies universally resort to transaction abortion—whether bilateral or coordinated through locking—degrading throughput under contention. Third, no prior work provides explicit dependency-track execution ordering, risking causality violations in multi-step workflows where parent transactions may be delayed or reordered. These gaps motivate CrossBuffer's design: achieving complete atomicity through lightweight state buffering that defers persistence without rollback overhead, resolving conflicts via unilateral reordering with age-based prioritization to reduce aborts, and maintaining causal consistency through DAG-based dependency tracking to preserve execution ordering across complex workflows.

3 Preliminaries and Models

3.1 Atomicity

Cross-chain transaction atomicity encompasses three levels of guarantees [13]. *Financial Atomicity (FA)* ensures that monetary transfers either complete fully or participants suffer no financial loss through compensatory refunds. *Semantic Atomicity (SA)* employs application-specific compensation logic to undo effects of partially executed workflows. *Complete Atomicity (CA)* guarantees that either all state transitions commit across participating blockchains, or the system reverts to its initial state as if no execution occurred.

Formally, let τ_i^j denote the state of blockchain Π_i at version j. A cross-chain execution E^{id} involving transactions on blockchains Π_i and $\Pi_{i'}$ triggers state transitions $\tau_i^j \xrightarrow{id} \tau_i^{j+1}$ and $\tau_{i'}^{j'} \xrightarrow{id} \tau_{i'}^{j'+1}$. We define:

Definition 1 (*Atomic State Transition*). Given state pair $(\tau_i^j, \tau_{i'}^{j'})$ accessed by E^{id}, atomic state transition holds if both transitions $\tau_i^j \xrightarrow{id} \tau_i^{j+1}$ and $\tau_{i'}^{j'} \xrightarrow{id} \tau_{i'}^{j'+1}$ eventually apply, or neither applies.

Definition 2 (*Serializable Atomic State Transition*). Given concurrent executions $\mathcal{E} = \{E^a, E^{a+1}, \ldots, E^{a'}\}$, if all executions satisfy atomic state transition and all blockchains commit state transitions in an identical serializable order, then $\mathcal{E}$ achieves serializable atomic state transition.

Complete atomicity extends financial atomicity by requiring *no state modifications* persist upon failure, rather than merely ensuring no financial loss despite state changes.

3.2 Causal Consistency

Causal consistency formalizes the intuitive notion that causally related operations must be observed in the same order by all participants [22]. The *happened-before* relation ($\rightarrow$) defines potential causality: (1) if events a and b occur in the same process with a preceding b, then $a \rightarrow b$; (2) if a is a message send and b its receipt, then $a \rightarrow b$; (3) transitivity: if $a \rightarrow b$ and $b \rightarrow c$, then $a \rightarrow c$. Events are *concurrent* if neither $a \rightarrow b$ nor $b \rightarrow a$ holds.

Definition 3 (*Causal Consistency*). A system provides causal consistency if for all causally related operations $op_1 \rightarrow op_2$, every process observes op_1 before op_2. Concurrent operations may be observed in different orders by different processes.

In cross-chain dApps with multi-step workflows, causal consistency ensures execution ordering integrity. When transaction tx_2 depends on outputs from tx_1 (i.e., $tx_1 \rightarrow tx_2$), all blockchains must process tx_1's state transitions before tx_2's, preventing inconsistencies from out-of-order execution.

3.3 System Model

Goal. This paper aims to achieve complete atomicity for cross-chain dApp executions while preserving causal consistency across dependent transactions, maintaining these properties even under concurrent execution scenarios.

Blockchain Infrastructure. We assume a finite collection of m heterogeneous blockchains $\Pi_1, \Pi_2, \ldots, \Pi_m$, each implementing Byzantine State Machine Replication (SMR) [23]. Each blockchain Π_i operates with a fault-tolerant consensus protocol tolerating Byzantine failures, ensuring:

- *Safety.* If two honest replicas output values v and v' at the same sequence number, then $v = v'$.
- *Liveness.* If a client submits request m, all honest replicas output m eventually.

Consensus protocols may follow synchronous, partially synchronous, or asynchronous timing assumptions. Blockchains can be permissionless or permissioned, each maintaining an immutable ledger of transactions and resulting state transitions. We assume adversaries can corrupt replicas and coordinate Byzantine behavior, drop or reorder network messages, but cannot violate the safety and liveness guarantees of the underlying SMR protocols.

Cross-Chain Execution Model. A cross-chain execution E^{id} consists of k dependent transactions $E^{id} = \{tx_i^{id} \mid i = 1, 2, \ldots, k\}$, where each tx_i^{id} executes on blockchain Π_i. Dependencies form a Directed Acyclic Graph (DAG)

$G = (V, E)$, where vertices V represent transactions and edges E encode pre-conditioning requirements. An edge $(tx_i^{id}, tx_j^{id}) \in E$ indicates tx_j^{id} depends on outputs from tx_i^{id}.

Cross-Chain Communication. Reliable authenticated communication between blockchains is provided by a Cross-Chain Communication (CCC) primitive satisfying:

- *Authenticity.* If transaction tx finalizes on source blockchain Π_s, any replica on destination blockchain Π_d can verify the state transitions via cryptographic finality proofs.
- *Reliability.* If tx finalizes on Π_s, all honest replicas in Π_d eventually receive and verify the finality proof.

CCC exposes two interfaces:

`CCC.route`$(src, dst, data)$ allows any process to submit finalized data from source src to destination dst;

`CCC.deliver`$(src, dst, data)$ enables verification of routed data authenticity at the destination. These abstractions encapsulate relay-based or light-client verification mechanisms [2,15] (Fig. 2).

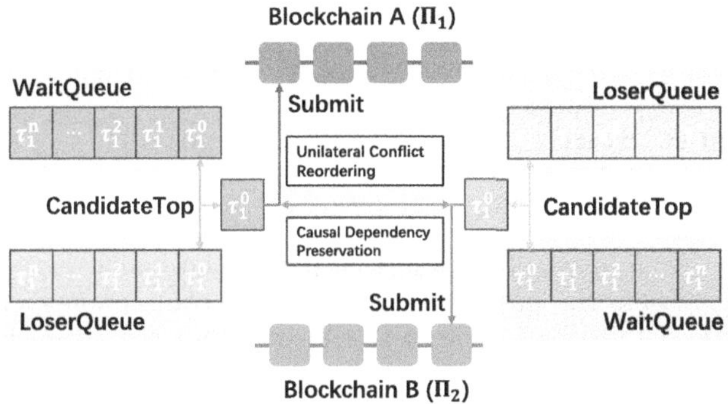

Fig. 2. Architecture of CrossBuffer

4 CrossBuffer Design

4.1 Revocable State Buffering

CrossBuffer introduces a state buffering mechanism before commitment to achieve complete atomicity without rollback overhead. The core insight is to maintain tentative state transitions in a managed queue structure rather than persisting them immediately to blockchain storage. Only after all participating blockchains confirm successful execution through authenticated proofs does the system commit buffered states to the permanent ledger. Failed executions simply result in queue removal without touching persistent storage, eliminating the

Algorithm 1. Revocable State Buffering (at blockchain Π_i)

1: **Init:**
2: $waitQueue \leftarrow \emptyset$; $round \leftarrow 0$; $committed \leftarrow \tau_i^0$
3: **function** EXECUTE(tx_i^{id}, ID)
4: $s \leftarrow$ transition($committed, tx_i^{id}$) // Apply transaction logic
5: $s.eid \leftarrow ID.eid$; $s.wait\_ok \leftarrow 0$; $s.birth\_round \leftarrow \bot$
6: $waitQueue$.enqueue(s) // Buffer tentative state
7: **emit** `CCC.route`(Π_i, allChains, ($\pi_{tx_i^{id}}, s.eid$))
8: **upon** event `CCC.deliver`(src, Π_i, ($\pi_{tx_{src}^{id}}, ID$))
9: $s \leftarrow waitQueue$.find($ID.eid$); $s.proofs \leftarrow s.proofs \cup \{src\}$
10: **if** $|s.proofs| = |ID.chains|$ **then**
11: $s.wait\_ok \leftarrow 1$ // Proofs collection complete
12: **if** $s = waitQueue$.peek() $\wedge$ $s.birth\_round = \bot$ **then**
13: $s.birth\_round \leftarrow round$ // Mark eligibility start
14: **end upon**
15: **function** ATTEMPTCOMMIT
16: $head \leftarrow waitQueue$.peek()
17: **if** $head.wait\_ok = 1$ **then**
18: $committed \leftarrow waitQueue$.dequeue() // Persist to storage
19: $round \leftarrow round + 1$
20: **emit** `CCC.route`(Π_i, allChains, (COMMIT, $head.eid$))
21: **function** CHECKTIMEOUTS
22: $s \leftarrow waitQueue$.peek(); $s.tries\_wait \leftarrow s.tries\_wait + 1$
23: **if** ($s.wait\_ok = 0 \wedge s.tries\_wait \geq L_{wait}$) $\vee$ $s.age \geq R$ **then**
24: $waitQueue$.dequeue()
25: **emit** `CCC.route`(Π_i, allChains, (ABORT, $s.eid$))

need for expensive rollback operations that plague checkpoint-based approaches. Algorithm 1 presents the protocol logic, omitting transaction-specific business logic and some details for brevity while focusing on the atomicity guarantee design.

The protocol operates on a FIFO queue *waitQueue* that buffers all tentative state transitions awaiting cross-chain confirmation. Each blockchain initializes with an empty queue, a committed state τ_i^0 representing the current persistent ledger state, and a global round counter *round* starting at zero (lines 1–2). The round counter increments with each successful commitment, providing a logical timeline for age-based prioritization in subsequent conflict resolution. Each candidate s in the queue carries metadata: a unique execution identifier $eid(s)$, a Boolean flag $wait\_ok(s)$ indicating whether all finality proofs have been collected, and $birth\_round(s)$ recording when the candidate first became eligible for commitment.

When transaction tx_i^{id} executes (lines 3–7), the system applies its business logic to produce a state transition s based on the most recent committed state (line 4). Rather than persisting immediately, the candidate initializes with $wait\_ok = 0$ and undefined $birth\_round = \bot$, then enqueues to *waitQueue* (lines 5–6). The blockchain generates a finality proof $\pi_{tx_i^{id}}$ certifying that tx_i^{id} has been executed and finalized through consensus, then broadcasts this proof to all participating chains via CCC (lines 7).

Upon receiving a finality proof from a remote chain (lines 8–14), the system locates the corresponding candidate and accumulates the proof in its collection set (line 9). Once proofs from all $|ID.chains|$ blockchains arrive (line 10), the candidate's $wait\_ok$ flag transitions to true (line 11), signaling readiness for commitment. If this candidate is at the queue head and has not yet been assigned a birth round, the protocol records the current $round$ as its $birth\_round$ (lines 13), marking the moment it became a valid commitment candidate.

The commitment logic (lines 15–20) enforces strict queue-head discipline: only the head candidate with $wait\_ok = 1$ can commit. When the head satisfies this condition (line 17), the protocol dequeues the state transition and persists it to permanent storage (line 18), increments the global round counter (line 19), and broadcasts a COMMIT message to all chains (line 20), notifying them to synchronize their commitment. This FIFO ordering ensures that state transitions commit in their execution sequence, maintaining temporal consistency across blockchains.

The timeout detection function (lines 21–25) implements liveness guarantees: when the head candidate fails to collect complete proofs within the lifetime threshold R rounds, or remains blocked at the queue head for more than L_{wait} consecutive rounds (line 23), the protocol removes the candidate (line 24) and broadcasts ABORT messages to all participating chains (lines 25) to trigger coordinated cleanup, ensuring liveness while preventing indefinite blocking.

By buffering tentative states until cross-chain consensus materializes, CrossBuffer achieves complete atomicity through selective commitment rather than compensatory rollback. Failed executions result in ephemeral queue removals that never touch persistent storage, fundamentally eliminating rollback overhead and enabling efficient abort-by-removal semantics.

4.2 Unilateral Conflict Reordering

While the buffering mechanism in Sect. 4.1 ensures complete atomicity for serial executions, practical deployments involve concurrent cross-chain transactions that introduce inter-chain conflicts when different blockchains commit conflicting state transitions in divergent orders. Existing approaches resolve such conflicts through bilateral abortion, where both parties abort upon detecting ordering inconsistencies, leading to cascading aborts and reduced throughput. CrossBuffer addresses this challenge by extending the buffering mechanism with a unilateral conflict reordering strategy inspired by optimistic concurrency control. Rather than bilateral abortion, the protocol unilaterally reorders the losing candidate into a priority queue ($loserQueue$) while preserving the winner's path, maintaining high concurrency through a dual-queue architecture where age-based prioritization enables fine-grained conflict resolution without sacrificing atomicity.

Algorithm 2 formalizes the conflict reordering protocol. Beyond *waitQueue* from Algorithm 1, each blockchain maintains a *loserQueue* priority heap storing reordered candidates and a $loserWinStreak$ counter tracking consecutive loser queue commitments to implement quota-based fairness, preventing indefinite starvation of the main queue(line 2). Each candidate s carries additional metadata: $earliest\_round(s)$ specifies the minimum eligible round (initialized to current $round$), and $tie(s)$ provides deterministic conflict resolution via hash over execution and chain identifiers. The *loserQueue* prioritizes candidates by lexicographic tuple $(age(s), isLoser = 1, tie(s))$ where $age(s) = round - birth\_round(s)$, ensuring older candidates receive preference with deterministic tiebreaking.

The protocol enforces single-candidate discipline through $candidateTop$ selection (lines 3–8). At each round, only one candidate may broadcast OK messages. The selection function first checks whether *waitQueue*'s head satisfies three criteria: complete proofs ($wait\_ok = 1$), temporal readiness ($round \geq earliest\_round$), and quota compliance ($loserWinStreak < K$) (lines 4–6). If satisfied, the head becomes $candidateTop$; otherwise, the protocol selects from *loserQueue* by extracting the highest-priority eligible candidate (lines 7–8). This ensures no concurrent conflicting OK messages originate from the same blockchain.

Upon receiving an OK message from a remote blockchain indicating its $candidateTop$ selection (lines 9–19), the local blockchain compares this remote choice against its own $candidateTop$ to detect inter-chain conflicts (line 11). When different blockchains select divergent candidates for commitment in the same round, a conflict arises. Rather than bilateral abortion, CrossBuffer performs unilateral reordering by age-based prioritization: the local blockchain removes the loser candidate, and reinserts it into *loserQueue* with age compensation Δ (lines 12–15). Setting $earliest\_round \leftarrow round + \Delta$ creates a cooling-off period preventing immediate re-conflict while preserving fairness (line 14). The blockchain broadcasts a tentative ABORT message to all participants signaling the conflict resolution outcome (lines 16). When there is no inter-chain conflicts, the system commits and updates structures based on queue source. Winners from *waitQueue* reset $loserWinStreak$ to zero (lines 23–25), while winners from *loserQueue* increment it (lines 26–28), implementing quota-based fairness that prevents loser monopolization. All surviving candidates age by one round capped at $R - 1$ (line 29), maintaining priority evolution.

Timeout handling extends to queue-head blocking (lines 30–37). When the head lacks proofs and exceeds L_{wait} consecutive waits (line 32), the protocol reorders it into *loserQueue* with compensation rather than immediate abortion (lines 33–34), allowing subsequent candidates to progress. Candidates exceeding lifetime R are removed with ABORT broadcasts for garbage collection (lines 35–37).

Through unilateral reordering, CrossBuffer transforms bilateral abortion into optimistic single-sided adjustment, achieving high concurrency while age-based prioritization, quota mechanisms, and deterministic tiebreaking ensure fairness,

Algorithm 2. Unilateral Conflict Reordering (at blockchain Π_i)

```
Init:
    waitQueue ← ∅; loserQueue ← ∅; loserWinStreak ← 0
function SELECTCANDIDATETOP
    top_w ← waitQueue.peek()
    if top_w ≠ ⊥ ∧ top_w.wait_ok = 1 ∧ round ≥ top_w.earliest_round then
        if loserWinStreak < K then return top_w
    top_l ← loserQueue.topByPriority()
    if top_l ≠ ⊥ ∧ round ≥ top_l.earliest_round then return top_l
    return ⊥
upon event CCC.deliver(src, Π_i, (OK, ID))
    remoteTop ← ID.eid
    if candidateTop ≠ ⊥ ∧ candidateTop.eid ≠ remoteTop then
        loser ← arg min_{x∈{candidateTop, remoteTop}}(x.age, x.isLoser, x.tie)
        loser.removeFrom(waitQueue ∪ loserQueue)
        loser.earliest_round ← round + Δ
        loserQueue.insert(loser)
        emit CCC.route(Π_i, allChains, (t-ABORT, loser.eid))
    else
        // Accumulate OK vote for execution remoteTop
end upon
function ATTEMPTCOMMIT
    candidateTop ← SELECTCANDIDATETOP()
    if candidateTop ≠ ⊥ ∧ allOKsReceived(candidateTop.eid) then
        if candidateTop ∈ waitQueue then
            loserWinStreak ← 0
            waitQueue.remove(candidateTop)
        else
            loserWinStreak ← loserWinStreak + 1
            loserQueue.remove(candidateTop)
        incrementAllAges()                    // Age all remaining candidates
function CHECKTIMEOUTS
    s ← waitQueue.peek(); s.tries_wait ← s.tries_wait + 1
    if s.wait_ok = 0 ∧ s.tries_wait ≥ L_wait then
        waitQueue.remove(s); s.earliest_round ← round + Δ
        loserQueue.insert(s)
    else if s.age ≥ R then
        waitQueue.remove(s)
        for dst ∈ s.eid.chains do emit CCC.route(Π_i, dst, (ABORT, s.eid))
```

prevent starvation, and maintain consistency across all blockchains without additional coordination.

4.3 Causal Dependency Preservation

The conflict reordering mechanism from Sect. 4.2 introduces causality violation risks when dependent executions exist. If execution E_a loses a conflict and enters *loserQueue* while its dependent E_b proceeds to commitment, the system commits E_b before its prerequisite E_a, violating causal consistency. CrossBuffer addresses this by modeling application workflows as directed acyclic graphs (DAGs) where edges represent causal dependencies, then extending eligibility criteria with a pending input counter *pend_in* that prevents descendants from committing before ancestors regardless of queue placement.

Algorithm 3 shows the dependency preservation protocol. Each candidate extends its state with three fields capturing DAG topology: *parents* stores references to causal predecessors, *children* maintains dependent successors to enable downstream notification, and *pend_in* counts uncommitted ancestors blocking eligibility (lines 1–2). When establishing dependencies, the protocol creates bidirectional linkage by simultaneously updating both the parent's children set and the child's parents set while incrementing the child's pending counter (lines 3–6). This symmetric design proves crucial for efficient propagation in both directions. The dependency-track selection logic integrates seamlessly with Sect. 4.2's candidate competition by adding $pend\_in = 0$ as a fourth eligibility criterion alongside proof completion, temporal readiness, and quota compliance (lines 7–10). This zero-pending-input requirement ensures that no candidate can become *candidateTop* while any ancestor remains uncommitted, elegantly preventing premature commitment through a simple counter check rather than expensive DAG traversals at selection time. When reordering a candidate s into *loserQueue* with adjusted *earliest_round*, the system immediately propagates this temporal displacement to all direct children by elevating any child's eligibility round that would otherwise allow premature competition (lines 11–17). This transitive propagation naturally extends across arbitrary DAG depths: when a grandparent is reordered, the parent's *earliest_round* increases, triggering child updates, which in turn may trigger grandchild adjustments through recursive application. The mechanism requires no explicit multi-hop traversal; instead, each reordering operation updates immediate children, and subsequent reorderings of those children automatically propagate constraints deeper into the dependency graph. Conversely, commitment triggers progressive unlocking by decrementing each child's *pend_in* counter (lines 18–22), enabling descendants to participate in competition as soon as all their prerequisites complete. This design achieves elegant causality preservation: dependent executions flow in correct order regardless of queue reordering events, while the age-based prioritization and unilateral conflict resolution from previous sections continue operating unimpeded, maintaining both semantic correctness and high throughput for complex workflows.

Through DAG modeling and transitive constraint propagation, CrossBuffer achieves both high concurrency and semantic correctness for complex multi-transaction workflows.

5 Correctness Analysis

CrossBuffer's correctness hinges on two fundamental properties: complete atomicity ensuring all-or-nothing commitment across blockchains, and causal consistency preserving dependency-induced ordering constraints. We formalize these

Algorithm 3. Causal Dependency Preservation (at blockchain Π_i)

```
Candidate Metadata Extension:
    s.parents ← ∅; s.children ← ∅; s.pend_in ← 0
function ESTABLISHDEPENDENCY(child, parent)
    child.parents ← child.parents ∪ {parent}
    parent.children ← parent.children ∪ {child}
    child.pend_in ← child.pend_in + 1
function SELECTCANDIDATETOP
    head ← waitQueue.peek()
    if head ≠ ⊥ ∧ head.wait_ok = 1 ∧ head.pend_in = 0 then
        if round ≥ head.earliest_round ∧ loserWinStreak < K then return head
    return selectFromLoserQueue()                    // With pend_in = 0 check
function REORDERWITHDEPENDENCY(s)
    s.removeFrom(waitQueue ∪ loserQueue)
    s.earliest_round ← round + Δ
    loserQueue.insert(s)
    for c ∈ s.children do                            // Propagate delay to dependents
        if c.earliest_round < s.earliest_round then
            c.earliest_round ← s.earliest_round
function ONCOMMIT(s)
    // Remove s from queue and commit state
    for c ∈ s.children do
        c.pend_in ← c.pend_in − 1                    // Enable child if ready
    incrementAllAges()
```

properties building upon the definitions established in Sect. 3, then outline proof strategies demonstrating CrossBuffer's guarantees under the dual-queue architecture with unilateral conflict reordering and DAG-based dependency preservation.

Complete Atomicity. Given a finite set of concurrent executions $\mathcal{E} = \{E_a, E_{a+1}, \ldots, E_{a'}\}$ executing across m blockchains $\Pi_1, \Pi_2, \ldots, \Pi_m$, CrossBuffer ensures that for any pair of blockchains, $\mathcal{E}$ eventually triggers serializable atomic state transitions—meaning either all participating blockchains commit a consistent subset $\mathcal{E}' \subseteq \mathcal{E}$ in identical order while aborting the remainder, or no state transitions occur. The proof strategy proceeds by contradiction through two cases: first establishing atomicity for isolated executions where commitment requires unanimous OK messages across all chains (any abortion message triggers coordinated cleanup via CCC reliability), then extending to concurrent scenarios where the single-candidate discipline enforced by *candidateTop* selection prevents conflicting OK broadcasts within each blockchain, while age-based prioritization in *loserQueue* ensures deterministic conflict resolution converges to consistent outcomes across all participants despite unilateral reordering.

Causal Consistency. For executions with declared dependencies forming a DAG $G = (V, E)$ where vertices represent executions and edges denote causal prerequisites, CrossBuffer guarantees that if execution E_b depends on E_a (i.e., $(E_a, E_b) \in E$), then E_a commits before E_b on all blockchains or both abort.

The proof leverages the *pend_in* counter mechanism: a candidate cannot achieve *candidateTop* status while any ancestor remains uncommitted ($pend\_in > 0$), and reordering operations transitively propagate *earliest_round* constraints through the children set, creating temporal barriers that prevent descendants from premature competition. This establishes a happens-before relation respecting the DAG topology regardless of queue placement or conflict-induced reorderings.

Detailed formal proofs of both properties appear in Appendix A, demonstrating that CrossBuffer's protocol design satisfies correctness under the assumptions of secure SMR-based blockchains and reliable authenticated cross-chain communication.

6 Implementation

We implement CrossBuffer within the Cosmos ecosystem, which provides modular infrastructure for deploying interconnected blockchains. The implementation leverages CosmWasm's smart contract environment to encode protocol logic without altering underlying blockchain code, while IBC's message relay capabilities fulfill the authenticated cross-chain communication requirements that CrossBuffer's coordination mechanisms depend upon. This development approach enables rapid prototyping and evaluation across multiple chain configurations without requiring modifications to core consensus implementations.

Our implementation instantiates m interoperable Cosmos blockchains, each running a CrossBuffer smart contract as the cross-chain coordination module alongside application-specific dApp contracts simulating business logic. The architecture separates concerns between protocol orchestration and application execution.

During operation, transactions are submitted to their respective blockchain's CrossBuffer module, which invokes the corresponding dApp contract to compute state transitions. The CrossBuffer module then manages these transitions through the dual-queue buffering algorithm, enforces conflict resolution via unilateral reordering with age-based prioritization, and maintains causal dependencies through DAG-based consistency preservation mechanisms. Cross-chain finality proofs and coordination messages exchange via IBC channels, enabling the protocol to achieve complete atomicity and causal consistency across this environment. The implementation validates CrossBuffer's feasibility while providing a foundation for performance evaluation under realistic blockchain consensus and network conditions.

7 Evaluation

7.1 Experimental Setup

The evaluation was conducted on an INSPUR SA5212 server equipped with two Intel Xeon Gold 6230 CPUs (20 cores, 2.10 GHz), 24×32 GB DDR4 RAM modules (2666 MHz), and two 960 GB solid-state drives. We deployed varying numbers of Cosmos blockchain instances (3, 6, and 9 chains) to assess CrossBuffer's behavior under different coordination scales. Each blockchain instance runs with Tendermint consensus configured for persistent storage using LevelDB, with relay infrastructure handling IBC message routing between chains.

The experimental workload simulates realistic concurrent conflict scenarios by varying the transaction submission interval from 10 to 60 s while injecting random delays under 5 s at client submission points to introduce temporal overlap. To evaluate dependency preservation mechanisms, we randomly inject 3 to 5 dependent transactions within every 10 transactions, where dependencies follow sequential ordering constraints reflecting common application patterns such as token transfers followed by purchases. We measure three key metrics: transaction latency from submission to final commitment, abortion rate indicating the fraction of transactions removed due to conflicts or timeouts, and gas consumption reflecting the computational cost of protocol operations including queue management and cross-chain message exchange.

7.2 Performance Analysis

The experimental results across Figs. 3a, 3b, and 3c reveal consistent patterns in CrossBuffer's behavior under varying contention levels. All three metrics exhibit strong correlation with transaction submission intervals and participating chain counts. Under high temporal overlap conditions with 10-second intervals, the 9-chain configuration demonstrates abortion rates around 37%, which decline substantially as intervals extend, while gas consumption and latency follow proportional trends. The 6-chain and 3-chain deployments show correspondingly reduced metric values across all dimensions. These patterns emerge from the protocol's reliance on cross-chain message exchange for coordination, where gas costs scale proportionally with the number of participating blockchains due to IBC message routing overhead. When submission intervals are sufficiently short relative to IBC round-trip latencies, multiple transactions execute concurrently and compete for candidateTop selection, leading to frequent conflict detection and unilateral reordering operations that elevate both abortion rates and processing delays. Conversely, longer intervals that span multiple IBC communication cycles reduce temporal overlap among candidates, allowing most transactions to complete proof collection and achieve commitment without encountering competing selections. Notably, all configurations display a transition zone between 30 and 40-second intervals where metrics stabilize. The dependency injection pattern introduces additional variance in latency measurements, as dependent transactions incur waiting periods for ancestor commitments regardless of their own proof collection status, particularly evident in high-contention scenarios where cascading delays propagate through dependency chains.

The evaluation demonstrates CrossBuffer's functional operation across multiple blockchain scales while revealing the protocol's sensitivity to workload characteristics. The unilateral reordering mechanism successfully resolves conflicts without requiring bilateral abortion, maintaining system progress even under

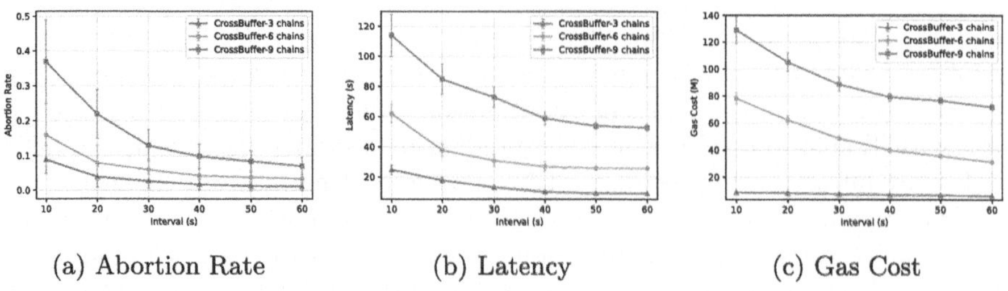

(a) Abortion Rate (b) Latency (c) Gas Cost

Fig. 3. CrossBuffer Under Conflicts.

substantial temporal overlap where competing candidates frequently undergo queue transitions. The dependency preservation logic correctly enforces causal ordering constraints through the pending input counter mechanism and transitive earliest round propagation, preventing premature commitment of dependent transactions throughout the tested scenarios. The resource consumption patterns reflect the computational overhead of queue management operations, dependency propagation, and cross-chain message exchange, with costs escalating under high contention due to increased reordering frequency and repeated coordination attempts for candidates navigating between wait and loser queues.

8 Conclusion

CrossBuffer, a cross-chain coordination protocol, ensures complete atomicity through a buffering-based approach combined with optimistic conflict resolution and dependency-track execution ordering. CrossBuffer introduces a dual-queue architecture where tentative state changes remain in managed buffers until all participating chains reach consensus, eliminating the need for costly rollback operations by committing only validated transitions. When conflicts arise among concurrent transactions, the protocol employs unilateral reordering with age-based prioritization rather than mutual abortion, allowing one transaction to proceed while repositioning the other for later retry. For transactions with causal dependencies, CrossBuffer leverages directed acyclic graph modeling to track prerequisite relationships and enforce commit ordering through counter-based eligibility checks and constraint propagation. These mechanisms have been validated through implementation on Cosmos blockchain infrastructure, where experimental evaluation demonstrates operational viability under varying workload characteristics, successfully coordinating concurrent conflicts and dependency chains while maintaining progression even under substantial conflicts. The design's correctness is further substantiated through formal analysis establishing theoretical guarantees for complete atomicity and causal consistency, with rigorous proofs accounting for the protocol's buffering, reordering, and dependency mechanisms to provide foundational assurance of reliability in distributed blockchain environments.

Acknowledgments. This paper is supported by the National Key R&D Program of China through project 2022YFB2702900, the Natural Science Foundation of China through projects U21A20467, U24B20144, 62572038 and 62272464, the Natural Science Foundation of Beijing-Tianjin-Hebei through projects 25JJJC0033, the Fundamental Research Funds for the Central Universities, the Research Funds of Renmin University of China (No. 202530187), and the Key R&D Program of Zhejiang Province (No. 2025C01084).

A Proofs of Correctness Properties

A.1 Proof of Complete Atomicity

Theorem 1 (Complete Atomicity). *Given a finite set of concurrent executions $\mathcal{E} = \{E_a, E_{a+1}, \ldots, E_{a'}\}$ on m distinct blockchains $\Pi_1, \Pi_2, \ldots, \Pi_m$, for any pair of blockchains $\Pi_i, \Pi_{i'}$, $\mathcal{E}$ eventually triggers serializable atomic state transition.*

Proof. We prove by contradiction under assumptions of secure SMR-coordinated blockchains and reliable CCC primitive satisfying authenticity and reliability properties.

Case 1: Single Execution. Let $E_k \in \mathcal{E}$ access states τ_i^j on Π_i and $\tau_{i'}^{j'}$ on $\Pi_{i'}$. Assume for contradiction that $\tau_i^j \xrightarrow{k} \tau_i^{j+1}$ commits on Π_i while $\tau_{i'}^{j'} \xrightarrow{k} \tau_{i'}^{j'+1}$ aborts on $\Pi_{i'}$.

Commitment on Π_i requires: (i) collecting finality proofs $\{\pi_{tx_{src}^{id}} \mid src \in ID.chains\}$ from all participating chains, (ii) achieving *candidateTop* selection with $wait\_ok = 1$, and (iii) receiving unanimous OK messages. By CCC reliability, Π_i receives proof from $\Pi_{i'}$. Conversely, abortion on $\Pi_{i'}$ necessitates broadcasting ABORT messages via CCC. By CCC reliability, these ABORT messages reach Π_i and prevent commitment, yielding $\tau_i^j \xrightarrow{k} \tau_i^{j+1}$ does not commit—a contradiction. Thus, $\exists$ blockchain equivocation, violating the secure SMR assumption.

Case 2a: Inconsistent Execution Sets. Let $\mathcal{E}_i = \{E \in \mathcal{E} \mid \tau_i \xrightarrow{E} \tau_i'\}$ denote the committed execution set on Π_i. Assume $\mathcal{E}_i \neq \mathcal{E}_{i'}$. Without loss of generality, $\exists E_b \in \mathcal{E}_i$ such that $E_b \notin \mathcal{E}_{i'}$.

For $E_b \in \mathcal{E}_i$, the commitment condition requires $\forall \Pi_j \in ID.chains$, Π_i receives $\mathtt{OK}(E_b)$ from Π_j, including $\Pi_{i'}$. For $E_b \notin \mathcal{E}_{i'}$, either: (i) $\Pi_{i'}$ never executed E_b, contradicting the execution model where $\forall \Pi_j \in ID.chains$, E_b triggers tx_j^{id}; or (ii) $\Pi_{i'}$ aborted E_b by broadcasting $\mathtt{ABORT}(E_b)$. In case (ii), CCC reliability ensures $\mathtt{ABORT}(E_b)$ reaches Π_i, preventing commitment—contradicting $E_b \in \mathcal{E}_i$. Therefore, $\mathcal{E}_i = \mathcal{E}_{i'}$.

Case 2b: Inconsistent Ordering. Let $\mathcal{E}_e = \{E \in \mathcal{E} \mid E \in \mathcal{E}_i \cap \mathcal{E}_{i'}\}$ denote the commonly committed subset. Assume $\exists E_a, E_b \in \mathcal{E}_e$ such that the commitment order on Π_i satisfies $E_a \prec_i E_b$ while on $\Pi_{i'}$ satisfies $E_b \prec_{i'} E_a$.

Let r_a^i denote the round at which Π_i commits E_a. The single-candidate discipline ensures $\forall r, |\{E \mid E = candidateTop_i(r)\}| = 1$. At round r_a^i, only E_a broadcasts $\mathtt{OK}(E_a)$ from Π_i. For $\Pi_{i'}$ to satisfy $E_b \prec_{i'} E_a$, $\Pi_{i'}$ must commit E_b at round $r_b^{i'} < r_a^i$ and subsequently send $\mathtt{OK}(E_a)$ at round r_a^i. This requires $\Pi_{i'}$ to broadcast $\texttt{OK}(E_a)$ when $E_a \neq candidateTop_{i'}(r_a^i)$, violating the protocol invariant that $\texttt{OK}(E) \Rightarrow E = candidateTop(r)$. This contradicts secure blockchain operation. Therefore, $E_a \prec_i E_b \Leftrightarrow E_a \prec_{i'} E_b$, establishing serializable atomic state transition.

A.2 Proof of Causal Consistency

Theorem 2 (Causal Consistency). *For executions forming a dependency DAG $G = (V, E)$, if E_b depends on E_a (i.e., $(E_a, E_b) \in E$), then E_a commits before E_b on all blockchains or both abort.*

Proof. Dependency establishment sets $E_a \in E_b.parents$, $E_b \in E_a.children$, and increments $E_b.pend\_in$. The eligibility criterion $pend\_in = 0$ prevents E_b from becoming *candidateTop* while E_a remains uncommitted, as $E_b.pend\_in \geq 1$ blocks its selection.

When E_a undergoes reordering, the protocol propagates temporal displacement: if $E_b.earliest\_round < E_a.earliest\_round$ after adjustment, the system elevates $E_b.earliest\_round$ to match. This temporal barrier ensures E_b cannot compete prematurely even after E_a commits and decrements $E_b.pend\_in$ to zero.

For multi-level dependencies $E_a \rightarrow E_b \rightarrow E_c$, reordering E_a increases $E_b.earliest\_round$, which upon E_b's subsequent reordering propagates to E_c. This transitive propagation extends through induction: base case (depth 1) holds by direct parent-child mechanism; inductive step assumes causality at depth d and shows the *pend_in* and *earliest_round* mechanisms ensure depth $d+1$ children wait for depth d parents, preserving transitivity. Therefore, Cross-Buffer maintains causal consistency across arbitrary DAG depths and conflict resolutions.

References

1. Ren, K., et al.: Interoperability in blockchain: a survey. IEEE Trans. Knowl. Data Eng. **35**(12), 12750–12769 (2023)
2. Han, P., Yan, Z., Ding, W., Fei, S., Wan, Z.: A survey on cross-chain technologies. Distrib. Ledger Technol. Res. Pract. **2**(2), 1–30 (2023)
3. Herlihy, M.: Atomic cross-chain swaps. In: Proceedings of the 37th ACM Symposium on Principles of Distributed Computing (PODC'18), pp. 245–254. ACM (2018)
4. Liu, Z., et al.: Hyperservice: interoperability and programmability across heterogeneous blockchains. In: Proceedings of the 26th ACM SIGSAC Conference on Computer and Communications Security (CCS'19), pp. 549–566. ACM (2019)
5. Wu, K., Ma, Y., Huang, G., Liu, X.: A first look at blockchain-based decentralized applications. Software Pract. Exp. **51**(10), 2033–2050 (2021)
6. Han, R., et al.: Vassago: efficient and authenticated provenance query on multiple blockchains. In: Proceedings of the 40th International Symposium on Reliable Distributed Systems (SRDS'21), pp. 132–142. IEEE (2021)
7. Wang, Y., et al.: A survey on metaverse: fundamentals, security, and privacy. IEEE Commun. Surv. Tutor. **25**(1), 319–352 (2022)

8. Herlihy, M., Liskov, B., Shrira, L.: Cross-chain deals and adversarial commerce. VLDB J. **31**(6), 1291–1309 (2022)
9. Lu, H., Jajoo, A., Namjoshi, K.S.: Atomicity and abstraction for cross-blockchain interactions. arXiv preprint arXiv:2403.07248 (2024)
10. Cai, Y., Cheng, R., Zhou, Y., Zhang, S., Xiao, J., Jin, H.: Enabling complete atomicity for cross-chain applications through layered state commitments. In: Proceedings of the 43rd International Symposium on Reliable Distributed Systems (SRDS'24), pp. 1–13. IEEE (2024)
11. Wood, G.: Polkadot: vision for a heterogeneous multi-chain framework. White Paper (2016)
12. Montgomery, H., et al.: Hyperledger Cactus whitepaper. Technical Report, Hyperledger (2021)
13. Falazi, G., Breitenbücher, U., Leymann, F., Schulte, S.: Cross-chain smart contract invocations: a systematic multi-vocal literature review. ACM Comput. Surv. **56**(6), 1–38 (2024). https://doi.org/10.1145/3638045
14. Thyagarajan, S.A., Malavolta, G., Moreno-Sanchez, P.: Universal atomic swaps: secure exchange of coins across all blockchains. In: Proceedings of the 43rd IEEE Symposium on Security and Privacy (SP'22), pp. 1299–1316. IEEE (2022)
15. Kwon, J., Buchman, E.: Cosmos whitepaper: a network of distributed ledgers. Technical Report, Interchain Foundation (2019)
16. Kung, H.-T., Robinson, J.T.: On optimistic methods for concurrency control. ACM Trans. Database Syst. **6**(2), 213–226 (1981)
17. Kokoris-Kogias, E., Jovanovic, P., Gasser, L., Gailly, N., Syta, E., Ford, B.: OmniLedger: a secure, scale-out, decentralized ledger via sharding. In: Proceedings of the 39th IEEE Symposium on Security and Privacy (SP'18), pp. 583–598. IEEE (2018)
18. Robinson, P., Ramesh, R.: General purpose atomic crosschain transactions. In: Proceedings of the 2nd Workshop on Blockchain Research & Applications for Innovative Networks and Services (BRAINS'21), pp. 61–68. ACM (2021)
19. Nissl, M., Sallinger, E., Schulte, S., Borkowski, M.: Towards cross-blockchain smart contracts. In: Proceedings of the IEEE International Conference on Decentralized Applications and Infrastructures (DAPPS'21), pp. 85–94. IEEE (2021)
20. Wang, W., Zhang, Z., Wang, G., Yuan, Y.: Efficient cross-chain transaction processing on blockchains. In: Proceedings of the 38th IEEE International Conference on Data Engineering (ICDE'22), pp. 2853–2866. IEEE (2022)
21. Garcia-Molina, H., Salem, K.: Sagas. In: Proceedings of the ACM SIGMOD International Conference on Management of Data, pp. 249–259. ACM (1987)
22. Lamport, L.: Time, clocks, and the ordering of events in a distributed system. Commun. ACM **21**(7), 558–565 (1978)
23. Lamport, L., Massa, M.: Cheap paxos. In: Proceedings of the 5th International Conference on Dependable Systems and Networks (DSN'04), pp. 307–314. IEEE (2004)

Enhancing Long-Range Security for Proof-of-Stake Consensus via Sampleable Verifiable Delay Functions

Xuecheng Lin[1,2], Decun Luo[1,2], Qianhong Wu[1,2], and Bo Qin[3](✉)

[1] School of Cyber Science and Technology, Beihang University, Beijing, China
[2] Hangzhou Innovation Institute of Beihang University, Hangzhou, China
[3] School of Information, Renmin University of China, Beijing, China
bo.qin@ruc.edu.cn

Abstract. Long-range attacks constitute a fundamental weakness of Proof-of-Stake (PoS) blockchains: once signing keys are leaked or obtained, fabricating a convincing alternative chain history becomes effectively costless. To mitigate this issue, we introduce a sampleable verifiable delay function (sVDF) that embeds compact, verifiable time samples into block headers and drives a time-aware fork-choice rule that lexicographically prioritizes cumulative sVDF iterations. We formalize the threat model and protocol interfaces, prove that our sVDF satisfies correctness, uniqueness, and sequentiality under standard cryptographic assumptions, and show that the augmented protocol increases the amount of sequential work required for a successful long-range forgery. Our experimental analysis indicates that moderate hardware heterogeneity and periodically refreshed anchors suffice to keep the catch-up probability low within realistic regimes. Our design is backward compatible, incurs modest bandwidth and verification overhead, and can serve as an additive defense for existing PoS blockchains.

Keywords: Proof-of-Stake · Long-range attacks · Verifiable Delay Functions · Consensus security

1 Introduction

Proof-of-Stake (PoS) has become a mainstream paradigm for achieving high throughput and energy-efficient blockchain consensus. Relative to Proof-of-Work (PoW) [19], PoS allocates block production rights in proportion to stake rather than raw computational work, thereby drastically reducing energy expenditure and hardware externalities while improving scalability and sustainability [17]. For example, Ethereum's "The Merge" transitioned the network from PoW to PoS and led to a dramatic reduction in network-wide energy consumption. Moreover, PoS designs can shorten time-to-finality and, in Byzantine Fault Tolerance (BFT)-style variants, even provide fast finality in permissionless settings.

W. Meng et al. (Eds.): ASSS 2025, CCIS 2903, pp. 54–74, 2026.
https://doi.org/10.1007/978-3-032-21600-7_4

However, replacing computational expenditure with stake weighting also creates a distinct attack surface. In many deployed PoS systems, once an actor holds the relevant signing key, producing a valid block entails near-zero marginal cost [3,11]. In particular, this economic asymmetry enables practical long-range attacks (LRAs). By amassing historical validator keys via leakage, resale, or posterior corruption, an adversary can retroactively sign a seemingly old and well-formed alternative history [6,14]. Such a fork threatens the authenticity of deep chain prefixes and impedes secure bootstrapping for newly joining or long-offline nodes.

The Long-Range Attack Problem. Informally, these LRAs exploit three properties commonly observed in PoS systems.

- *Near-zero marginal block production cost.* [3,11,17] Unlike PoW, producing a valid PoS block requires merely holding the corresponding credentials (signing keys) and performing negligible computation.
- *Historical key leakage or sale.* [6,8] Over extended horizons, keys can be lost, exfiltrated, sold, or bribed from honest parties. An adversary can accumulate a substantial corpus of such historical keys.
- *No endogenous, verifiable time base.* [3,6,16,18] With past keys, an adversary can backdate a seemingly old and long alternative history at negligible extra cost. Without an internal time anchor, newcomers or long-offline nodes cannot reliably tell such forgeries from the honest chain.

Therefore, these properties enable the canonical LRA: by amassing obsolete yet valid signing keys, an adversary can cheaply backdate a fork whose apparent length or weight outstrips the honest chain. In the absence of an endogenous, publicly verifiable time base, newcomers bootstrapping from untrusted peers may accept the forgery as canonical [14].

Why are Existing Defenses Insufficient? Nowadays, both academia and industry have proposed various defense mechanisms against LRAs, each incurring distinct trade-offs among security, efficiency, and usability.

- *Checkpointing and social-layer finality* [6]. Periodic checkpoints or socially coordinated finality can block the acceptance of alternative histories older than the most recent checkpoint. However, they introduce out-of-band trust, which entails designating authorities responsible for issuing and acknowledging checkpoints and risks eroding permissionless decentralization.
- *Key-evolving signatures (KES)* [11,17]. KES reduces the value of old keys by evolving secrets over time, but it burdens operations and still assumes honest erasure; retained or later-recovered keys can bypass it.
- *External anchoring* [2,18]. Anchoring PoS state into an external PoW chain or trusted ledger yields a tamper-evident timeline and stronger long-range resistance, at the cost of extra trust, anchoring latency, and nontrivial operational overhead.

These observations point to the need for an *internal, publicly verifiable* notion of elapsed time that preserves permissionless deployment. In contrast, we target an endogenous, publicly verifiable time base that requires no new trust roots and drops into prevailing PoS designs.

1.1 Our Approach

We propose to *internalize* elapsed time within the ledger by introducing a sampleable VDF (sVDF) into the standard PoS protocol and its chain-selection rule. Specifically, our approach is as follows:

- The sVDF is designed to be sampleable so that progress can be observed and verified within normal block cadence. Proofs are short and verification is fast. The bandwidth and processor overhead for honest nodes remain modest.
- Each block carries a succinct sVDF time sample that contains an output value, a proof, and a step count. The sample is bound to an input that is derived from the parent header in a public and deterministic way. Honest validators advance a local sVDF clock continuously. When proposing a block, they take a sample at the current step and publish the output, the proof, and the step count with the block. Verifiers derive the input from the header and check the sample using the proof.
- We define chain *weight* as the sum of the per-block step counts committed along a branch. The fork choice prefers the branch with the greater accumulated sVDF time. Because VDF evaluation is inherently sequential and resists parallel acceleration, an adversary who fabricates history must carry out substantial sequential work to keep a forged fork competitive.

This construction combines an internal notion of verifiable time grounded in VDF progress with a fork choice that remains compatible with stake-based designs. It enables PoS protocols to reject retroactive forks that do not reflect genuine elapsed VDF time, even when the adversary controls many historical signing keys.

1.2 Contributions

We introduce VDF-anchored time chains that internalize a sVDF into standard PoS block structure and fork choice, providing an endogenous, publicly verifiable notion of elapsed time without new trust roots or consensus re-engineering. This imposes quantifiable sequential work on retroactive forgeries to mitigate long-range attacks while preserving compatibility with prevailing designs and low verification overhead. In summary, our contributions are as follows:

- *Problem articulation and formal goals.* We formalize the long-range threat in a PoS setting that models (i) adversarial acquisition of historical keys and (ii) realistic network assumptions for bootstrapping nodes. We set out precise security goals—consistency, liveness, and long-range resistance—for any PoS augmentation intended for practical deployment.
- *sVDF-based verifiable time chain.* We introduce a sVDF integration that lets each block carry a succinct, verifiable time sample. We define a chain-weight metric that aggregates cumulative sVDF iterations and show how to embed sVDF sampling into standard PoS block production with minimal protocol churn.

- *Security analysis.* Under standard VDF sequentiality and uniqueness assumptions, and under a realistic adversarial model (including posterior corruption or key leakage), we prove that an adversary must perform sequential VDF work proportional to the honest chain's accumulated time to make a forged fork dominant. This lifts the economic and temporal cost of LRAs to the point where they are impractical for rational adversaries; we characterize quantitative bounds on the required effort.

1.3 Paper Roadmap

Section 2 reviews related work; Sect. 3 formalizes the system and threat model; Sect. 4 presents the protocol design; Sect. 5 analyzes security; Sect. 6 discusses evaluation; Sect. 7 concludes the paper.

2 Related Work

This section situates our work within consensus foundations, PoS-specific long-range risks and defenses, VDF primitives and deployments, and then positions our contribution.

2.1 Consensus Foundations and PoS Security

Theoretical analyses of longest-chain style protocols originate from the Bitcoin backbone framework [15], which formalizes common-prefix, chain-growth, and chain-quality properties and underpins many later analyses. The Sleepy model [20] generalizes synchrony and availability assumptions to capture churn and partial participation. Within PoS, Ouroboros and its successors [3,11,17] provide rigorous persistence and liveness guarantees under adaptive corruptions and realistic network assumptions, including robust bootstrapping from genesis. In parallel, committee and BFT families such as Algorand [16], Tendermint [5], and HotStuff [25] achieve fast finality with quorum certificates at Internet scale. Alternative metastable designs (the Avalanche family [22]) demonstrate high-throughput probabilistic finality via repeated subsampling. The Ethereum beacon chain specification [9] combines a longest-chain fork-choice (LMD-GHOST) with a finality gadget named Casper FFG [8] in a deployed, large-scale PoS setting.

2.2 Long-Range Attacks in PoS and Existing Defenses

Unlike PoW, PoS makes block production near-zero marginal cost once keys are available, enabling retroactive signing of "old but valid" histories and thus long-range attacks (LRAs) [6,14]. Surveys synthesize risks and mitigations [13,24]. Defenses fall into three broad streams with distinct trade-offs: (i) social or protocol checkpoints and weak subjectivity windows [6], which require operator diligence and introduce trust/coordination assumptions; (ii) fast-finality gadgets (e.g., Casper FFG [8] atop LMD-GHOST, or HotStuff-derived designs [25]), which limit the depth of reversible history but still require careful handling of key compromises and validator set changes; and (iii) external anchoring into PoW or trusted ledgers, which creates a tamper-evident time base at the cost of cross-chain trust, latency, and operational overhead (e.g., Babylon [18]). A complementary direction hardens bootstrapping by publishing succinct commitments or witness sets to constrain admissible histories (e.g., Winkle [1]) or by checkpointing PoS into Bitcoin via modern primitives (e.g., Pikachu [2]). These methods strengthen long-range resistance but either rely on extra trust roots or impose new operational dependencies.

2.3 Verifiable Delay Functions in Blockchain Systems

Verifiable Delay Functions (VDFs) enforce inherently sequential work while permitting succinct, fast verification [4]. Practical schemes due to Wesolowski [23] and Pietrzak [21] offer complementary trade-offs and have matured through extensive engineering. Importantly, VDFs can be built over unknown-order groups without a trusted setup (e.g., class groups of imaginary quadratic fields), mitigating RSA ceremony concerns; operational experience at scale corroborates this path [10]. Beyond their intrinsic sequentiality, VDFs are compelling for decentralized randomness beacons: the RANDAO+VDF construction reduces last-reveal bias and has shaped the design space of production beacons [7].

In deployed systems, Chia combines Proof-of-Space with a timelord network that continuously produces VDF proofs to pace block production and supply unbiased randomness, with inexpensive verification by all nodes [10]. Beyond randomness, several works integrate VDFs into leader election and fork-choice. PoSAT redesigns chain-based PoS by gating lotteries with VDF progress, embedding a cryptographic notion of elapsed time directly into fork-choice [12]. While compelling, PoSAT is a new protocol rather than a drop-in reinforcement for existing deployments. In parallel, external anchoring approaches export time to Bitcoin (e.g., Babylon [18]) to harden long-range safety and accelerate unbonding, at the cost of cross-chain availability and liveness assumptions.

We differ from full protocol redesigns and cross-chain anchoring by proposing a modular augmentation: embed sVDF time-samples into blocks and account for cumulative iterations in fork-choice. This yields an endogenous, publicly verifiable notion of elapsed time that raises the sequential cost of retroactive forgery without introducing new trust roots, and remains compatible with prevailing chain-based and committee/BFT PoS designs. We show that a forged fork requires sequential VDF work commensurate with the honest chain's accumulated time under standard uniqueness and sequentiality assumptions.

3 System Model

In this section, we present a formal system and threat model for an sVDF-based PoS blockchain. For clarity, we list the notation used in this paper, as summarized in Table 1.

Table 1. Notations.

Symbol	Meaning
λ	The security parameter
Δ	Network synchrony bound
$t \in \mathbb{N}$	Slot index
$\mathcal{V}_t$	Active validator set at slot t
$w_t(v)$	Stake of validator v at slot t
W_t	Total stake at slot t
$C \preceq C'$	C is a prefix of C'
$\mathrm{trim}_k(C)$	Remove the last k blocks of C
$\|x\|$	Bit-length of x
$\varepsilon(\cdot)$	Negligible function
ρ	Weak-subjectivity period
k	Confirmation depth / common-prefix parameter
τ	Per-block sVDF step count
T	Accumulated sVDF iterations (chain time-weight)
B_{anc}	Trusted anchor (checkpoint) block
t_{anc}, $t^\star$	Anchor timestamp, current time
$\mathcal{A}$	The Adversary
α	Adversarial online stake bound
α_t	Online corrupted stake fraction at slot t
$\mathcal{C}_t$	Corrupted validator set at slot t
QC	Quorum certificate (when a BFT gadget is present)

3.1 Basic Model

First, the system consists of validators. Validators participate in block production; The probability of each validator being selected as the block producer is proportional to its staked tokens. Every validator maintains a local chain as a tree of blocks rooted in a designated genesis block. Once a new validator joins the system for the first time or an old validator rejoins after being offline, it must choose a canonical chain based on information they receive from the network.

We write blockchain $C \preceq C'$ to denote that C is a prefix of C', $\text{trim}_k(C)$ to denote removing the last k blocks from C, $|x|$ for the bit-length of x, and $\varepsilon(\cdot)$ for a negligible function.

Next, we abstract the underlying PoS as a six-tuple $\Pi = \langle \mathcal{V}, \mathcal{S}, \mathsf{G}, \mathcal{R}, \mathcal{F}, \mathcal{I} \rangle$, where the components are:

- $\mathcal{V}$(*Validator set*): A set of validators' public keys together with their corresponding stake weights. Upon receiving a new block, a validator verifies its validity (including signatures and basic structural constraints) and, when eligible, proposes a new block.
- $\mathcal{S}$(*State space*): The system state space includes the chain state, the stake distribution, and any protocol-level randomness or metadata required by the PoS mechanism. Each block header at least contains a parent hash and the randomness seed(s) used to derive eligibility in the corresponding slot, and may additionally carry a quorum certificate if a BFT-style finality gadget is present.
- $\mathcal{R}$(*Randomness*): A public randomness beacon derived from on-chain data or combined contributions from validators provides per-slot seeds for leader or committee sampling. We assume that the PoS-derived randomness outputs are unpredictable.
- G(*Block generation*): Block-production eligibility is determined by $\mathcal{R}$. A participating node proposes either a block that satisfies the basic validity predicate or $\varnothing$, while other honest validators, upon verification, accept the block and update $\mathcal{S}$ accordingly.
- $\mathcal{F}$(*Fork-choice rules*): A deterministic rule selects a unique canonical chain among competing branches, subject to both safety and liveness constraints. We abstract this via a weight function, yielding a globally determined fork-choice rule.
- $\mathcal{I}$(*Incentives mechanism*): An additional incentive mechanism is introduced to specify how validators are rewarded or penalized for their actions. In particular, $\mathcal{I}$ is responsible for ensuring that honest participation—following the protocol, remaining online, and building on the canonical chain—is a stable equilibrium. Additionally, we need to consider the operational overhead incurred by all parties involved in the agreement process (such as hardware operation, etc.).

This abstraction is broad enough to capture chain-based PoS protocols (e.g., longest-chain variants), BFT-style designs with quorum certificates, and hybrid systems that combine both. Our augmentation in later sections will operate purely at the interface between G and $\mathcal{F}$, leaving stake accounting and randomness generation unchanged.

We assume standard cryptographic primitives: the hash function used in the protocol is collision-resistant, and the signature scheme is existentially unforgeable under chosen-message attacks.

Additional assumptions related to verifiable time will be stated explicitly when we introduce our concrete construction.

This abstraction provides a unified framework for describing PoS mechanisms and supports modular, additive enhancements. In particular, our sVDF layer integrates as a time-weighting add-on while preserving the underlying stake accounting and randomness generation. Time in the system advances in discrete slots $t \in \mathbb{N}$. At slot t, the active validator set is $\mathcal{V}_t$, validator v has stake $w_t(v) \geq 0$, and total stake is $W_t = \sum_{v \in \mathcal{V}_t} w_t(v)$.

3.2 Network and Adversary Model

Communication proceeds in a Δ-synchronous model, namely, any message broadcast by an honest party at slot t is received by all honest recipients no later than $t + \Delta$. Messages are mutually authenticated over point-to-point authenticated channels.

Time in the system advances in discrete slots $t \in \mathbb{N}$. At slot t, the active validator set is $\mathcal{V}_t$, validator v has stake $w_t(v) \geq 0$, and total stake is $W_t = \sum_{v \in \mathcal{V}_t} w_t(v)$.

We consider a probabilistic polynomial-time adversary (PPT) $\mathcal{A}$ in a Δ-synchronous network who attempts to deceive honest nodes by crafting alternative chains, particularly for newcomers and long-offline nodes. Unless stated otherwise, $\mathcal{A}$ respects standard cryptographic assumptions, and its online stake is bounded by α. We endow $\mathcal{A}$ with the following capabilities:

- *Adaptive online corruption.* At any slot t, $\mathcal{A}$ may corrupt $\mathcal{C}_t \subseteq \mathcal{V}_t$ with fraction $\alpha_t = \left(\sum_{v \in \mathcal{C}_t} w_t(v)\right)/W_t \leq \alpha$ (e.g., $\alpha < 1/2$ for Nakamoto-style or $\alpha < 1/3$ with a BFT finality gadget).
- *Synchronous network model.* $\mathcal{A}$ may eavesdrop, reorder, and delay messages by at most Δ slots.
- *Past-key exposure.* $\mathcal{A}$ may obtain signing keys of validators that have exited and fully unbonded outside the weak-subjectivity window ρ, allowing retroactive signatures on historical epochs.

We assume that $\alpha_t \leq \alpha$ for all t, where $\alpha < 1/2$ for longest-chain style PoS protocols and $\alpha < 1/3$ when a BFT finality gadget is in use.

3.3 Long-Range Attack Experiments

We formalize adversarial goals via two complementary security experiments that capture common-prefix violations and finalized-checkpoint conflicts, respectively.

Experiment $\mathsf{LRA}^{\mathrm{CP}}_{\Pi,\rho,k}(\mathcal{A})$ – *Common-Prefix Violation via Long-Range Fork.* The parameters are listed bellow: security parameter λ; synchrony bound Δ; online adversarial stake bound α; confirmation depth k; weak-subjectivity period ρ; PoS protocol Π with fork-choice $\mathcal{F}$.

1 **Setup.** Challenger $\mathcal{C}$ initializes Π and runs an honest execution up to time $t^\star$ under Δ-synchrony with adversarial online stake $\leq \alpha$. Let C be the honest main chain at $t^\star$.

2 **Past-key release.** $\mathcal{C}$ provides $\mathcal{A}$ with the set $\mathsf{SK}_{\text{past}}$ of signing keys belonging to validators that were active only at times $\leq t^\star - \rho$; these validators have fully unbonded and are considered outside the weak-subjectivity window.
3 **Anchor.** A rejoining node $\mathcal{N}$ holds a trusted anchor block B_{anc} on C with $t^\star - t_{\text{anc}} \leq \rho$.
4 **Forgery.** Using $\mathsf{SK}_{\text{past}}$ and admissible scheduling, $\mathcal{A}$ constructs an alternative history C' (from genesis or from a height before B_{anc}) that passes all local validity checks of Π.
5 **Adoption test.** The validator $\mathcal{V}$ applies $\mathcal{F}$ to $\{C, C'\}$. Then we define $\mathsf{BadCP} := \left[\text{trim}_k(C) \npreceq C' \ \vee \ \text{trim}_k(C') \npreceq C\right]$. The experiment outputs 1 iff $\mathcal{N}$ adopts a chain inconsistent with common-prefix at depth k; else 0.

The adversarial advantage in this experiment is defined as $\text{Adv}^{\text{CP}}_{\Pi,\rho,k}(\mathcal{A}) = \Pr[\mathsf{LRA}^{\text{CP}}_{\Pi,\rho,k}(\mathcal{A}) = 1]$.

Experiment $\mathsf{LRA}^{\text{FIN}}_{\Pi,\rho}(\mathcal{A})$ — *Finality Conflict via Long-Range Fork.* Applies if Π exports a finality gadget with a finalized predicate specific to the implementation. Steps 14 are identical. In Step 5, let X denote the latest finalized anchor $\mathcal{N}$ within ρ, the experiment outputs 1 iff, according to the native finality rule of Π, $\mathcal{N}$ accepts a finalized checkpoint X' that conflicts with X; otherwise 0.

The adversarial advantage is $\text{Adv}^{\text{FIN}}_{\Pi,\rho}(\mathcal{A}) = \Pr[\mathsf{LRA}^{\text{FIN}}_{\Pi,\rho}(\mathcal{A}) = 1]$.

3.4 Security Goals

Long-Range Attack Resistance. We say that a PoS protocol Π achieves long-range attack resistance with parameters (ρ, k), denoted $\mathsf{LRS}_\Pi(\rho, k)$, if every PPT adversary $\mathcal{A}$ has only negligible advantage in both experiments defined above.

Formally, for all PPT $\mathcal{A}$, $\text{Adv}^{\text{CP}}_{\Pi,\rho,k}(\mathcal{A}) \leq \varepsilon(\lambda)$, and whenever Π exports a finality predicate, $\text{Adv}^{\text{FIN}}_{\Pi,\rho}(\mathcal{A}) \leq \varepsilon(\lambda)$.

Intuitively, given a trusted anchor that is at most ρ slots old, no polynomial-time adversary armed with historical keys should be able to (except with negligible probability) rewrite a prefix of depth k or produce a conflicting finalized history that a correctly-bootstrapping node would accept.

When we focus on one of the two lenses in isolation, we write $\mathsf{LRS}^{\mathsf{CP}}_\Pi(\rho, k)$ and $\mathsf{LRS}^{\mathsf{FIN}}_\Pi(\rho)$ to emphasize common-prefix or finality safety, respectively.

4 Protocol Design

In this section, building on the model defined in Sect. 3, we present an sVDF-augmented PoS protocol. We integrate an sVDF into the PoS protocol by: (i) lifting the Wesolowski VDF to a sampleable, stateful verifiable delay primitive; (ii) extending it to block headers so that each block carries succinct time samples, while the fork-choice rule accounts for accumulated sequential work; and (iii) specifying the block generation and verification algorithms of the protocol.

4.1 From Wesolowski VDF to sVDF

We begin by briefly recalling the basic construction of the Wesolowski Verifiable Delay Function (VDF), and then explain how to extend it into a sampleable, stateful VDF primitive. Let $N = pq$ denote an RSA modulus with unknown factorization. For any input $x \in \mathrm{QR}_N$ and delay parameter $T \in \mathbb{N}$, the VDF evaluation is

$$y = x^{2^T} \bmod N.$$

To obtain a succinct proof, derive a prime $\ell \leftarrow H_\ell(x\|T\|y)$ and write $2^T = q\ell + r$ with $0 \leq r < \ell$.

The prover outputs $\pi = x^q \bmod N$, and the verifier checks

$$y \stackrel{?}{=} \pi^\ell \cdot x^{2^r} \bmod N.$$

Evaluation necessarily performs T sequential squarings, whereas verification is efficient: one modular exponentiation with an ℓ-bit exponent and one with roughly $\log_2 r$ bits. Soundness and uniqueness follow from the hidden-order assumption for N and the hash-to-prime mapping.

Building on this, we adopt the notion of cumulative work from PoW and design a VDF-based cumulative elapsed-time mechanism, which makes it difficult to counterfeit the chain's "time accumulation". This mechanism extends the Wesolowski VDF into a standardized, sampleable interface engineered to support continuous accumulation, dynamic updates, and public verifiability. The interface design is as follows:

- $\mathsf{pp} \leftarrow \mathsf{Setup}(1^\lambda)$: Generate public parameters for a hidden-order group (e.g., RSA modulus N with unknown factorization) and fix the hash-to-prime function H_ℓ; output pp.
- $\sigma \leftarrow \mathsf{Init}(\mathsf{pp}, x)$: Initialize the local state for iterative squaring on input $x \in \mathrm{QR}_N$. The state maintains $\sigma = (x, y, k)$ with $y = x$ and step counter $k = 0$.
- $\sigma' \leftarrow \mathsf{Iter}(\sigma)$: Update $y \leftarrow y^2$, $k \leftarrow k+1$; perform one sequential squaring step advancing the computation by one unit of delay.
- $(y, \pi, k) \leftarrow \mathsf{Sample}(\mathsf{pp}, \sigma)$: Return the current output and a Wesolowski proof attesting that $y = x^{2^k}$ at step k.
- $\{0, 1\} \leftarrow \mathsf{Verify}(\mathsf{pp}, x, y, \pi, k)$: Derive $\ell \leftarrow H_\ell(x\|k\|y)$, write $2^k = q\ell + r$, and check $y \stackrel{?}{=} \pi^\ell \cdot x^{2^r} \bmod N$; accept iff the equality holds.

4.2 Bootstrap PoS via sVDF

We augment a generic PoS protocol with sVDF. Building on a PoS protocol modeled as the sextuple $\Pi = \langle \mathcal{V}, \mathcal{S}, \mathsf{G}, \mathcal{R}, \mathcal{F}, \mathcal{I} \rangle$, the sVDF-augmented protocol is $\Pi^+ = \langle \mathcal{V}^+, \mathcal{S}^+, \mathsf{G}^+, \mathcal{R}^+, \mathcal{F}^+, \mathcal{I}^+ \rangle$. Our goal is to make only minimal changes so that each block carries a succinct per-block time sample and the fork-choice rule accounts for cumulative sequential work.

$\mathcal{V} \Rightarrow \mathcal{V}^+$. Each validator continuously evaluates a local sVDF instance in the background. When it receives a newly produced block, it temporarily pauses

Algorithm 1. The G^+'s Propose and Validate Procedures

procedure PROPOSE(B_i)
  Compute x_i after passing the verification of block B_{i-1}, initialize $\sigma \leftarrow \mathsf{Init}(\mathsf{pp}, x_i)$.
  Run Iter continuously while waiting for proposal-slot eligibility.
  Upon eligibility, let the current counter be t, set $\tau_i \leftarrow t$ and obtain $(y_i, \pi_i) \leftarrow \mathsf{Sample}(\mathsf{pp}, \sigma)$.
  Assemble header with $(x_i, \tau_i, y_i, \pi_i)$ and broadcast the block.
end procedure
procedure VALIDATE(B_i)
  Check base protocol validity, including parent, signatures, randomness usage.
  Recompute x_i from the parent sample y_{i-1} and the parent hash.
  Verify block via $\mathsf{Verify}(\mathsf{pp}, x_i, y_i, \pi_i, \tau_i) = 1$.
  Enforce hygiene bounds $\tau_{\min} \leq \tau_i \leq \tau_{\max}$.
  If all checks pass, mark B_i valid, otherwise reject.
end procedure

sampling and invokes Verify to validate the sVDF sample embedded in the block header. Upon accepting the block, it re-initializes or continues its local sVDF state relative to the new tip.

$\mathcal{S} \Rightarrow \mathcal{S}^+$. We incorporate the sVDF public parameters $\mathsf{pp} = (N, H_\ell, H_G)$ into the global ledger state, for example, in the genesis block. For each block B_i, we place a time sample $\langle x_i, \tau_i, y_i, \pi_i \rangle$ into block header, where τ_i is the iteration count at sampling. Also, we define an optional cached branch weight $\mathrm{TW}(\mathcal{C}) = \sum_{B_i \in \mathcal{C}} \tau_i$. Each block header adds fields $(x_i, \tau_i, y_i, \pi_i)$ where τ_i is the iteration count at sampling. Optional hygiene bounds $\tau_{\min} \leq \tau_i \leq \tau_{\max}$ mitigate spam (reject out-of-range samples). Blocks may omit a sample (interpreted as $\tau_i = 0$) for backward compatibility.

$\mathcal{R} \Rightarrow \mathcal{R}^+$. We keep the randomness beacon (VRF/RANDAO) unchanged. We bind its per-block output into the sVDF input as auxiliary data (see below), but do not modify how randomness is generated or consumed.

$\mathsf{G} \Rightarrow \mathsf{G}^+$. We add input binding, proof generation, and proof validation to the block production and validation pipeline. First, for input binding, given child block B_i with parent B_{i-1}, we define

$$x_i \;=\; H_G\big(y_{i-1} \;\|\; H(\mathrm{parent}(B_i)) \;\|\; \mathrm{aux}_i\big) \;\in\; \mathrm{QR}_N,$$

where y_{i-1} is the predecessor's sVDF output, $H(\cdot)$ hashes the parent header, and aux_i may include the proposer identity or beacon output. This lineage binding prevents cross-fork replay. Second, for block production and validation, we design a proposer procedure G^+.Propose and a validator procedure G^+.Validate as in Algorithm 1.

$\mathcal{F} \Rightarrow \mathcal{F}^+$. Let $\mathcal{F}$ be the base rule (e.g., longest-chain, GHOST, or finality overlay).

We define the cumulative time weight of a chain $\mathcal{C}$ as $\mathrm{TW}(\mathcal{C}) = \sum_{B_j \in \mathcal{C}} \tau_j$. Then we define the time-aware rule used at bootstrap:

$$\mathcal{F}^{+}(\{\mathcal{C}_j\}) \;:=\; \arg\max_{\mathcal{C}_j} \Big(\mathrm{TW}(\mathcal{C}_j),\; \mathcal{F}(\mathcal{C}_j) \Big).$$

That is, the above rule prioritizes a larger accumulated time and uses $\mathcal{F}$ to break ties. This is the only behavioral change at the consensus layer.
$\mathcal{I} \Rightarrow \mathcal{I}^{+}$. To mitigate free-riding and to encourage dense yet bounded sampling, the incentive layer may grant a small bonus to blocks that carry valid sVDF samples within hygiene bounds and/or deem blocks with invalid samples ineligible for rewards.

These are hygiene-oriented, optional measures.

4.3 Why This Resists Long-Range Attacks

We summarize the core intuition, which will be formalized in Sect. 5.

- **Replay is fork-specific.**
  Due to input binding and sVDF uniqueness, a valid sample (y_i, π_i, τ_i) for one ancestry cannot be reused under a different ancestry, except with negligible probability.
- **History requires time.**
  Producing a chain C with time weight $\mathrm{TW}(C)$ requires $\Omega(\mathrm{TW}(C))$ dependent squarings along its lineage; shortcuts would violate VDF sequentiality.
- **Old keys alone do not buy time.**
  Posterior corruption grants signatures but not sVDF progress: computing signatures on a forged history is cheap, but computing valid sVDF samples for that history requires sequential work.
- **The bootstrapper prefers honest time.**
  A rejoining node compares the honest chain C_H and an adversarial fork C_A via $\mathrm{TW}(\cdot)$.
  If the adversary has not done at least the additional squarings needed to close the time-weight gap (up to small jitter), the time-aware fork choice $\mathcal{F}^{+}$ selects C_H.

Informally, let $\Delta_T := \mathrm{TW}(C_H) - \mathrm{TW}(C_A)$ measured post-anchor, and let $\delta \geq 0$ capture network jitter and sampling variance.

If the adversary performs fewer than $\Delta_T - \delta$ dependent squarings after the anchor, a correctly bootstrapping node selects C_H with probability $1 - \mathrm{negl}(\lambda)$.

5 Security Analysis

We analyze the security of the proposed sVDF layer and the PoS augmentation that integrates time-samples into headers and fork-choice. We begin by analyzing the intrinsic properties of the sVDF primitive and formally proving that its security is inherited from the underlying Wesolowski VDF. We then show that, when grafted onto a base PoS protocol via the sextuple interface, our modification preserves base safety and liveness, while introducing long-range resistance in the weak-subjectivity model.

5.1 Assumptions and Setting

We assume that the underlying VDF is instantiated using the Wesolowski construction over an unknown-order group (e.g., RSA class groups) and satisfies the following properties in the Random Oracle Model (ROM):

- **Correctness:** Honest evaluation and verification always succeed.
- **Uniqueness:** For any (x, k), there exists at most one (y, π) satisfying the verifier equation.
- **Sequentiality:** Any PPT adversary that outputs a valid proof for k iterations without performing k dependent squarings breaks the underlying Adaptive Root or Strong RSA assumption.

5.2 Security of the sVDF

An sVDF is a stateful interface $sVDF = (Setup, Init, Iter, Sample, Verify)$ where $sVDF.Iter$ performs one dependent squaring and increases the local counter $k \leftarrow k+1$, and $sVDF.Sample$ proves the current state (x, y, k) without rewinding the computation.

The sVDF *does not* change (a) the group, (b) the hardness assumptions, (c) the proof relation, or (d) the verification equation. It *only* exposes a controlled interface to *when* a proof can be requested (at the current counter k), and *how* the prover packages the transcript (state σ with (x, y, k)). Thus all algebraic and cryptographic assumptions remain identical to the baseline VDF.

Correctness. For all (x, y, π, k) honestly generated by the sVDF,

$$\Pr[\mathsf{Verify}(\mathsf{pp}, x, y, \pi, k) = 1] = 1.$$

Uniqueness. For fixed (x, k), there exists at most one pair (y, π) such that $\mathsf{Verify}(\mathsf{pp}, x, y, \pi, k) = 1$.

A second distinct pair implies either a discrete-root collision in QR_N or a collision in the hash-to-prime function $H_\ell(x \parallel k \parallel y)$.

Sequentiality. Let $\mathrm{time}_\mathcal{A}$ denote the number of dependent squarings performed by an adversary $\mathcal{A}$. Define

$$\mathsf{Adv}^{\mathsf{seq}}_{\mathcal{A}}(\lambda) = \Pr\left[\mathsf{Verify}(\mathsf{pp}, x, y, \pi, k) = 1 \ \wedge \ \mathrm{time}_\mathcal{A} < k\right].$$

For all PPT $\mathcal{A}$, $\mathsf{Adv}^{\mathsf{seq}}_{\mathcal{A}}(\lambda) \leq \mathrm{negl}(\lambda)$.

Sample Consistency. Let $\sigma = (x, y, k)$ be an internal state obtained by repeated invocations of Iter.

Any sample $(y', \pi', k') \leftarrow \mathsf{Sample}(\mathsf{pp}, \sigma)$ with $k' > k$ must reflect at least $k' - k$ additional sequential squarings; otherwise $\mathcal{A}$ breaks VDF sequentiality.

Theorem 1 (Security of sVDF). *If the underlying VDF is correct, unique, and sequential under the Adaptive Root or Strong RSA assumption, then the sVDF interface inherits correctness, uniqueness, and sequentiality in the ROM.*

Any PPT adversary that breaks sVDF sequentiality with advantage $\epsilon(\lambda)$ can be converted into an adversary that breaks the underlying VDF with advantage at least $\epsilon(\lambda)/q_{\mathsf{sample}}$, where q_{sample} is the number of intermediate samples.

Proof. A reduction $\mathcal{B}$ simulates the sVDF interface for $\mathcal{A}$ using access to the VDF challenger. Whenever $\mathcal{A}$ outputs a valid (x, y, π, k) with fewer than k dependent squarings, $\mathcal{B}$ forwards this as a violation of the underlying VDF's sequentiality. Each sample corresponds to one VDF proof; the loss in advantage is at most linear in q_{sample}.

5.3 Compatibility with the Base PoS Protocol

Let a PoS consensus protocol $\Pi = \langle \mathcal{V}, \mathcal{S}, \mathsf{G}, \mathcal{R}, \mathcal{F}, \mathcal{I} \rangle$ satisfy CP and liveness under standard assumptions. Our augmentation Π^+ (i) adds a verifiable time sample value to each block and (ii) defines a time-aware fork-choice maximizing $\mathrm{TW}(C) = \sum_{B_i \in C} \tau_i$, tie-breaking by $\mathcal{F}$. Stake accounting, eligibility, and incentives remain unchanged.

Lemma 1 (Preservation of base safety and liveness). *If Π satisfies CP and liveness under (α, Δ), then Π^+ also satisfies CP and liveness under (α, Δ).*

Validity Monotonicity. $Valid_{\Pi^+} \subseteq Valid_{\Pi}$: every Π^+-valid block is Π-valid; conversely, a Π-valid block that fails $Verify(x_i, y_i, \pi_i, \tau_i)$ is invalid in Π^+.
Fork-Choice Refinement. $\mathcal{F}^+$ denote the Π^+ fork choice and $\mathcal{F}$ the base Π choice. If $TW(C) = TW(C')$, then $\mathcal{F}^+(\{C, C'\}) = \mathcal{F}(\{C, C'\})$. If $TW(C) > TW(C')$, then $\mathcal{F}^+(\{C, C'\}) = C$.
Projected Execution. Erase sVDF fields and replace the fork choice $(TW, \mathcal{F})$ by $\mathcal{F}$ to project any Π^+ execution to a Π execution. By validity monotonicity, the accepted blocks in Π^+ are a subset of the valid blocks of Π. By fork-choice refinement, tie cases exactly match $\mathcal{F}$, and non-tie cases *strengthen* selection without contradicting $\mathcal{F}$. Hence, any CP property proven for Π transfers to Π^+. Liveness follows since eligibility, synchrony, and verification remain polynomial-time and unchanged in nature; honest blocks that appear in Π continue to appear and extend in Π^+.

5.4 Long-Range Resistance of Π^+

We now work in the weak-subjectivity model of Sects. 3: a rejoining node has an anchor B_{anc} of age at most ρ. The adversary may obtain obsolete keys (outside ρ), delay and reorder messages by up to Δ, and supply an alternative chain C_A. Each block B_i binds its sVDF input via

$$x_i := H_G\big(y_{i-1} \parallel H(\mathrm{parent}(B_i)) \parallel \mathrm{aux}_i\big) \in \mathrm{QR}_N,$$

which prevents cross-fork replay. The fork choice prefers larger $\mathrm{TW}(\cdot)$, tie-breaking by $\mathcal{F}$. We restate and formalize three lemmas.

Lemma 2 (Fork specificity). *Fix a parent header* parent(B_i) *and predecessor output* y_{i-1}. *For any* τ_i, *there exists at most one accepting pair* (y_i, π_i) *for* (x_i, τ_i). *The same* (y_i, π_i, τ_i) *cannot validate under a different ancestry (i.e., with different* parent(B_i) *or* y_{i-1}*) except with negligible probability.*

Proof. For fixed ancestry, x_i is fixed; uniqueness of the sVDF yields at most one valid (y_i, π_i) for (x_i, τ_i). Reusing the same sample under different ancestry requires either H_G or H to collide, which occurs with negligible probability in the ROM.

Lemma 3 (Work-to-weight lower bound). *Let* C *be any chain with valid sVDF samples* $\{(x_i, y_i, \pi_i, \tau_i)\}$. *Producing* C *requires* $\Omega(\mathrm{TW}(C))$ *dependent calls to* Iter *along its lineage.*

Proof. Each accepted sample (y_i, π_i, τ_i) certifies that the prover has advanced from x_i by exactly τ_i sequential squarings. Summing over blocks gives a lower bound of $\sum_i \tau_i = \mathrm{TW}(C)$ dependent squarings; otherwise, one can assemble a chain with time weight $\mathrm{TW}(C)$ using fewer than $\mathrm{TW}(C)$ squarings, contradicting sVDF sequentiality and sample consistency.

Lemma 4 (Obsolete keys do not advance time). *Posterior corruption grants signatures but not sVDF progress: computing signatures on an alternative history is cheap, but computing valid sVDF samples for that history requires sequential work as in Lemma 3.*

Proof. The sVDF input x_i depends only on public data $(y_{i-1}, \mathrm{parent}(B_i), \mathrm{aux}_i)$ and pp.

Possessing signing keys for historical validators does not help compute y_i or π_i faster than squaring; any shortcut would again contradict sequentiality.

We can now relate post-anchor sequential work to the success probability in the long-range experiments of Sect. 3.3.

Let C_H be the honest chain starting from the anchor and C_A any adversarial chain constructed in the experiment $\mathsf{LRA}^{\mathsf{CP}}_{\Pi^+,\rho,k}(\mathcal{A})$. Let

$$\Delta_T := \mathrm{TW}(C_H) - \mathrm{TW}(C_A)$$

denote the time-weight gap measured strictly post-anchor, and let $\delta \geq 0$ cover network jitter and sampling noise.

Theorem 2 (CP-LRA security of Π^+). *In the experiment* $\mathsf{LRA}^{\mathsf{CP}}_{\Pi^+,\rho,k}(\mathcal{A})$, *suppose the adversary performs fewer than* $\Delta_T - \delta$ *dependent squarings after the anchor. Then the probability of a* k*-deep common-prefix violation is negligible in* λ. *Equivalently,*

$$\mathsf{Adv}^{\mathsf{CP}}_{\Pi^+,\rho,k}(\mathcal{A}) \leq \mathrm{negl}(\lambda)$$

unless $\mathcal{A}$ *invests post-anchor sequential work at least* $\mathrm{TW}(C_H) - \delta$.

Proof. Consider a successful common-prefix violation in $\mathsf{LRA}^{\mathsf{CP}}_{\Pi^+,\rho,k}$. By Lemma 2, the adversarial chain C_A must contain fresh valid samples; by Lemma 3, producing these samples requires at least $\mathrm{TW}(C_A)$ dependent squarings. If $\mathrm{TW}(C_A) < \mathrm{TW}(C_H) - \delta$, then the time-weighted fork choice $\mathcal{F}^+$ selects C_H, and the bootstrapping node cannot adopt a conflicting chain at depth k.

Any attempt to induce adoption of C_A while performing fewer than $\Delta_T - \delta$ additional squarings amounts to either forging time weight (breaking sVDF sequentiality) or violating CP in the projected Π execution—both negligible under our assumptions.

Theorem 3 (FIN-LRA security of Π^+). *If Π exports a finality predicate, then in the experiment $\mathsf{LRA}^{\mathsf{FIN}}_{\Pi^+,\rho}(\mathcal{A})$ any adversary that makes a rejoining node accept a finalized checkpoint conflicting with its ρ-fresh finalized anchor must perform post-anchor sequential work $\Omega(\mathrm{TW}(C_H))$, except with negligible probability.*

Proof. We apply the same reasoning as in Theorem 2, now restricted to chains that contain conflicting finalized checkpoints.

The fork-choice and finality rules of Π^+ project to those of Π, while the time-weight constraint enforces that any chain overtaking the honest finalized history must match or exceed its TW, requiring comparable sequential work post-anchor.

Finally, we summarize the long-range safety of the augmented protocol.

Theorem 4 (Long-range safety of Π^+). *Under the sVDF/hash assumptions of Sect. 5.1 and the base common-prefix and liveness of Π, the augmented protocol Π^+ satisfies $\mathsf{LRS}_{\Pi^+}(\rho, k)$ as defined in Sect. 3.4.*

In the experiments $\mathsf{LRA}^{\mathsf{CP}}_{\Pi^+,\rho,k}$ and $\mathsf{LRA}^{\mathsf{FIN}}_{\Pi^+,\rho}$, any PPT adversary with obsolete keys succeeds (i.e., causes a common-prefix or finality violation) with at most negligible probability unless it expends post-anchor sequential work at least $\mathrm{TW}(C_H) - \delta$.

Proof. Combine Lemma 1 (preservation of base CP/liveness) with Theorem 2 (CP-LRA security) and Theorem 3 (FIN-LRA security), and then invoke the definition of $\mathsf{LRS}_{\Pi^+}(\rho, k)$ from Sect. 3.4.

6 Evaluation

To evaluate the sVDF-augmented PoS design, we develop Python scripts for simulations. They track the cumulative sVDF iterations, called the time weight (TW). Our analysis focuses on how this accumulated value affects the capability of a long-range adversary to overtake the honest chain during bootstrap.

6.1 Experimental Setup

Rather than emulating full consensus, we model only per-branch time weight accumulation, which is sufficient for the time-aware fork-choice (Sect. 4).

Parameters are chosen to be realistic yet scale-free: only ratios matter for outcomes because TW increases linearly with the per-second squaring rate. Unless otherwise stated, we use:

- Slot time $S = 12$ seconds. The validators sample the running sVDF at proposal time, so TW grows with wall-clock time regardless of empty slots.
- Honest squaring rate r_H (steps/s) and adversarial rate $r_A = f \cdot r_H$ with hardware advantage factor $f \in \{1.0, 1.2, 1.5, 2.0, 3.0\}$. Only the factor f affects relative outcomes.
- Per-sample iteration count τ is modeled as Gaussian noise around its mean $\mu = r \cdot S$ with coefficient of variation cv $\in [0.0, 0.1]$ and truncated to be non-negative; this captures jitter in local clocks and scheduling while preserving sequentiality on average.
- Hygiene bounds for block samples: $\tau_{\min} = 0.8\,\mu$ and $\tau_{\max} = 1.2\,\mu$ by default; out-of-range samples would be rejected (Sect. 4).
- Weak-subjectivity window $\rho \in \{12, 24, 72\}$ hours (anchor freshness). A rejoining node trusts a checkpoint at most ρ hours old.
- Adversary start delay $d \in \{0, 6, 12\}$ hours after the anchor: the earliest time the adversary can begin post-anchor sVDF evaluation on its fork (e.g., due to key collection latency).

We study two questions: *(Q1)* Given $f > 1$, how quickly can a long-range adversary catch up in TW from an initial gap? *(Q2)* For a fixed anchor freshness ρ, what is the probability that the adversary can present a TW-dominant fork to a rejoining node? For intuition, when both sides start at the anchor and run continuously, the deterministic catch-up time (neglecting jitter) is

$$t_c \approx \frac{\max\{0, \mathrm{TW}_H(0) - \mathrm{TW}_A(0)\}}{r_A - r_H}$$

whenever $r_A > r_H$; if $r_A \leq r_H$, catching up is impossible without additional advantages. Our simulator measures the distribution of t_c with jitter and the finite-slot sampling effect.

6.2 Evaluation Results

Catch-up Probability vs Horizon. In Fig. 1, we sweep the time horizon (how long an adversary has to work post-anchor) and report the probability of TW catch-up within that horizon across trials. Two regimes appear: (i) for $f \leq 1.2$, catch-up is rare within 72h even with $d = 0$; (ii) for $f \geq 1.5$, catch-up becomes likely unless d is substantial or the node's anchor is very fresh ($\rho \leq 24$h). This highlights an operational guidance: keep anchors fresh (small ρ) and encourage homogeneous validator hardware to limit realistic f.

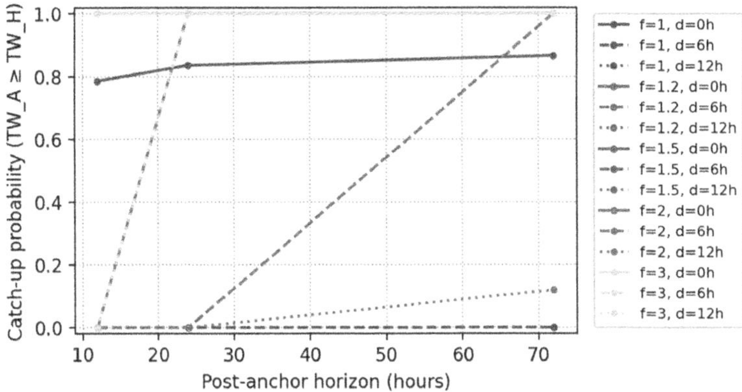

Fig. 1. Catch-up probability within a given post-anchor horizon for various hardware factors f and start delays d (aggregated across $\rho \in \{12, 24, 72\}$h).

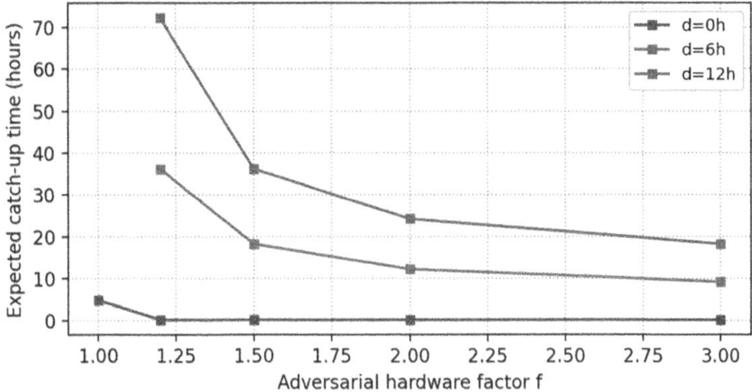

Fig. 2. Expected catch-up time $\mathbb{E}[t_c]$ vs adversarial hardware factor f.

Expected Catch-up Time . Figure 2 plots the expected catch-up time $\mathbb{E}[t_c]$ (truncating at 96h if not achieved) versus the hardware factor f. The empirical curve aligns with the simple bound $t_c \approx \Delta_0/(r_A - r_H)$, where Δ_0 is the initial TW gap induced by any adversary delay d. For $f \leq 1.2$, $\mathbb{E}[t_c]$ exceeds typical ρ; for $f \geq 2$, catch-up is fast unless d is large. This quantifies the "sequential cost to rewrite" intuition: either the adversary needs outsized hardware or must start immediately after the anchor to be competitive.

The sVDF TW rule transforms LRA feasibility into an explicit sequential-work race after the anchor; keeping hardware heterogeneity modest ($f \leq 1.2$) and anchors fresh ($\rho \leq 24$h) keeps catch-up probability low; and if an ecosystem expects powerful specialized hardware, operators should tighten ρ or publish more frequent social checkpoints as a backstop. Our scripts allow re-running with deployment-specific S, r_H, and expected f distributions without changing the methodology.

7 Conclusion

We presented a practical, backward-compatible augmentation to Proof-of-Stake consensus that embeds sampleable Verifiable Delay Function (sVDF) samples into block headers and uses cumulative sVDF iterations as a primary fork-choice weight. Under standard unknown-order and random-oracle assumptions we prove the sVDF interface preserves correctness, uniqueness, and sequentiality, and we show formally that any adversary attempting a long-range rewrite must expend sequential work proportional to the honest chain's accumulated sVDF time. Our simulation-based evaluation confirms that with modest hardware assumptions and reasonably fresh anchors the probability of adversarial TW catch-up is low across realistic horizons, while verification and bandwidth costs remain small. The mechanism is intentionally modular: it does not alter stake accounting or core randomness, and can be deployed as an additive defense layer alongside existing operational practices.

Acknowledgments. This paper is supported by the National Key R&D Program of China through project 2022YFB2701600, the Key R&D Program of Zhejiang Province 2025C01084, the Natural Science Foundation of China through projects U21A20467, U24B20144, 62572038, 62272464, the Natural Science Foundation of Beijing-Tianjin-Hebei through projects 25JJJC0033, and the Fundamental Research Funds for the Central Universities, the Research Funds of Renmin University of China(No. 202530187), and Big Data and Responsible Artificial Intelligence for National Governance, Renmin University of China.

References

1. Azouvi, S., Danezis, G., Nikolaenko, V.: Winkle: Foiling long-range attacks in proof-of-stake systems. In: Proceedings of the 2nd ACM Conference on Advances in Financial Technologies (AFT '20), pp. 189–201. Association for Computing Machinery, New York (2020). https://doi.org/10.1145/3419614.3423260
2. Azouvi, S., Vukolić, M.: Pikachu: Securing pos blockchains from long-range attacks by checkpointing into bitcoin pow using taproot. In: Proceedings of the 2022 ACM Workshop on Developments in Consensus (ConsensusDay '22), pp. 53–65. Association for Computing Machinery, New York (2022). https://doi.org/10.1145/3560829.3563563
3. Badertscher, C., Gaži, P., Kiayias, A., Russell, A., Zikas, V.: Ouroboros genesis: Composable proof-of-stake blockchains with dynamic availability. In: Proceedings of the 2018 ACM SIGSAC Conference on Computer and Communications Security (CCS '18), pp. 913–930. Association for Computing Machinery, New York (2018). https://doi.org/10.1145/3243734.3243848
4. Boneh, D., Bonneau, J., Bünz, B., Fisch, B.: Verifiable delay functions. In: Advances in Cryptology – CRYPTO 2018, Proceedings, Part I. Lecture Notes in Computer Science, vol. 10991, pp. 757–788. Springer, Cham (2018). https://doi.org/10.1007/978-3-319-96884-1_25
5. Buchman, E.: Tendermint: Byzantine Fault Tolerance in the Age of Blockchains. Master's thesis, University of Guelph, Guelph, Ontario, Canada, June 2016. http://hdl.handle.net/10214/9769, master's thesis

6. Buterin, V.: Explanation of weak subjectivity. Ethereum Blog (2014). https://blog.ethereum.org/2014/11/25/proof-stake-learned-love-weak-subjectivity/
7. Buterin, V., Drake, J., et al.: Minimal vdf randomness beacon. Ethereum Research Forum (2018). https://ethresear.ch/t/minimal-vdf-randomness-beacon/3566
8. Buterin, V., Griffith, V.: Casper the friendly finality gadget. arXiv preprint arXiv:1710.09437 (2017). https://arxiv.org/abs/1710.09437
9. Buterin, V., et al.: Ethereum consensus layer specifications. GitHub repository (2024). https://github.com/ethereum/consensus-specs
10. Chia Network: Chia timelords and vdfs. Chia Network Documentation (2023). https://docs.chia.net/chia-blockchain/architecture/timelords/
11. David, B., Gaži, P., Kiayias, A., Russell, A.: Ouroboros praos: An adaptively-secure, semi-synchronous proof-of-stake blockchain. In: Advances in Cryptology – EUROCRYPT 2018, Proceedings, Part II. LNCS, vol. 10821, pp. 66–98. Springer, Cham (2018). https://doi.org/10.1007/978-3-319-78375-8_3
12. Deb, S., Kannan, S., Tse, D.: Posat: proof-of-work availability and unpredictability, without the work. In: Financial Cryptography and Data Security, FC 2021, Revised Selected Papers, Part II. LNCS, vol. 12676, pp. 104–128. Springer, Heidelberg (2021). https://doi.org/10.1007/978-3-662-64331-0_6
13. Deirmentzoglou, E., Papakyriakopoulos, G., Patsakis, C.: A survey on long-range attacks for proof of stake protocols. IEEE Access **7**, 28712–28725 (2019). https://doi.org/10.1109/ACCESS.2019.2901858
14. Ethereum Foundation: Long range attacks. Ethereum Blog (2014). https://blog.ethereum.org/2014/05/15/long-range-attacks-the-serious-problem-with-adaptive-proof-of-work/
15. Garay, J.A., Kiayias, A., Leonardos, N.: The bitcoin backbone protocol: Analysis and applications. In: Advances in Cryptology – EUROCRYPT 2015, Proceedings, Part II. LNCS, vol. 9057, pp. 281–310. Springer, Heidelberg (2015). https://doi.org/10.1007/978-3-662-46803-6_10
16. Gilad, Y., Hemo, R., Micali, S., Vlachos, G., Zeldovich, N.: Algorand: Scaling byzantine agreements for cryptocurrencies. In: Proceedings of the 26th Symposium on Operating Systems Principles (SOSP '17), pp. 51–68. Association for Computing Machinery, New York (2017). https://doi.org/10.1145/3132747.3132757
17. Kiayias, A., Russell, A., David, B., Oliynykov, R.: Ouroboros: A provably secure proof-of-stake blockchain protocol. In: Advances in Cryptology – CRYPTO 2017, Proceedings, Part I. LNCS, vol. 10401, pp. 357–388. Springer, Cham (2017). https://doi.org/10.1007/978-3-319-63688-7_12
18. Li, F., Zhang, L., et al.: Babylon: Reusing bitcoin mining to enhance proof-of-stake security. arXiv preprint arXiv:2207.08392 (2022). https://arxiv.org/abs/2207.08392
19. Nakamoto, S.: Bitcoin: A peer-to-peer electronic cash system. Self-published white paper (2008). https://bitcoin.org/bitcoin.pdf, original white paper; not a 2024 reprint
20. Pass, R., Shi, E.: The sleepy model of consensus. In: Advances in Cryptology – ASIACRYPT 2017, Proceedings, Part II. LNCS, vol. 10625, pp. 380–409. Springer, Cham (2017). https://doi.org/10.1007/978-3-319-70697-9_14
21. Pietrzak, K.: Simple verifiable delay functions. In: 10th Innovations in Theoretical Computer Science Conference (ITCS 2019). Leibniz International Proceedings in Informatics (LIPIcs), vol. 124, pp. 60:1–60:15. Schloss Dagstuhl – Leibniz-Zentrum für Informatik, Dagstuhl, Germany (2019). https://doi.org/10.4230/LIPIcs.ITCS.2019.60

22. Team Rocket: Snowflake to avalanche: A novel metastable consensus protocol family for cryptocurrencies. Whitepaper (2018). https://avax.network/whitepapers
23. Wesolowski, B.: Efficient verifiable delay functions. In: Advances in Cryptology – EUROCRYPT 2019, Proceedings, Part III. LNCS, vol. 11478, pp. 379–407. Springer, Cham (2019).https://doi.org/10.1007/978-3-030-17659-4_13
24. Xu, J., Wang, C., Jia, X.: A survey of blockchain consensus protocols. ACM Computing Surveys **55**(13s) (Jul 2023). https://doi.org/10.1145/3579845
25. Yin, M., Malkhi, D., Reiter, M.K., Gueta, G.G., Abraham, I.: Hotstuff: Bft consensus with linearity and responsiveness. In: Proceedings of the 2019 ACM Symposium on Principles of Distributed Computing (PODC '19), pp. 347–356. Association for Computing Machinery, New York (2019). https://doi.org/10.1145/3293611.3331591

KG-Engine: A Compliance Evaluation Framework for Cryptographic Schemes Based on Ontology-Driven Knowledge Graphs

He Liujing[1], Pan Chenchen[1], Han Runze[1], and Zhao Yue[2](✉)

[1] Hainan University, Haikou, China
[2] National Key Laboratory of Security Communication, Chengdu, China
yuezhao@foxmail.com

Abstract. With the rapid advancement of digital transformation and artificial intelligence technologies, the importance of data security has become increasingly prominent. Among these, the compliance evaluation of cryptographic schemes has emerged as a critical defense line for safeguarding data security due to its significance. The core challenge lies in translating ambiguous standards described in natural language into logical assertions that can be processed by computers. Among existing approaches, manual evaluation suffers from inefficiency and incomplete coverage; rule-based methods lack deep modeling of domain concepts; and machine learning methods offer good scalability but struggle with interpretability. While knowledge graph technology holds potential to integrate the strengths of these approaches, its application in cryptographic scheme compliance evaluation remains an under-explored domain. Addressing these issues, this paper proposes KG-Engine, an automated evaluation framework based on ontology-driven knowledge graphs. This framework leverages a formalized ontology of cryptographic misuse and compliance evaluation to construct a precise semantic framework. Within this framework, declarative mapping rules transform raw data into structured knowledge graphs. Based on this graph, automated and explainable compliance detection is achieved through logical reasoning mechanisms involving entity linking, graph traversal, context awareness, and risk attribution. Experimental results demonstrate that KG-Engine significantly outperforms traditional baseline methods in detection precision, recall, and F1 score, while effectively identifying compound risks. This provides an effective solution for advancing data security compliance evaluation from "human-driven" to "intelligence-driven."

Keywords: Ontology · knowledge graph · compliance evaluation

1 Introduction

Driven by the dual forces of digital transformation and the rapid advancement of artificial intelligence technologies, data security has become a core responsibility and legal obligation for organizations worldwide. As a critical component in safeguarding data security, the importance of compliance evaluations for cryptographic solutions is increasingly prominent. The continuous improvement of laws and the rapid transformation of

W. Meng et al. (Eds.): ASSS 2025, CCIS 2903, pp. 75–87, 2026.
https://doi.org/10.1007/978-3-032-21600-7_5

technology have made the standards for compliance evaluation increasingly strict and the complexity continuously rising.

In recent years, research on cryptographic scheme compliance evaluation methods has evolved from "static conformity determination" to "dynamic risk quantification". The core challenge lies in translating compliance standards expressed in ambiguous natural language into logical assertions that can be processed by computers. Early compliance evaluations relied on manual expert audits and deductive reasoning [2]. Although this method can identify deep-seated design flaws with profound domain knowledge, its process is characterized by low efficiency, strong subjectivity, and difficulty in comprehensively covering the vast amount of implementation code and interaction logic in modern complex software systems [3].

With the rise of automated scanning tools and dynamic testing, tool-driven quantitative evaluation has become the mainstream approach for cryptographic compliance evaluation. Achieving automated, quantifiable understanding of cryptographic semantics remains a core challenge in compliance evaluation. Current research in tool-driven quantitative evaluation is progressively shifting from keyword matching toward context-aware analysis.Meng [4] proposed the Contrastive Learning-Driven Hierarchical Clustering Model (TICL) to jointly optimize semantic similarity and hierarchical structure, enabling the formation of a more reasonable hierarchy in the embedding space. However, the classification basis still relies on distributed similarity rather than semantic rules. Ershov [5] proposed the "Compliance-as-Code" framework, which maps regulatory provisions to executable graph database rules and integrates language models to enable regulatory question-answering and compliance verification. However, this approach relies on manual annotation for relationship identification, which remains a limitation. The Hypert model proposed by Yun [6] utilizes the Hearst schema to retrain BERT, achieving improved performance in attribute-species relationship recognition. However, the logical verifiability and interpretability of the hierarchical structure it generates remain key challenges and difficulties in current research. Traditional rule-based or statistical methods can efficiently extract facts but often lack deep modeling of domain conceptual systems. Machine learning-based approaches, while offering good scalability, heavily depend on the quality and scale of labeled data for performance, and their decision-making processes are frequently "black boxes" [7]. In the field of cryptography, where security requirements are extremely stringent, this may introduce unpredictable risks and errors. Therefore, a new technology is needed to synthesize the strengths of these approaches, enabling more efficient, comprehensive, and precise compliance evaluations for cryptographic schemes. The emergence of knowledge graph technology offers new possibilities for integrating these strengths. As a semantic network capable of effectively expressing and linking complex relational data, knowledge graphs have demonstrated unique value in cybersecurity [8], privacy protection [9], and cryptographic misuse [10]. However, knowledge graphs across different domains cannot be mutually adapted. The systematic application of knowledge graphs in cryptographic compliance evaluation remains an under-explored direction. Existing methods still exhibit significant shortcomings in areas such as the fine-grained semantic representation of cryptographic policy provisions and the logical mapping between cryptographic techniques and management requirements, making it difficult to support automated compliance determination in complex cryptographic environments.

Therefore, constructing an automated evaluation framework oriented toward cryptographic compliance requirements, integrating formal semantic modeling with interpretable reasoning, holds significant and urgent importance for enhancing the precision, adaptability, and effectiveness of cryptographic compliance evaluations. In light of this, this paper proposes a novel evaluation framework, KG-Engine. The main contributions of this paper are summarized as follows:

1. We propose an automated evaluation framework named KG-Engine, which establishes a comprehensive technological system encompassing ontology modeling, knowledge graph construction, and intelligent reasoning. This framework achieves precise semantic mapping and association from legal provisions and technical standards to specific operational configurations, effectively addressing the limitations of existing methods in semantic granularity and domain adaptability.
2. This framework achieves a paradigm shift in evaluation from reliance on manual expertise to automated knowledge reasoning. By converting implicit compliance knowledge into executable rules and graph queries, it enables automated validation of cryptographic configurations and traceability of violations, fundamentally overcoming the bottlenecks of manual approaches in efficiency, consistency, and scalability.
3. Experimental validation demonstrates that the KG-Engine framework significantly outperforms traditional baseline methods in cryptographic compliance detection tasks. In complex risk scenarios, it accurately deconstructs multi-entity association logic to achieve precise attribution of risk root causes. This framework provides reliable technical support for compliance evaluation applications in organizational data security governance during the AI era.

2 Method Design

2.1 Overall Plan

This chapter proposes a novel evaluation framework, KG-Engine, as shown in Fig. 1. Its core approach involves constructing knowledge graphs based on ontologies and leveraging automated reasoning tools to perform evaluations, thereby enabling automated compliance evaluations of cryptographic schemes.

This study first constructs a formal ontology for evaluating cryptographic misuse and compliance, endowing it with a semantic framework and logical constraints. Building upon this foundation, a corresponding knowledge graph is developed, transforming the ontology's logic into a knowledge graph structure. This elevates the knowledge graph from a "data network" to a "semantic network" and a "logical network." Finally, the knowledge graph leverages automated reasoning tools to automatically detect non-compliant issues and identify potential risks based on ontology semantics and logical rules, thereby enabling efficient compliance evaluation. Based on the above description, this chapter will focus on three core components: the construction and representation of formalized ontology, the instantiation of knowledge graphs, and the logical reasoning process for conducting compliance evaluations within this framework.

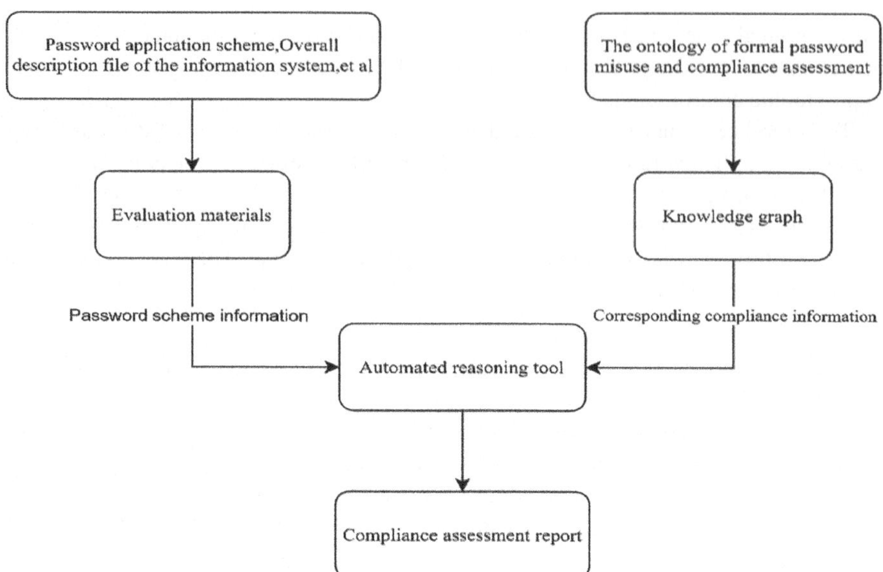

Fig. 1. KG-Engine evaluation Framework

2.2 Construction and Representation of Formal Ontologies

This section forms the foundation of this evaluation framework. Ontology construction involves the collection and organization of preliminary materials to clearly define core concepts, attributes, and relationships. This establishes a structured semantic framework for the knowledge graph.

Data Collection and Organization. This study extensively gathered academic materials from diverse sources and formats. These include papers from domestic and international core journals, proceedings from major conferences, university theses, authoritative research reports, and technical white papers. Covering a broad range of disciplines and research levels, these materials provide rich reference material for subsequently defining core concepts, attributes, and relationships.

Define Core Entities and Concepts. The knowledge graph in this study uses nodes to represent various entities related to cryptographic misuse, weak implementation of cryptographic policies, and compliance evaluations. To ensure the graph's structured and standardized nature, we constructed a corresponding ontology to clarify the scope of research and define key entities. The construction of the ontology is based on typical cryptographic algorithms as its core foundation. Building upon this foundation, it extends to cover a rich array of related concepts, such as cryptographic algorithms, misuse patterns, vulnerability cases, and their potential security consequences. Additionally, it incorporates various concepts related to compliance evaluation, including compliance standards and compliance requirements. The overall core concepts and entity examples are illustrated in Fig. 2.

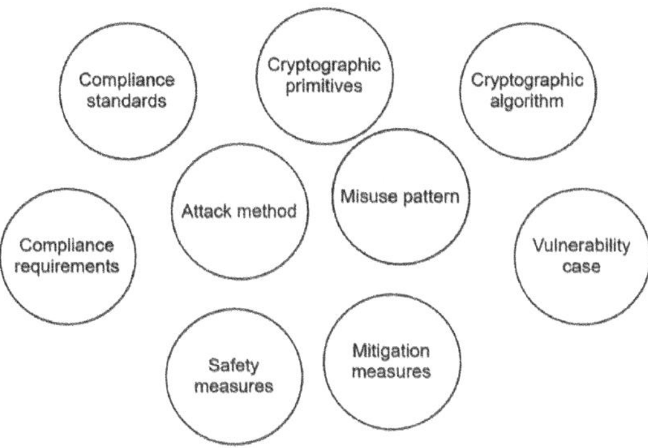

Fig. 2. The overall core concepts and entity examples are illustrated.

Define Attributes and Constraints. To further enrich the semantic layers of the knowledge graph and enhance its computability, we have defined a comprehensive set of attributes for the core concepts of the ontology. Examples of core concepts and attributes are shown in Table 1. By attaching structured attributes to concepts, the knowledge graph is elevated from a conceptual network to a deep knowledge repository. This not only enhances its descriptive capabilities but also provides direct criteria for rule-based inference engines: inference engines can automatically identify potential risks by verifying compliance with key length requirements, ensuring operational modes meet scenario security demands, and more.

Table 1. Examples of Overall Core Concepts and Attributes

Core concept	Related attributes
Cryptographic primitives	name, type, key length, output length
Cryptographic algorithm	specific name, detailed description, working mode
Misuse pattern	mode name, description, severity, relevant CWE ID
Attack method	attack name, description
Vulnerability case	CVE ID, description, affected software/systems, severity
Mitigation measures	name, description
Compliance standards	standard name, version, organization
Compliance requirements	require ID, description, specific requirement text

Define Relationships Between Different Entities. To construct a complete knowledge graph, beyond entities and attributes, the semantic relationships between them must be explicitly defined. Ontologies play a central role in this process. By formally defining various types of relationships, they ensure consistency and accuracy in how these relationships are expressed within the knowledge graph. Examples of core relationships between different entities are shown below:

Property Relationship: Such as "hasWeakness", it used to associate a cryptographic primitive or operation with its corresponding misuse pattern, indicating that the primitive or operation possesses a specific security weakness.

Causal Relationship: Such as "canLeadTo", it used to associate a misuse pattern with an attack method it may trigger, establishing a causal chain between misuse behavior and security threats.

Mitigation Relationship: Such as "mitigatedBy", it used to associate a misuse pattern with countermeasures or best practices that can mitigate it, providing security improvement solutions.

Functional Relationship: Such as "uses", it used to associate a cryptographic operation with the cryptographic primitives it invokes, indicating the operation's dependency on the primitives.

Compliance Relationship: Such as "violates", it used to associate a specific cryptographic misuse pattern with the compliance requirements or security standards it contravenes.

Specification Relationship: Such as "requires", it used to declare specific security controls or correct cryptographic practices that a compliance requirement must include or depend upon.

2.3 Instantiation Generation of Knowledge Graphs

Knowledge graph instantiation is a critical step in transforming raw data into structured, semantic knowledge representations, laying the foundation for subsequent applications of automated reasoning tools. Given that the target data sources exist in structured formats, this paper primarily employs declarative mapping rules to accomplish instantiation generation. Declarative mapping is a method that defines the correspondence between data schemas and target ontology schemas through logical rules. Through the instantiation process, we can map entities, properties, and relationships from data sources to the ontology framework of a knowledge graph, generating RDF triples that adhere to ontology constraints. This not only renders data machine-readable and understandable but also provides rich starting points and logical foundations for automated reasoning tools. Automatic reasoning tools can leverage these triples and ontology rules to detect logical consistency within the knowledge graph and identify potential contradictions and errors, thereby enabling efficient and precise compliance evaluations.

2.4 Conduct Logical Reasoning for Compliance Evaluation

The logical reasoning for compliance evaluation follows a formal ontology as its guiding principle, sequentially executing four key steps: entity linking and semantic understanding, graph traversal and association mining, context-aware risk attribution, and generation of interpretable compliance reports. This approach abandons traditional linear pattern matching in favor of multi-step deep analysis based on knowledge graphs. It elevates compliance evaluation from superficial matching to knowledge-driven logical reasoning, significantly enhancing detection accuracy, comprehensiveness, and interpretability.

Entity Linking and Semantic Understanding. The first step in logical reasoning is the semantic interpretation of code elements. KG-Engine employs entity recognition and linking technology to map strings within code to predefined nodes in the knowledge graph, thereby achieving the transformation from syntactic symbols to semantic concepts. This step provides an accurate semantic foundation for subsequent reasoning and serves as a critical prerequisite for achieving context-aware processing.

Graph Traversal and Association Mining. Building upon entity links, the engine activates its core inference mechanism—exploring the network structure of the knowledge graph to uncover complex latent relationships between entities. Its core approach involves starting from linked nodes, traversing the graph along corresponding relationships to locate all associated nodes, thereby forming a risk association network. This step not only identifies direct, obvious risks but also reveals indirect, deep-seated risk connections.

Context-Aware Risk Attribution. After acquiring rich contextual information, the engine makes intelligent decisions based on graph semantics and code context to accurately filter risks and determine their root causes. This approach mimics human expert judgment to effectively distinguish genuine risks, potential correlations, and semantic noise. By filtering out distracting elements like comments, it focuses analysis on actual risk triggers and precisely attributes root causes to specific code entities.

Explainable Compliance Reports. The ultimate value of logical reasoning lies in the explainability and actionability of its conclusions. KG-Engine's output is not a black-box conclusion but a transparent, traceable evaluation report. Its core approach ensures the final report clearly identifies "risk locations," "triggered misuse patterns," and "primary root causes of risk in compound risk scenarios," forming a complete chain of evidence. This ensures transparency and verifiability throughout the reasoning process. Developers not only receive the results but also understand the underlying "why," enabling efficient remediation. This explainability represents a key advantage of applying logical reasoning to rigorous compliance evaluation scenarios.

3 Experiment

To comprehensively and rigorously evaluate the effectiveness and advanced nature of the proposed KG-Engine, this study designed and conducted a series of experiments.

3.1 Experimental Setup

All experiments in this study were conducted on a standard server (Intel Core i7 CPU, 16GB RAM). The core logic of the evaluation engine and related data processing workflows were implemented in a Python 3.8 environment, while the knowledge graph was deployed on the Neo4j graph database.

The cryptographic compliance knowledge graph relied upon in this experiment was pre-constructed, encapsulating a comprehensive model of cryptographic misuse. The schema layer contains 163 MisuseCategory nodes and 61 MisusePattern nodes. These nodes form a risk hierarchy through the IS_SUBCATEGORY_OF and IS_EXAMPLE_OF relationships. The data layer is built through automated keyword extraction. It includes more than 770 CryptoEntity nodes. Over 1,000 INVOLVES_ENTITY relationships link these entities to misuse patterns. Together, they form a complex knowledge network for cryptographic compliance, as shown in Fig. 3. (Since a complete knowledge graph comprises thousands of knowledge elements, its global view becomes difficult to clearly present in visualization due to the high overlap of nodes and edges. Therefore, this diagram only captures a representative slice of the data layer.)

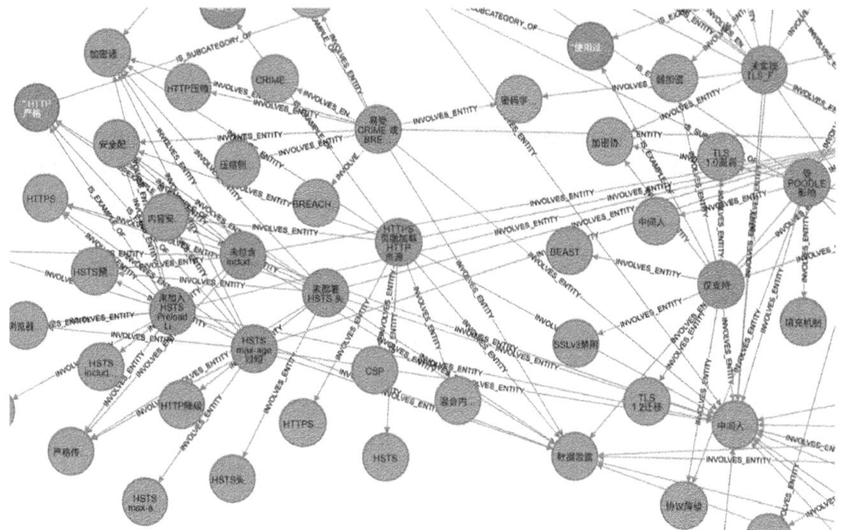

Fig. 3. Representative Slice of the Cryptographic Compliance Knowledge Network.

3.2 Experimental Results

To ensure standardized and reproducible evaluation, this study constructed a dedicated Java code snippet test dataset. This dataset covers typical cryptographic misuse scenarios, containing both compliant and non-compliant samples. Deceptive keywords were intentionally introduced into the comments or strings of some compliant samples to simulate real-world noise, thereby comprehensively testing the robustness of the evaluation method. For performance metrics, this study employs standard classification task evaluation indicators from information retrieval and machine learning: precision, recall, and F1 score.

KG-Engine Detection Performance. To objectively evaluate KG-Engine's performance, this study introduces a keyword-matching-based baseline method as a comparative reference. This baseline model represents a widely adopted and computationally efficient traditional detection approach. We selected this baseline to establish a clear and comparable performance reference point. This ensures that the subsequent performance comparison can address a central question effectively. Compared with a mature and practical tool-driven quantitative evaluation method, does the introduction of a sophisticated knowledge engine—rather than relying solely on model extraction—yield a statistically significant improvement in performance?

We conducted a comprehensive performance evaluation of KG-Engine and the aforementioned baseline methods on the predefined dataset. Both approaches scanned all code snippets in the test set and compared their detection results against the ground truth facts in the dataset to compute precision, recall, and F1 scores. This experimental design ensures fairness in the evaluation process and reproducibility of the results. It also establishes a representative and strong baseline, which provides a conservative and reliable foundation for any conclusion regarding performance gains. The experimental results are shown in Table 2.

Table 2. Performance of the two methods on the test set

Method	Precision	Recall	F1-Score
Keyword-Based Baseline	0.63	0.46	0.53
KG-Engine(Ours)	0.95	0.81	0.88

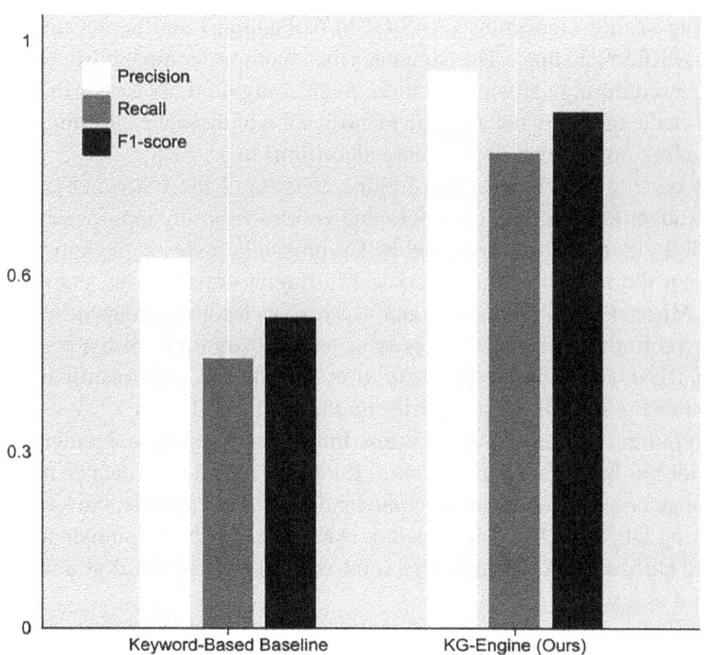

Fig. 4. Performance Comparison of the Two Methods on the Test Dataset

As observed in Fig. 4, which visualizes the performance of both methods on the test set, KG-Engine significantly outperforms the keyword-based baseline method across all three metrics: precision, recall, and F1 score.

Specifically, KG-Engine achieved an accuracy rate of 0.95, significantly higher than the baseline method's 0.63. This gap underscores the critical role of knowledge graphs in suppressing false positives. The baseline method, lacking contextual awareness, frequently misreports annotations or keywords within text. In contrast, KG-Engine effectively filters semantic noise through entity linking and graph relationship inference, enabling more reliable judgments. Meanwhile, in terms of recall, KG-Engine achieves a score of 0.81, which is significantly higher than the baseline value of 0.46. This result indicates that KG-Engine provides a clear advantage in coverage. By leveraging the systematically organized misuse patterns and entity associations in the knowledge graph, KG-Engine is able to identify a broader and more subtle set of risk cases. In terms of the overall performance metric, the F1 score of KG-Engine reaches 0.88, representing a substantial improvement over the baseline value of 0.53. This result systematically validates, from a statistical perspective, the necessity and effectiveness of incorporating a knowledge structure to enhance code risk detection. Taken together, the quantitative evaluation strongly demonstrates the accuracy and comprehensiveness of our approach in the task of cryptographic compliance evaluation.

Analysis of Composite Risk Identification Capability. To validate KG-Engine's ability to identify composite cryptographic risks, this paper designs a typical hybrid configuration scenario as an analysis case. In this scenario, the system dynamically initializes a set of encryptors based on configuration files, simultaneously incorporating secure algorithms (AES/GCM/NoPadding) and deprecated algorithms (DES/CBC/PKCS5Padding). This simulates the common "compatibility configuration" pattern observed during software iteration. Such configurations harbor high risks, with the critical challenge being the accurate identification of insecure algorithms (e.g., DES) while excluding interference from secure algorithms (e.g., AES).

The processing workflow of KG-Engine consists of the following key steps. The engine first identifies multiple cryptographic entities from the input, such as AES and DES, and links them to the corresponding CryptoEntity nodes in the knowledge graph. Starting from the identified entity nodes, KG-Engine traverses the graph to trace all associated MisusePattern nodes. The analysis reveals a complex dependency network:

The CryptoEntity {name: 'DES'} is associated with multiple misuse patterns, including "using DES/3DES symmetric encryption algorithms" and "insufficient ECC key length," indicating that DES itself carries multiple potential risks.

The CryptoEntity {name: 'AES'} is also linked to several misuse patterns. However, this does not imply that AES is insecure. Rather, it reflects the deeper mechanism of the knowledge graph in representing contextual risks. For example, the keywords in the pattern "using DES/3DES..." may include AES because the recommended mitigation is to replace DES with AES. Thus, AES is introduced in this context as a risk mitigation measure, not as a source of risk.

Despite the complex connections in the knowledge graph, KG-Engine does not simply list all associated nodes. Instead, it attributes risks based on the core entities that trigger them. In this case, the reasoning path of the compound risk scenario of KG-Engine is visualized, as shown in Fig. 5. since the code directly invokes the DES algorithm, the engine accurately attributes the root cause of the risk to the DES entity and highlights "using DES/3DES symmetric encryption algorithms" as the directly relevant misuse pattern. AES is referenced only in the mitigation recommendation and is not falsely reported as a risk source.

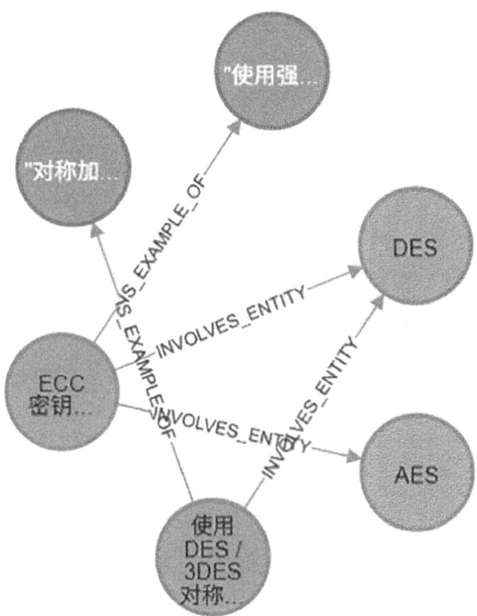

Fig. 5. KG-Engine's Inference Path Visualization for a Composite Risk Scenario

This case demonstrates that KG-Engine can leverage the semantic associations and contextual reasoning of the knowledge graph to achieve precise risk identification and attribution in compound algorithm configurations. It effectively distinguishes between risky and secure entities, highlighting its practical value in complex cryptographic risk evaluation.

4 Conclusion

This paper addresses the need for automation and intelligence in cryptographic compliance evaluation by proposing an ontology-driven knowledge graph evaluation framework, KG-Engine.

At the theoretical modeling level, we constructed an ontology for cryptographic misuse and compliance evaluation. The ontology defines core entities, properties, and semantic relationships, providing a unified semantic framework for structured knowledge representation. This approach overcomes the limitations of existing models, which often lack semantic constraints and domain adaptability.

At the method development level, we introduced a knowledge graph construction approach that integrates process-attribute generation with declarative mapping rules.

This enables accurate transformation from raw data to semantic knowledge, effectively enhancing the dynamism and consistency of the knowledge graph.

At the reasoning mechanism level, we designed a four-stage logical inference process, including entity linking, graph traversal, context-aware reasoning, and interpretable report generation. This elevates compliance evaluation from shallow pattern matching to deep knowledge-driven reasoning, significantly improving the accuracy, interpretability, and traceability of the evaluation.

Experimental results demonstrate the exceptional effectiveness of the KG-Engine framework: in cryptographic compliance detection tasks, it achieves precision, recall, and F1 scores of 0.95, 0.81, and 0.88, respectively, significantly outperforming traditional baseline methods. In complex risk scenarios, it accurately deconstructs multi-entity association logic to achieve precise attribution of risk root causes. This research establishes a comprehensive technical system encompassing ontology modeling, graph construction, and intelligent reasoning, providing a reusable and scalable automated solution for cryptographic compliance evaluation.

Acknowledgments. The work was supported by the National Key Laboratory of Security Communication Foundation under grant No. 6142103042401, Sichuan Science and Technology Innovation Talent Program under grant No. 2024JDRC0007.

References

1. China Academy of Information and Communications Technology: China Academy of Information and Communications Technology Data Governance Research Report - Research on the Legal System of Network Data Security Management (2024), https://aigc.idigital.com.cn/djyanbao/%E3%80%90%E4%B8%AD%E5%9B%BD%E4%BF%A1%E9%80%9A%E9%99%A2%E3%80%91%E6%95%B0%E6%8D%AE%E6%B2%BB%E7%90%86%E7%A0%94%E7%A9%B6%E6%8A%A5%E5%91%8A%EF%BC%882024%E5%B9%B4%EF%BC%89-2025-01-23.pdf, last Accessed 24 Nov 2025
2. State Cryptography Administration: Expert Interpretation|Ma Yuan: Establishing a Sound Security Evaluation System for Commercial Cryptography Applications to Promote Standardized Use of Commercial Cryptography, https://www.oscca.gov.cn/sca/xxgk/2023-05/31/content_1061054.shtml, last accessed 24 Nov 2025
3. Wang, C.: Farewell to static passwords: how AI builds "living" security Defenses? Inf. Secur. Commun. Secur. (9), 11–18 (2025). https://doi.org/10.3969/j.issn.1009-8054.2025.09.002
4. Meng, Y., Zhai, S., Chai, Z., et al.: Which is better? Taxonomy induction with learning the optimal structure via contrastive learning. Knowl.-Based Syst. **304**, 112405 (2024)
5. Ershov, V.: A case study for compliance as code with graphs and language models: Public release of the regulatory knowledge graph. arXiv **preprint**, arXiv:2302.01842 (2023).
6. Yun, G., Lee, Y., Moon, A.S.: & et al.: Hypert: hypernymy-aware BERT with Hearst pattern exploitation for hypernym discovery. J. Big Data. **10**(1), 141 (2023)
7. Heidary, K., Atluri, V., Bland, J.: Performance evaluation of machine learning algorithms in reduced dimensional spaces. J. Cyber Secur. **6**(0), 69–87 (2024). https://doi.org/10.32604/JCS.2024.051196
8. Zhong, X., Yang, G., Shan, L.: A review of cybersecurity knowledge graph research. Inf. Warfare Technol. **3**(05), 19–29 (2024)

9. Zhang, S., Zhan, H., Li, X., et al.: Research review on cybersecurity knowledge graph construction and application. J. Cyberspace Secur. Sci. **2**(03), 79–106 (2024). https://doi.org/10.20172/j.issn.2097-3136.240307
10. Wu, J., Xu, W., Pan, L., et al.: Construction and analysis of a knowledge graph for cryptographic misuse vulnerabilities. Electron. Technol. **54**(06), 100–103 (2025)

Automated Program Repair Based on Large Language Model and Mask Templates

Xiaohan Wu, Lili Bo(✉), Xiaohan Jiang, and Yuting He

College of Information and Artificial Intelligence (College of Industrial Software), Yangzhou University, Yangzhou 225000, China
lilibo@yzu.edu.cn

Abstract. Most of the automated program repair (ARP) approaches are learning-based techniques. They treat bug fixes as a neural machine translation task by translating incorrect code into correct code. However, these approaches rely heavily on high-quality bug-fixing pairs and may spend expensive training costs. To alleviate the problems, in this paper, we present TemRepair, a new approach based on mask templates and Large Language Model (LLM), which generate patches through zero-shot learning. First, eight categories of mask templates are summarized by manually analyzing 2,000 bug-fixing pairs, such as modifying method invocation expressions, altering variables, and adjusting operators. Then, mask lines are produced using mask templates, and together with the method context as well as the comments, are input to the Large Language Model (InCoder) to predict the masked sections. Finally, the generated patches are deduplicated and verified. Experimental results on the Defects4J dataset show that, TemRepair can generate 67 correct patches, indicating its superiority over the state-of-the-art approaches.

Keywords: automated program repair · Large Language Model · patch generation · mask templates

1 Introduction

Currently, various automated program repair techniques have emerged. These techniques automatically generate patches to fix bugs, thereby relieving researchers from the burdensome task of manual debugging. Traditional program repair methods can be categorized based on patch generation strategies into approaches based on heuristic search [1], manual repair templates [2, 3], semantic constraints [4], and statistical analysis [5]. Although the widely used template-based methods in earlier stages could generate patches with high accuracy, they heavily relied on the quality of the templates and were only capable of repairing specific types of errors, making them difficult to apply on a large scale. With the advancement of machine learning and deep learning technologies, researchers have begun to explore learning-based patch generation methods, which frame the patch generation process as a translation task—translating the original buggy code into correctly repaired code.

However, learning-based methods face two major challenges. (1) Difficulty in acquiring high-quality training data. Traditional models rely on high-quality pairs of buggy

W. Meng et al. (Eds.): ASSS 2025, CCIS 2903, pp. 88–99, 2026.
https://doi.org/10.1007/978-3-032-21600-7_6

code and repaired code for training. However, such data are not easily obtainable, and bug-fix commits often contain unrelated edits—such as refactoring or new feature implementations—which introduce noise into the training dataset. (2) Expensive training resources and substantial computational overhead. Learning-based methods are often characterized by a massive number of parameters. To capture syntactic and semantic patterns from vast code corpora, the training phase of these models necessitates significant graphical processing unit (GPU) power, storage capacity, and time investment [6].

To address the challenges, this paper proposes TemRepair, a method that integrates simple mask templates with Large Language Models (LLMs) under a zero-shot learning setting to directly generate patches. It eliminates the need for high-quality repair templates or additional training as well as fine-tuning on repair pairs. Specifically, through manual analysis of 2,000 bug-fixing pairs, we summarize eight categories of mask templates, covering common types such as modifying method invocation expressions, altering variables, and adjusting operators. These templates are used to generate masked lines that replace the buggy lines, which—along with the buggy method code and contextual comments—are fed into a large language model (InCoder) to predict the masked content and generate patches. Finally, the generated patches undergo deduplication and validation, including compilation and testing, to ensure their correctness and reliability. Experimental results demonstrate that TemRepair generates 67 correct patches on the Defects4J [7] dataset, improving the efficiency of software bug fixes, and outperforms existing methods in the accuracy of patch generation.

2 Related Work

Large Language Models (LLMs) generate logically consistent code segments by comprehending code context, thereby providing effective patches or repair suggestions for automated program repair. Xia et al. [8] proposed AlphaRepair, the first cloze-style APR approach, which directly leverages large language code models without requiring fine-tuning or retraining on historical bug fixes. It predicts correct code to repair bugs and supports multiple programming languages. Fan et al. [9] observed that large language models (e.g., Codex) can generate code for programming tasks and investigated the role of APR techniques in enhancing their reliability. Peng et al. [10] introduced TypeFix, which integrates repair templates to improve the effectiveness of prompts, covering approximately 75% of type errors and enhancing the performance of LLMs in bug fixes. Lutellier et al. proposed CoCoNuT [11], a context-aware neural machine translation architecture that processes erroneous code and contextual code separately, extracts hierarchical features, and integrates them through learning to repair various code defects.

3 Our Approach: TemRepair

In this section, we present TemRepair, a program repair method based on mask templates and large language models. Fig. 1 illustrates the workflow of TemRepair, which consists of two main phases: masked line designation and patch generation. The phase of masked line designation comprises two steps, which focus on fault localization and creating masked code lines using templates, whereas the patch generation phase includes three steps, aiming to produce, deduplicate, and validate candidate patches.

Step 1: Fault Localization. In our evaluation, we assume perfect fault localization (i.e., the exact buggy line is given) to fairly compare with other APR tools. The entire method containing the buggy line and its comments are then extracted. Subsequently, extract the entire method code containing the buggy line (or buggy lines), along with the method comments. Here, the method code constitutes the "contextual code", providing the LLM with the full structural and semantic scope necessary for understanding the bugs and generating a coherent patch.

Step 2: Masked Line Generation. For each identified erroneous line, the Javaparser library [12] is employed to perform syntactic analysis, through which key code elements—including parameters, method calls, and expressions—are identified. Based on this analysis, the appropriate mask templates are applied to generate multiple candidate masked lines. Each masked line, in which specific elements are replaced with the <mask> token, is then combined with the complete method code and associated comments to form the input sequence for the code generation model (InCoder).

Step 3: Patch Generation. We use the InCoder-6B model. The input is the masked code, and the model is tasked with predicting the $<mask>$ content. 50 candidates are generated per mask using a temperature of 0.8 and top-p sampling of 0.95 to encourage diversity.

Step 4: Patch Deduplication. The generated patches are re-examined to eliminate those identical to the original buggy code or duplicates among the generated candidates.

Step 5: Patch Validation. The patches are validated by compiling each candidate patch and verified against the corresponding test suite. Patches that pass all tests are output as valid repairs.

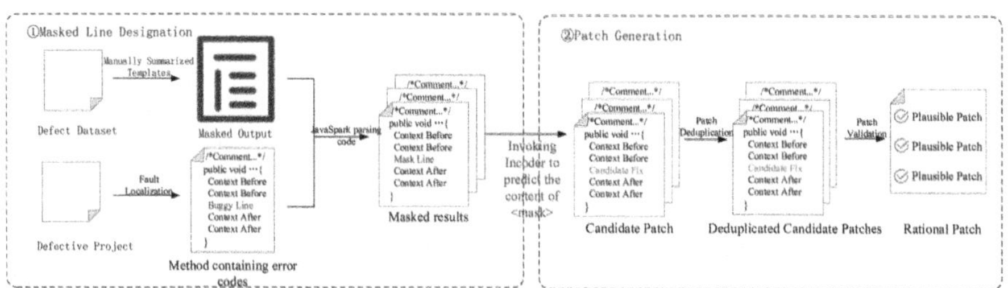

Fig. 1. Overview of TemRepair

3.1 Mask Template Extraction

To enhance repair efficiency and accuracy, this paper systematically investigates bug-fixing pairs and manually summarizes repair templates. For the enhancement of repair efficiency and accuracy, a systematic investigation of defect-repair code pairs is conducted, leading to the manual summarization of repair templates. We collected and organized the training dataset from CURE [13], which comprises a total of 2,000 bug-fixing pairs. Each row in this bug dataset represents one instance, formatted as follows: buggy line <*CTX* > context repaired line. Only the buggy lines and repaired lines were retained for manual analysis and summarization.

Upon inspection, it was found that 439 bug-fixing pairs involved multi-line repair additions. Since multi-line modifications are often challenging to repair effectively, only single-line modification patterns were considered. After excluding these 439 instances, the remaining 1,561 pairs were systematically summarized and categorized, resulting in eight types of mask templates, as presented in Table 1.

To ensure the reliability of the manually summarized mask templates, this study employed Cohen's Kappa coefficient [14] to verify inter-rater agreement in data labeling. Cohen's Kappa coefficient is a statistical measure used to assess the level of agreement between two raters for categorical items. The formulas are defined as follows:

$$p_{i+} = \sum_{j=1}^{k} \mathrm{p}_{ij} \tag{1}$$

$$p_{+j} = \sum_{j=1}^{k} \mathrm{p}_{ij} \tag{2}$$

Cohen's Kappa coefficient is defined as:

$$x = \frac{p_o - p_e}{1 - p_e} \tag{3}$$

Where $p_o = \sum_{i=1}^{k} \mathrm{p}_{ii}$ represents the observed proportion of agreement.

In this study, the third and fourth authors served as raters. Cohen's Kappa [15] coefficient was used to evaluate the agreement between the two raters. During the initial phase, when approximately 5% of the bug-fixing pairs were independently labeled, the Kappa coefficient was approximately 0.25. After training and label refinement between the raters, a follow-up pilot study involving 10% of the data was conducted, resulting in a Kappa coefficient of approximately 0.55. Through continuous discussion and calibration using representative examples, the Kappa coefficient for each category eventually exceeded 0.90. A thorough review of the final conclusions allowed comprehensive validation of the accuracy and applicability of the research findings. The results are summarized in Table 2.

A detailed analysis of the eight template types reveals that MP1 (modifying method-invocation expressions) is the most prevalent, accounting for 43.0% (671/1, 561) of all patches. This indicates that altering method invocations is the dominant repair pattern in software bug fixes. By contrast, MP8 (deleting statements) is the least common, representing only 2.2% (35/1, 561), suggesting that simply removing statements is rarely employed as a repair strategy.

3.2 Patch Generation

To generate replacement patches for buggy code lines, our study employs the InCoder model to generate code for each input mask. InCoder completes the masked portion of the code using the natural language description of the buggy method. It utilizes the

Table 1. Eight Types of Mask Templates

Category	Category Description	Mask Template	Mask Template Description
MP1	Modify Method-Invocation Expression	- method(arg1, arg2) MP1.1 + method(<mask>, arg2) MP1.2 + method(arg1, arg2, <mask>) MP1.3 + method(arg1) MP1.4 + <mask>(arg1,arg2) MP1.5 + <mask>(method(arg1, arg2)) MP1.6 + (arg1, arg2)	MP1.1: Replacing a method parameter with <mask> MP1.2: Adding a method parameter with <mask> MP1.3: Deleting a method parameter MP1.4: Replacing a method name with <mask> MP1.5: Adding an invoked method name with <mask> MP1.6: Deleting a method name
MP2	Modify Variable	- ...var1... + ...<mask>ssss...	MP2: Replacing a variable with <mask>
MP3	Modify Operator	- exp1 op exp2 + exp1 <mask> exp2	MP3: Replacing an operator with <mask>
MP4	Modify Numeric Type	- T1 var. + <mask> var	MP4: Replacing a data type with <mask>

MP5	Modify Conditional Expression	- if(confition_exp 1 op 1 condition_exp2){
		+ MP5.1 - if(<mask> op 1 condition_exp2){
		+ MP5.2 - if(condition_exp1 op 1 condition_exp2 op 2 < mask>)
		+ MP5.3
		– if(condition_exp1){
			MP5.1: Modifying a conditional expression with <mask>
			MP5.2: Adding a conditional expression with <mask>
			MP5.3: Deleting an existing condition

(*continued*)

contextual code behavior that precedes and follows the mask. Taking the example of *str.getChars* (0, *strLen*, *buffer*, *size*) from Fig. 2, assuming perfect fault localization, the masked line is generated by replacing the buggy code line according to the mask template. Since MP8 involves statement deletion rather than code generation, only the first seven mask templates are considered. The original faulty code is *str.getChars* (0,

Table 1. (*continued*)

Category	Category Description	Mask Template	Mask Template Description

MP6	Add Missing Statement	MP6.1 + return <mask>
		MP6.2 + try{
		< mask >;...
		+}catch(Exception e){...}
		MP6.3 + if (<mask>){
		Statement;
		+}
		MP6.4 + <mask>
			MP6.1: Adding a return statement
			MP6.2: Adding a try-catch block
			MP6.3: Adding a conditional expression
			MP6.4: Adding an arbitrary statement

MP7	Replace Statement	- statement + <mask>	MP7: Replace Statement
MP8	Delete Statement	- statement - statement	MP8: Delete Statement

Table 2. Statistical distribution of eight types of mask templates

Template ID	MP1	MP2	MP3	MP4	MP5	MP6	MP7	MP8
Count	671	205	41	143	59	263	144	35

strLen, *buffer*, *size*), where 0, *strLen*, *buffer*, and *size* are parameters, and *str* is the string object invoking the *getChars* method.

Following the MP1 mask template, the parameters of the erroneous statement are masked first. For instance, masking the first parameter 0 generates the masked line: *str.getChars* (*<mask > <mask > <mask>*).

After generating all masked lines, the InCoder model is invoked to automatically complete the masked code segments. Leveraging its bidirectional nature, InCoder integrates the structural and logical relationships of the code surrounding the mask—both before and after—to generate patches that align with the overall semantics. In this study, masking is applied to specific parts of a single line of code (e.g., parameters, variable names) or specific regions spanning multiple lines (e.g., conditional expressions, loop structures). Ultimately, InCoder generates replacement lines based on the mask templates, producing a series of initial patches (as illustrated in Fig. 2).

3.3 Patch Deduplication

Since an erroneous line may contain only one error, many positions might not actually be faulty. Consequently, the generated patched code may be identical to the original code. As illustrated in Fig. 2, patches ①, ③, ④, ⑤, and ⑥ are the same as the original erroneous line, indicating that these locations may not be where the error occurred. Patches identical to the original erroneous line are clearly unlikely to be correct and should therefore be

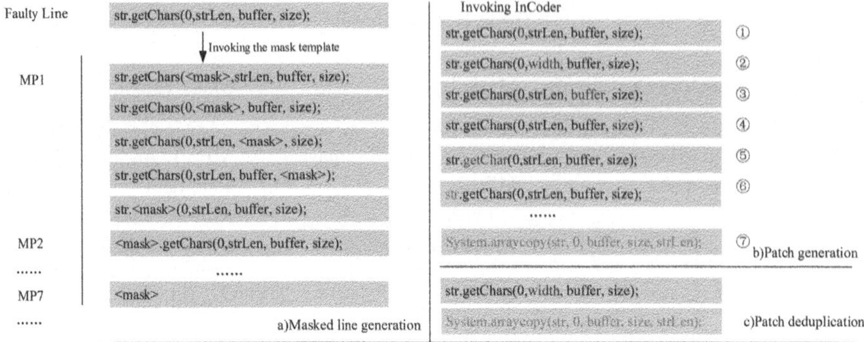

Fig. 2. An Example of Patch Generation Process

removed. Additionally, some patches, although generated from different mask templates, may ultimately produce the same patched code. For instance, even if different templates are invoked, they may still generate identical patch content. Such duplicate patches also require deduplication.

After deduplication, only one unique correct patch remains in Fig. 2, that is patch ②.

As shown in Fig. 2, without patch deduplication, the originally correct patch was ranked second. After deduplication, its ranking ascends to first place, surpassing other patches and becoming the optimal choice. The importance of patch deduplication lies in eliminating redundant validation efforts and avoiding duplicated work. Without deduplication, the same erroneous code may generate multiple duplicate and incorrect patches, necessitating independent validation for each patch. This increases both the workload and time costs. Through patch deduplication, obviously erroneous and duplicate patches can be filtered out first. This significantly reduces the validation workload, improves repair efficiency, and saves time and resources. Therefore, patch deduplication is essential. It not only enhances repair efficiency and reduces validation efforts but also conserves time and resources.

3.4 Patch Validation

The patch validation process is implemented by executing a test suite. For multiple candidate patches generated, each undergoes validation sequentially. First, the candidate patch is applied to the buggy code, and an attempt is made to compile it to generate an executable program. If the compilation succeeds, it indicates that the patch possesses basic syntactic correctness and structural integrity; if the compilation fails, the patch is directly discarded. For patches that pass compilation, it is observed whether they can pass all test cases. If a patch passes all test cases, it is considered a plausible patch. For plausible patches, further manual inspection is conducted. After verification by manual review without discrepancies, the patch is deemed a correct patch. If none of the candidate patches pass validation, the next suspicious location in the report is selected, and the patch generation model is used again to generate new candidate patches for validation. This process repeats until a plausible and correct patch is identified.

The manual inspection is solely for the final, definitive classification of "**Correct**" patches, ensuring they are semantically equivalent to the human-written patches. This step is a common practice in APR research for ground-truth validation and does not affect the fully automated process of generating, compiling, and testing the patches to identify "**Plausible**" candidates.

4 Experimental Evaluation

4.1 Design of Experimental Questions

RQ1: How many bugs in Defects4J can TemRepair repair?

RQ2: How effective TemRepair is compared with the state-of-the-art APR tools?

RQ3: How do different configurations affect the performance of TemRepair?

We demonstrate the effectiveness of TemRepair by comparing it with state-of-the-art learning-based APR tools. We assume perfect fault localization results are known, as this eliminates the impact of fault localization and better reflects the patch generation capability of each APR tool.

4.2 Experimental Dataset

For evaluation, we conducted experiments on the widely used dataset Defects4J. Defects4J is an extensively utilized benchmark dataset in the fields of program repair and fault localization. It comprises a series of real-world open-source Java projects with known software bugs, including well-known open-source projects such as Apache Commons Math, JFreeChart and Joda-Time. Each project version includes a set of known bugs manually labeled and documented by developers or researchers. We adopted the widely used Defects4J version 1.2, which contains 395 bugs from six different projects. Consistent with prior learning-based tools [13], all experiments were allocated a patch repair time limit of 5 h.

4.3 Experimental Results and Analysis

Research Question 1. Assuming the statement-level bug locations are known and directly provided to TemRepair for patch generation, the results are shown in Table 3. Among 395 bugs in the Defects4J benchmark, TemRepair generated plausible patches for 102 bugs, 67 of which were correct.

Table 3. Number of patches TemRepair generated

Item	Chart	Closure	Lang	Math	Mockito	Time	Total
Count	8/11	19/26	14/20	20/36	3/3	3/6	67/102

Research Question 2. Table 4 shows the comparison results of TemRepair with existing APR approaches using perfect bug localization. TemRepair achieved the best performance by correctly repairing 67 bugs, demonstrating its effectiveness in large-scale bug fix under ideal localization conditions. Furthermore, we evaluated the number of unique bugs repaired exclusively by TemRepair. As shown in Fig. 3, TemRepair repaired 11 unique bugs—3 more than TBar (the second-best template-based method) and significantly outperformed learning-based approaches (e.g., CURE, CoCoNuT). This highlights the superiority of TemRepair in handling complex bugs and suggests its potential for integration with other techniques to increase correct patch generation.

Table 4. Comparison with the existing APR approaches based on perfect bug localization

Project	TemRepair	CURE[14]	CoCoNuT[11]	PROPR[16]	DLFix[17]	Simfix[18]	SequenceR[19]
Chart	8	10	7	5	5	3	3
Closure	19	14	9	11	11	6	3
Lang	14	9	7	8	8	9	3
Math	20	19	16	13	13	11	4
Mockito	3	4	4	1	1	0	0
Time	3	1	1	2	2	0	0
Total Correct	67	57	44	41	40	29	13

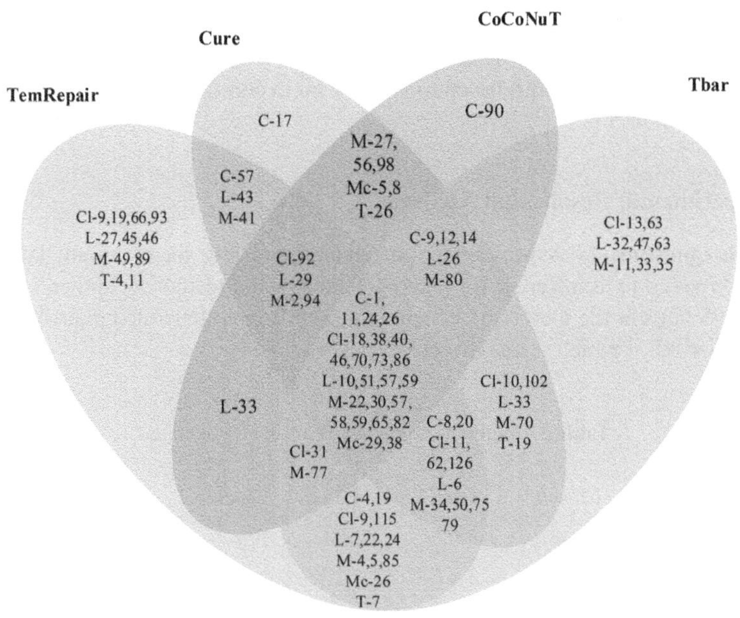

Fig. 3. Venn diagrams of correct patches

Fig. 4 illustrates a conditional statement bug (from Defects4J 1.2) that only TemRepair could fix. The original buggy code *if (expPos < decPos)* lacked a boundary check for string length. The repaired version added a new condition *expPos > str.length()* to prevent index overflow. Template-based and learning-based APR methods failed here due to limitations in training data coverage. TemRepair succeeded because its mask template MP5 (designed for conditional expression modification) guided the model to inject *<mask >* at critical positions (e.g., *if (expPos < decPos < <mask>)*). The subsequent mask prediction leveraged InCoder's pre-trained knowledge to generate contextually valid patches without requiring repair-specific training data.

```
  if(expPos > -1) {
-     if(expPos < decPos) {
+     if(expPos < decPos || expPos > str.length()) {
          throw new NumberFormatException(str + " is not a valid number.");
      }
      dec = str.substring(decPos + 1, expPos);
  }
```

Fig. 4. Examples of bug fixing in Defects4J 1.2

Research Question 3. Fig. 5 shows the result of comparing the ranking of correct patches before and after deduplication (dashed lines indicate average ranks). Without deduplication, the average rank was 58.12. After deduplication, it improved to 39.46 (a 32.12% reduction). This strategy filters out redundant/incorrect patches early, significantly elevating correct patches in the candidate list.

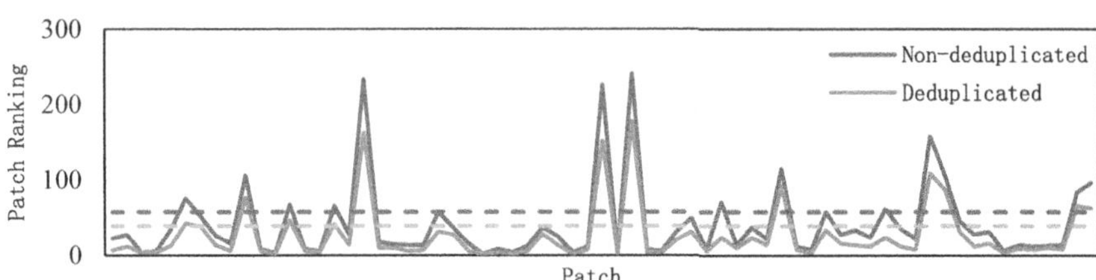

Fig. 5. Ranking result of the correct patches before and after deduplication

Furthermore, we analyzed the contribution of each template category. Unsurprisingly, the most frequently applied template, MP1 (Modify Method-Invocation), also contributed to the highest number of correct patches. However, we observed that templates like MP5 (Modify Conditional Expression), despite a lower overall frequency, were crucial for fixing specific, complex bugs that other templates could not address, demonstrating the complementary value of our diverse template set.

Take the bug Math41 in Defects4J for example, the original loop for (*int* $i = 0$; $i < weights.\ length$; $i{+}{+}$) required multi-edit repairs (changing start index and termination condition). The single mask template of TemRepair prioritized high-quality patches, enabling efficient repair for complex multi-edit scenarios.

4.4 Threats to Validity

1) Internal Threats

Manual design of mask templates may not cover all patterns of bugs. Furthermore, the inherent randomness of large language models could cause instability in mask predictions. Both factors may affect patch accuracy and ranking consistency.

2) External Threats

Defects4J, while representative in Java APR research, covers limited types and scenarios of bugs. In addition, version discrepancies in language models may impact reproducibility.

5 Conclusion

In this paper, we propose TemRepair, a method combining mask templates with LLMs to generate patches. Evaluated on Defects4J, TemRepair generated 67 correct patches, outperforming state-of-the-art APR tools. This demonstrates its potential for practical deployment in automated software maintenance.

While the current templates are effective in this work, manual template engineering may not cover all repair patterns, especially for complex, multi-line fixes or other programming languages. Future work will explore automated mining of templates from larger and more diverse codebases to enhance generalizability.

Acknowledgments. This work was supported by the National Natural Science Foundation of China (62002309) and the Teaching Reform Project of Yangzhou University (YZUJX2020-D15).

Disclosure of Interests. The authors have no competing interests.

References

1. Murphy-Hill, E., Zimmermann, T., Bird, C., et al.: The design of bug fixes. In: 2013 35th International Conference on Software Engineering (ICSE), pp. 332–341. IEEE (2013)
2. Peng, Y., Gao, S., Gao, C., et al.: Domain knowledge matters: improving prompts with fix templates for repairing python type errors. In: Proceedings of the 46th IEEE/ACM International Conference on Software Engineering, pp. 1–13 (2024)
3. Liu, K., Koyuncu, A., Kim, D., et al.: TBar: revisiting template-based automated program repair. In: Proceedings of the 28th ACM SIGSOFT International Symposium on Software Testing and Analysis, pp. 31–42 (2019)
4. Nguyen H D T, Qi D, Roychoudhury A, et al. Semfix: program repair via semantic analysis[C]//2013 35th International Conference on Software Engineering (ICSE). IEEE, 2013: 772–781.

5. Bhattacharya, P., Neamtiu, I.: Bug-fix time prediction models: can we do better? In: Proceedings of the 8th Working Conference on Mining Software Repositories, pp. 207–210 (2011)
6. Chen, Q., Li, D., Zhao, M., et al.: Learning-based automated program repair: a systematic litera-ture review. Complex Syst. Model. Simul. (2025)
7. Just, R., Jalali, D., Ernst, M.D.: Defects4J: a database of existing faults to enable controlled testing studies for Java programs. In: Proceedings of the 2014 International Symposium on Software Testing and Analysis, pp. 437–440 (2014)
8. Xia, C.S., Zhang, L.: Less training, more repairing please: revisiting automated program repair via zero-shot learning. In: Proceedings of the 30th ACM Joint European Software Engineering Conference and Symposium on the Foundations of Software Engineering, pp. 959–971 (2022)
9. Fan, Y., Xia, X., Lo, D., et al.: Chaff from the wheat: characterizing and determining valid bug reports. IEEE Trans. Softw. Eng. **46**(5), 495–525 (2018)
10. Peng, Y., Gao, S., Gao, C., et al.: Domain knowledge matters: improving prompts with fix tem-plates for repairing python type errors. In: Proceedings of the 46th Ieee/Acm International Conference on Software Engineering, pp. 1–13 (2024)
11. Lutellier, T., Pham, H.V., Pang, L., et al.: Coconut: combining context-aware neural translation models using ensemble for program repair. In: Proceedings of the 29th ACM SIGSOFT International Symposium on Software Testing and Analysis, pp. 101–114 (2020)
12. JavaParser Community. JavaParser: Analyse, transform and generate your Java codebase[EB/OL]. https://javaparser.org/
13. Chen, Z., Kommrusch, S., Monperrus, M.: Neural transfer learning for repairing security vulnerabilities in c code. IEEE Trans. Softw. Eng. **49**(1), 147–165 (2022)
14. Guha, S., Rastogi, R., Shim, K.: CURE: an efficient clustering algorithm for large databases[J]. ACM SIGMOD Rec. **27**(2), 73–84 (1998)
15. Vieira, S.M., Kaymak, U., Sousa, J.M.C.: Cohen's kappa coefficient as a performance measure for feature selection. In: International Conference on Fuzzy Systems, pp. 1–8. IEEE (2010)
16. Gissurarson, M.P., Applis, L., Panichella, A., et al.: Propr: property-based automatic program repair. In: Proceedings of the 44th International Conference on Software Engineering, pp. 1768–1780 (2022)
17. Li, Y., Wang, S., Nguyen, T.N.: Dlfix: context-based code transformation learning for automated program repair. In: Proceedings of the ACM/IEEE 42nd International Conference on Software Engineering, pp. 602–614 (2020)
18. Yang, C.: Accelerating redundancy-based program repair via code representation learning and adaptive patch filtering. In: Proceedings of the 29th ACM Joint Meeting on European Software Engineering Conference and Symposium on the Foundations of Software Engineering, pp. 1672–1674 (2021)
19. Chen, Z., Kommrusch, S., Tufano, M., et al.: Sequencer: sequence-to-sequence learning for end-to-end program repair. IEEE Trans. Softw. Eng. **47**(9), 1943–1959 (2019)

A NIC-Host Binding Method for Scalable Authentication via EEPROM Read/Write Access

Fei Wang[1], Jielong Liu[1(✉)], Zhihan Zheng[2], Ruqi Zhang[2], Mu Mu[2], and Yu-An Tan[2]

[1] Institute of Information Technology of National Immigration Administration, Beijing, China
ljdrgn@163.com

[2] School of Cyberspace Science and Technology, Beijing Institute of Technology, Beijing, China
tan2008@bit.edu.cn

Abstract. As the development of communication networks, mobile nodes or personal workstations are allowed to gain access to the Internet anywhere and at any time. Facing the threats of various malicious attacks, access authentication is the key mechanism to be strengthened because it is mainly used to prevent illegal nodes from accessing network services. Existing access authentication mechanisms often rely on hardware-level binding to prevent attackers from bypassing the authentication system by replacing hardware. However, hardware-level binding often introduces additional hardware cost or requires hardware modifications to the device, hindering its large-scale deployment. In this paper, we propose a host-network interface card (NIC) binding method, which utilizes the read and write operations of the NIC's Electrically Erasable Programmable Read-Only Memory (EEPROM) to achieve hardware-level binding. This approach runs the binding process via external media to obtain the host's hardware fingerprint and maintain it in the EEPROM region. The authentication process will use the EEPROM read and write operations to obtain the hardware fingerprint to determine whether the binding relationship is established. Qualitative analysis shows that the proposed approach effectively mitigates security risks while eliminating the need to modify the device hardware, demonstrating good adaptability and the potential for widespread deployment.

Keywords: Binding technology · Access authentication · Network interface card · EEPROM

1 Introduction

With the deepening development of informatization, the scale of enterprise networks and public networks continues to expand. Network access security has

W. Meng et al. (Eds.): ASSS 2025, CCIS 2903, pp. 100–114, 2026.
https://doi.org/10.1007/978-3-032-21600-7_7

gradually become an indispensable core component of information security systems.

Existing access authentication mechanisms primarily rely on account-password combinations or digital certificates. Although these methods can prevent unauthorized access to a certain extent, they still exhibit significant shortcomings in practical applications. Account-password-based authentication lacks sufficient security. As the most traditional authentication method, accounts and passwords are vulnerable to leakage and brute-force attacks. In enterprise scenarios, some employees tend to use weak passwords or reuse the same password across multiple systems. Once credentials are compromised, attackers can easily gain access to the network. Moreover, account passwords are often stored in local files or server databases, making them susceptible to theft by trojans, phishing attacks, or insider threats. Digital certificate-based authentication is complex to manage and still carries risks. While digital certificates can enhance authentication security by verifying the legitimacy of devices or users, they rely heavily on the integrity of the certificate files themselves. If a certificate is illegally copied, attackers can spoof legitimate devices and bypass network authentication. Additionally, the processes of certificate issuance, renewal, and revocation are cumbersome, requiring enterprises to establish comprehensive certificate management mechanisms. This not only increases operational costs but also causes inconvenience during usage.

Moreover, existing authentication mechanisms generally lack hardware-level binding capabilities. Traditional architectures primarily depend on host-based account systems or operating system environments, with little direct enforcement of the one-to-one correspondence between hosts and network interface cards (NICs). This means attackers can simply replace the NIC to circumvent the authentication system and initiate new authentication requests with the new card. For large enterprise networks, this vulnerability allows unauthorized devices to bypass authentication through simple physical means, posing serious security risks. Hardware-level security solutions are feasible but come with high costs. Existing solutions such as Trusted Platform Module (TPM)[1] chips, smart cards [9], and dedicated hardware encryption modules [11] can achieve strong device-level binding. However, these solutions often require additional hardware procurement or modification of existing terminals, resulting in high costs and complex deployment. This makes large-scale promotion in enterprise or public networks impractical.

Authentication based MAC address is a method that enables simple deployment by obtaining the MAC address via a standard programming interface, so it is suitable for terminals and Internet of Things (IoT) devices enabling simple deployment, which makes it suitable for terminals and IoT devices. However, MAC addresses are highly susceptible to forgery and tampering, cannot resist MAC spoofing attacks, and the binding relationship is relatively fragile.

In summary, existing authentication mechanisms present a significant technology gap: they either rely on high-cost, complex-to-deploy dedicated hardware (like TPM or smart cards) for high security , or they depend on easily forged or tampered identifiers (like MAC addresses) for low-cost deployment. This leaves current solutions unable to simultaneously satisfy the three key requirements of security, low cost, and scalability. Therefore, there is an urgent need for a new approach that leverages existing hardware resources to achieve a one-to-one, verifiable hardware-level binding between hosts and NICs without incurring extra costs, thereby enhancing both the security and reliability of network access.

To address this gap, this paper proposes a host-NIC binding method based on NIC's Electrically Erasable Programmable Read-Only Memory (EEPROM) read/write operations. The novelty of this approach lies in its creative use of the ubiquitous but often overlooked EEPROM storage region on the NIC, achieving a strong hardware-level binding effect-previously requiring dedicated hardware like TPM-without any additional hardware procurement or modification.It combines binding technology with authentication control technology to achieve hardware-level binding between hosts and NICs. The authentication result serves as a prerequisite for Network Access Control (NAC) or Authentication, Authorization, and Accounting (AAA) [8] authentication, effectively preventing unauthorized devices from bypassing authentication by replacing NICs. Specifically, this paper aims to answer the following research questions:

1. How can a strong, one-to-one hardware-level binding between a host and its NIC be established to prevent unauthorized NIC replacement attacks, *without* incurring the high costs and deployment complexity of dedicated hardware like TPM or smart cards?
2. How can the existing EEPROM on a NIC—a ubiquitous but often underutilized component—be securely leveraged to store an encrypted host fingerprint and verify this binding during the authentication process?

In a nutshell, this paper brings the following contributions:

1) We propose a binding method that stores an encrypted host fingerprint in the NIC's EEPROM, establishing a one-to-one hardware-level binding relationship between the host and the NIC. This approach addresses the limitation of existing authentication mechanisms in preventing NIC replacement.
2) To ensure that fingerprint data cannot be forged or copied, this approach adopts an asymmetric encryption mechanism and writes the encrypted host fingerprint to the NIC EEPROM during the binding phase, effectively mitigating security risks associated with account password or certificate leakage.
3) This approach requires no additional hardware and fully leverages the existing NIC EEPROM and operating system tools to achieve hardware-level binding between hosts and NICs. Compared with existing approaches based on TPM or smart cards, it significantly reduces deployment costs, making it a cost-effective choice for large-scale enterprises and organizations.
4) This approach can seamlessly integrate with existing NAC/AAA systems, 802.1X protocol, and EAP-TLS authentication, and can also be extended to various scenarios such as cloud platforms and zero-trust architectures, demonstrating excellent adaptability and scalability.

The remainder of this article is organized as follows: Section 2 introduces the preliminary situation related to NICs, binding technology and access authentication technology. The detailed architecture of the proposed approach and threat model are described in Sect. 3. Section 4 gives the implementation details of the proposed scheme. Section 6 reviews the related work. Finally, we draw the conclusion in Sect. 7.

2 Background

2.1 Network Interface Card

A NIC is a hardware component that enables a computer to connect to a network to achieve data communication. It provides a physical interface and performs essential operations including data transmission, reception, encoding, decoding, and encapsulation.

A NIC's structure combines physical interfaces, Physical Layer (PHY), and memory to ensure efficient, secure, and scalable network communication. Each NIC is assigned a unique Media Access Control (MAC) address, a 48-bit identifier permanently stored in its ROM during manufacturing. This address ensures every networked device has a distinct identity, which is critical for network communication and security. EEPROM is usually used to store the MAC address of the NIC, some configuration information of the NIC, etc. It is equivalent to the BIOS of the NIC and is very important for the initialization and configuration of the NIC.

2.2 Binding Technology

Binding technology restricts commercial software with intellectual property (IP) rights to only on specific hardware devices in order to efficiently protect IPs from being copied or used without authorization. In the proposed scheme, a dedicated binding program will be invoked via external media when the device is first activated or the NIC is replaced, completing the binding between the host and the NIC. The binding program checks whether the operating system version, user permissions, and dependent tools meet the requirements. At the same time, the host's unique hardware identification information such as the hard disk serial number, CPU Universally Unique Identifier (UUID), and motherboard UUID is collected, and a fixed-length host fingerprint is generated through a hash algorithm (e.g., SHA-256). The binding program uses the private key to encrypt the fingerprint, generate ciphertext, and write it to the NIC EEPROM through the `ethtool -E` interface. After the write operation is completed, a readback operation is immediately performed to verify the correctness of the write result. If the preset number of times is exceeded, an error is recorded and the process terminates. The binding technology is only executed once when the device is first enabled or the NIC is replaced, and the binding result is valid for a long time.

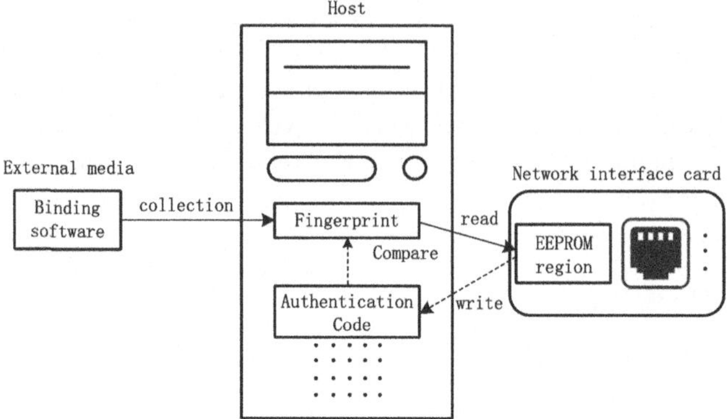

Fig. 1. System model.

2.3 Authentication Control Technology

Access authentication is the first line of network defense, which is responsible for identifying the legitimacy of nodes accessing the network and preventing illegal nodes from accessing the network[12]. In the proposed scheme, a authentication control program will be invoked each time the host boots or the network interface card is enabled to verify the binding relationship. The authentication control program first collects the current host hardware information to generate a fingerprint. It then reads the stored fingerprint ciphertext from the EEPROM and decrypts it using the public key to obtain the binding fingerprint. The decrypted result is then compared with the current host fingerprint. If the results match, the network interface card is allowed to operate normally and enter the NAC/AAA authentication process. If they do not match, the authentication control program on the host side blocks the network interface card from further network communication, preventing the host's access request from entering the NAC/AAA authentication process and causing it to be rejected.

3 System Model and Threat Model

3.1 System Overview

The system structure of the proposed method is shown in Fig. 1. When the device is first activated or the NIC is replaced, the external medium will run a binding program to collect host hardware information and generate a host fingerprint. The host provides unique identification information such as the hard disk serial number, CPU UUID, and motherboard UUID, and a fixed-length host fingerprint is generated using a hash algorithm. The authentication control program verifies the binding relationship when the host is booted, and the EEPROM storage region on the NIC is used to store the encrypted host fingerprint.

The interaction between the system components is as follows: the binding program runs through the external medium when first activated, generates the host fingerprint, and writes it to the EEPROM storage region. The authentication control program runs each time the host is booted, reads the binding fingerprint from the EEPROM region, and compares it with the host fingerprint generated in real time. The comparison result determines whether the NIC is allowed to continue working, thereby determining whether the host can enter the NAC/AAA access authentication process.

3.2 Threat Model

In this article, we apply the widely used DolevYao[3] threat model into the security of the proposed method. The adversary is completely in control of the communication channel between the host and the NIC. She is able to eavesdrop, modify, delete messages exchanged between the host and the NIC, as well as insert any false messages.

In our system, we assume the channel between the host and the external media to be a secure channel. Additionally, we assume that the adversary has limited physical access to the NIC. By limited physical access, we exclude physical attacks for the forensic examination of NIC EEPROM from the threat model.

4 Implementation

In this section, we describe the implementation details of the proposed solution, including the implementation of binding technology and authentication control technology.

4.1 Binding Process

As shown in Algorithm 1, when a device is first activated or the NIC is replaced, the user can run the binding program using external media (e.g., a Universal Serial Bus flash drive). The program first performs an environment check to confirm that the operating system version, user permissions, and dependent tools meet the requirements. The binding program then collects the host's unique hardware identification information, such as the hard drive serial number, CPU UUID, and motherboard UUID. This hardware information can be concatenated in a preset order or generated using accumulation, exclusive-or, or weighted combination to form a comprehensive identification string. To avoid conflicts caused by varying lengths of different hardware information, delimiters or normalization can be added after concatenation.

This combined identification string is hashed to generate a fixed-length host fingerprint. After the fingerprint is generated, it is encrypted using the private key to generate a fingerprint ciphertext. The binding program then calls an operating system tool (e.g., the `ethtool -E` interface) to write the ciphertext to the NIC's EEPROM region. After writing is complete, the program immediately reads back the EEPROM contents and compares them byte-by-byte with the original ciphertext to ensure the integrity and correctness of the written data.

Algorithm 1: Binding code in external media.

```
Function Binding:
    Gnerate fingerprint;
    Encrypt the fingerprint using the private key;
    while less than the maximum number of rewrites do
        Write the ciphertext into the EEPROM of the NIC;
        Reread the EEPROM of the NIC;
        if ciphertext fails to be written then
            continue;
        else
            break;
        end
    end
return
```

If the comparison fails, it automatically performs a preset number of retries, for example, three. If failures occur after exceeding the maximum number of retries, the program records an error log, including the time of failure, the NIC model, and the reason for the failure, and terminates the binding process. After successful binding, the external media is removed. The binding result is permanent and persists even after a host reboot or changes in the network environment.

4.2 Authentication Control

As shown in Algorithm 2, the authentication control program automatically runs each time the host boots or the network interface card is enabled. The program again collects the current host's unique hardware identification information and concatenates or combines it using the same rules as the binding phase (e.g., concatenation in a fixed order, concatenation with delimiters, or accumulation/XORing) to generate a real-time host fingerprint. This processing rule must remain consistent with the binding phase; otherwise, the fingerprints will be inconsistent.

The authentication control program then reads the previously written fingerprint ciphertext from the network interface card's EEPROM and decrypts it using the public key to obtain the binding fingerprint. To enhance security, the decryption process can employ multi-threaded authentication or include a checksum to prevent data tampering during the reading process.

The program compares the real-time host fingerprint with the decrypted binding fingerprint. This comparison can be performed for byte-by-byte equality or, in specific implementations, with a certain amount of redundant check bits. If the two match, the binding relationship is considered established, the network interface card is allowed to operate normally, and access authentication processes such as NAC/AAA are initiated. If the two match, the binding relationship is considered invalid, and the authentication control program on the

Algorithm 2: Authentication code in the host.

```
Function Authentication:
    Gnerate fingerprint;
    Read the fingerprint from the EEPROM of the NIC;
    Decrypt the fingerprint using the public key;
    if the fingerprint consistent with the current host's then
        Allow access to the network;
    else
        Deny access to the network;
return
```

host side prevents the network interface card from further network communication, thereby denying the host's access request. At the same time, the system will generate an exception log, recording key information including timestamp, host hardware parameters, NIC model, comparison results, etc., and report it to the network security management platform through syslog or API when necessary for subsequent security audit and tracking.

4.3 Prototype

We have integrated the proposed method into an independent software, which is a NIC customization tool for Linux operating system. The software's core function is to read and write the NIC's EEPROM through the `ethtool -e` and `ethtool -E` interfaces. The software uses a universal interface to read and write the NIC EEPROM, and does not require modification of the NIC driver. For the software to work properly, the system kernel version must be 2.6.32 or later, and the NIC EEPROM must be at least 512 bytes.

By writing the host's unique fingerprint to the NIC, the software transforms the generic NIC into a customized one, ultimately achieving one-to-one binding verification between the host and the NIC. To achieve this goal, the software includes the following six sub-functions:

1) Software configuration.
2) Software execution environment detection.
3) List NICs with EEPROM free space.
4) Generate host fingerprint (plain text).
5) Write host fingerprint (cipher text) for NIC-Host Binding.
6) Check NIC-host binding status.

The software configuration process involves two steps:

1) Setting a password, which is embedded in the fingerprint reader software.
2) Generating a public-private key pair. The public key is embedded in the fingerprint reader software.

The software execution environment detection process includes three steps:

Table 1. Commands and fingerprint sources

Commands	Fingerprint source
`lsblk -no SERIAL /dev/sda`	hard drive serial number
`dmidecode -s processor-uuid`	CPU UUID
`dmidecode -s system-uuid`	motherboard UUID

1) First, obtain the Linux kernel version through the `uname -r` command and verify whether it meets 2.6.32 and above. This version and subsequent kernels have more stable storage read and write support for `ethtool -E`.
2) Then, use the `dpkg -l | grep ethtool` (Debian system) or `rpm -qa | grep ethtool` (RHEL system) command to check whether the ethtool tool is installed. If it is not installed, the user will be automatically prompted to install it through the `apt-get install ethtool` or `yum install ethtool` command.
3) Finally, check the current running user permissions. Since the NIC hardware operation requires root permissions, if it is detected that the ordinary user is running, a pop-up window will be prompted and the system will be guided to switch to the root account.

To achieve accurate reading and writing of NIC, it is necessary to list the physical NIC that can be read and written and obtain key hardware parameters, avoiding virtual NIC (e.g., virbr0 and docker0) or NIC that do not support storage reading and writing software. This process mainly includes three steps:

1) Obtain a list of all NICs in the system.
2) Use `ethtool -e` command to read all EEPROMs of NICs.
3) List all NICs with 512 bytes of free space and their free address ranges.

In order to obtain the core fingerprint source of the host and NIC binding, the software is responsible for collecting the host's unique identification fingerprint, including: hard disk serial number, CPU UUID, and motherboard UUID. The commands for obtaining the above fingerprints are listed in Table 1. The result of obtaining the serial number of the physical hard disk through `lsblk -no SERIAL /dev/sda` is shown in Fig. 2. The result of obtaining the motherboard's information is shown in Fig. 3.

The core operation of the software for NIC customization is to securely write the host's fingerprint into the NIC's EEPROM while avoiding overwriting its critical operational fingerprint. This function is only accessible to users with a specific password, preventing any user from rebinding the NIC to a different host by rewriting the fingerprint. Based on the results of environmental detection and fingerprint generation process, the software selects a NIC that meets the conditions and writes the fingerprint into the free space of the EEPROM. The running results are shown in Fig. 4. It mainly involves the following five steps:

1) Before writing, it is necessary to check whether the fingerprint has been saved in the NIC EEPROM. If the fingerprint has been saved, the user should be prompted to overwrite it.
2) The software requires the user to enter a predetermined specific password. If the password is incorrect, the write function will not be executed.
3) The 32-byte host fingerprint is encrypted using the private key to obtain the ciphertext data of the fingerprint.
4) The write command template is: `ethtool -E NIC name magic magic value offset starting offset address length data length value hexadecimal data`. The software converts the ciphertext data of the fingerprint into the hexadecimal format supported by ethtool. If the fingerprint length exceeds the maximum length that the NIC can write at a time, it will automatically split it into multiple segments for writing (each segment length does not exceed 64 bytes).
5) After writing, the free space is read from the NIC and compared with the written fingerprint. It prompts whether the write is successful.

```
[root@uos-server bit910]#
[root@uos-server bit910]# lsblk -o NAME,SERIAL
NAME      SERIAL
sda       50026B72829A6524
|-sda1
|-sda2
sdb       WFM37NBS
|-sdb1
|-sdb2
|-sdb3
```

Fig. 2. Hard disk serial number acquisition results.

Finally, the software can read the written host fingerprint ciphertext data from the NIC EEPROM, decrypt it and compare it with the host's own fingerprint. If the fingerprints are the same, the binding status is normal, otherwise, the binding relationship between the NIC and the host is not established. This function specifically includes the following four steps:

1) First, call the function 3.4 to generate the fingerprint of the host.
2) Read the fingerprint ciphertext data in the NIC.
3) Use the public key to decrypt the ciphertext data to obtain the fingerprint plaintext data stored in the NIC.
4) Compare the fingerprints obtained in steps 1 and steps 3. If they are the same, the binding status is correct, otherwise the binding is incorrect.

To support reproducibility, the prototype software described in this section is available from the corresponding author upon reasonable request.

```
[root@uos-server bit910]#
[root@uos-server bit910]# dmidecode -t baseboa rd
 # dmidecode 2.9
SMBIOS 2.5 present.

Handle 0x0200, DMl type 2, 9 bytes
Base Board Information
 Manufacturer: Dell Inc.
 Product Name:0K649H
 Version: A00
 Serial Number: ..CN697028790626.

Handle 0x0A00, DMl type10,10 bytes
On Board Device 1 Information
 Type: Video
 Status: Enabled
 Description: Embedded ATI ES1000 Video
On Board Device 2 Information
 Type: Ethernet
 Status: Enabled
 Description: Embedded Broadcom 5708 NIC 1
On Board Device 3 Information
 Type: Ethernet
 Status: Enabled
 Description: Embedded Broadcom 5708 NIC 2
```

Fig. 3. Motherboard information acquisition results.

5 Comparative Analysis and Discussion

To validate the proposed method and demonstrate its advantages, this section provides a comparative analysis against existing hardware-level security solutions. While detailed performance benchmarks (e.g., binding and authentication latency) are considered future work, the successful implementation of the prototype described in Section 4.3 on a standard Linux environment (Kernel 2.6.32+ and ethtool) confirms the practical feasibility of our approach.

The primary advantages of our method—low cost, high scalability, and strong security—are highlighted in Table 2. We compare our EEPROM-based solution with mainstream mechanisms mentioned in this paper, including TPM-based solutions [1], Smart Cards [9], MAC Address binding, and PUF-based methods [7,14].

6 Related Work

In this section, we review previous studies related to our work. Specifically, we discussed various existing access authentication and binding technologies.

6.1 Access Authentication

Access authentication is a crucial technology to identify the legitimacy of nodes that will access the network, and to prevent illegal ones. LSAA[2] is a lightweight and secure access authentication scheme that can achieve several security functionalities, including mutual authentication, session-key establishment, identity

```
[root@uos-server bit910]#
[root@uos-server bit910]# ethtool-i enp1s0f0 driver: txgbe
Jersion: 1.3.6.4uos
firmware-version: 0x00020010
expansion-ron-version:
bus-info: 0000:01:00.0
supports-statistics: yes
supports-test: yes
supports-eepron-access:yes
supports-reg1ster-dump: yes
supports-priv-flags:yes
[root@uos-server bit910]# ethtool -e enp1s0f0 offset 0length 10
Dffset  Values
------  ------
x0000:  0040 a5 5a 00 00 00 00 0000
[root@uos-server bit910]# unane -a
Linux uos-server 4.19.90-2409.6.0.0297.101.ue120.x86_64 #1 SMP led Jul 2 19:39:26 CST 2025 x86
[root@uos-server bit910]#lsb_release
No LSB nodules are available.
[root@uos-server bit910]# lsb_release -a
No LSB nodules are available.
Distributor ID: Uos
Description:    UOS Server 20
Release:        20
Codenane:       fuyu
```

Fig. 4. Results of interaction with the EEPROM.

privacy protection, and perfect forward/backward secrecy (PFS/PBS). IMAS[13] is a secure and lightweight access authentication scheme for space-air-ground integrated networks (SAGINs). The introduction of multicast communication for re-authentication message transmission in access authentication can significantly reduce the authentication delay and signaling overhead during the handover process. Further qualitative analysis shows that IMAS has good security features and can meet various security requirements. Zheng et al. [15] adopts a secure access authentication scheme between vehicles and roadside units (RSUs) based on blockchain technique. The solution allows vehicles to anonymously use pseudonyms for vehicle-to-vehicle (V2V) and vehicle-to-infrastructure (V2I) communications in a non-fully trusted environment. Blockchain technology effectively achieves transparency in vehicle identity authentication and announcements. AAA-WSN[10] is an anonymous access authentication scheme for wireless sensor networks in big data environments, which not only achieves strong security services such as user anonymity and mutual authentication, but also performs the perfect forward secrecy feature with high level of efficiency. LAA[6] is an access authentication scheme for massive IoT devices (IoTDs) in space information network (SIN).This scheme contains two types of lattice-based authentication protocols, designed respectively for massive IoTDs and a single IoTD.

6.2 Binding

Existing research on binding technology mainly focuses on the field of software IP protection. Fischer et al. [4] present a software-hardware binding mechanism that combines hardware fingerprints with Boolean logic to protect IP of embedded software. This approach requires no additional hardware and relies only on relatively simple software updates. Lee et al. [5] present a software-hardware binding technique that uses hardware intrinsic security properties of devices

Table 2. Qualitative Comparison of Hardware-Level Binding Mechanisms

Comparison Dimension	Our Method (EEPROM)	TPM-based	Smart Card-based	MAC Address-based	PUF-based
Additional Hardware Cost	**None**	High	High	None	Low (Varies)[1]
Deployment Complexity	**Low** (Software only)	High (Hardware integration)	High (Management overhead)	Low	High (Integration)
Security (vs. NIC Replacement)	**High**	High	High	**Very Low**	High
Security (vs. Spoofing)	**High** (Encrypted)	High	High	**Very Low**	Very High
Scalability	**High**	Low (Cost barrier)	Low (Cost barrier)	High (but insecure)	Medium

[1]PUF leverages existing hardware, but integration and characterization can be complex.

being protected. This approach guarantees that only manufacturers can perform their hardware and software binding. GlueZilla[7] is a system that achieves software-hardware binding through Physical Unclonable Functions (PUFs) of user-space rowhammer. This system converts the binary program in memory at runtime so that it behaves correctly only on the real target machine to which it was bound at compile time. When run on any other machine, the program will behave differently. To protect IPs from being cloned, copied, or used with unauthorized integration, Zhang et al. [14] propose a binding-based mechanism to restrict IP's execution only on specific FPGA devices. This approach embeds a PUF customized for the FPGA in every registered FPGA device and uses the PUF response to activate a finite-state machine (FSM) that is added into the original IPs .

Unlike the existing software-hardware binding mechanism, our approach leverages NIC EEPROM to enhance security without relying on additional hardware features such as PUF, which significantly reduces costs.

7 Conclusion

In this paper, we proposed a novel binding method that achieves one-to-one hardware-level binding between the host and the NIC. The key insight was to store the encrypted host fingerprint in the NIC EEPROM. We further presented the detailed binding and authentication process of the proposed approach. We showed the design of the binding technology and authentication control technology, explaining how these technologies could be used to complete access authentication mechanism.

However, we acknowledge several limitations in the current approach. First, the method's feasibility depends on the NIC EEPROM having sufficient available free space (e.g., at least 512 bytes for our prototype) [Section 4.3], which may not be guaranteed on all NIC models. Second, EEPROM hardware has a finite number of write cycles; while our binding process is designed as a one-time operation, frequent re-binding on the same device could theoretically become an issue. Third, as defined in our threat model (which is based on the Dolev-Yao model [3]), the method is not designed to defend against sophisticated physical attacks involving direct forensic examination or hardware-level manipulation of the EEPROM chip itself [Section 3.2]. Finally, the implementation relies on specific operating system tools and kernel support (e.g., Linux kernel 2.6.32+ and ethtool) [Section 4.3], requiring a compatible software environment.This method does not rely on additional hardware and significantly reduces costs compared to existing hardware-level binding methods, making it suitable for large-scale enterprise and organizational deployments.

References

1. Arthur, W., Challener, D., Goldman, K.: A practical guide to TPM 2.0: using the new trusted platform module in the new age of security. Springer Nature (2015)
2. Cao, J., et al.: Lsaa: a lightweight and secure access authentication scheme for both ue and mmtc devices in 5g networks. IEEE Internet Things J. **7**(6), 5329–5344 (2020). https://doi.org/10.1109/JIOT.2020.2976740
3. Dolev, D., Yao, A.: On the security of public key protocols. IEEE Trans. Inf. Theory **29**(2), 198–208 (1983)
4. Fischer, B., Dorfmeister, D., Ferrarotti, F., Penz, M., Kargl, M., Zeinzinger, M., Eibensteiner, F.: Software-hardware binding for protection of sensitive data in embedded software. In: Proceedings of the 40th ACM/SIGAPP Symposium on Applied Computing. pp. 570–577 (2025)
5. Lee, R.P., Markantonakis, K., Akram, R.N.: Binding hardware and software to prevent firmware modification and device counterfeiting. In: Proceedings of the 2nd ACM International Workshop on cyber-Physical System Security, pp. 70–81 (2016)
6. Ma, R., Cao, J., Feng, D., Li, H.: Laa: lattice-based access authentication scheme for iot in space information networks. IEEE Internet Things J. **7**(4), 2791–2805 (2020). https://doi.org/10.1109/JIOT.2019.2962553
7. Mechelinck, R., Dorfmeister, D., Fischer, B., Volckaert, S., Brunthaler, S.: Gluezilla: efficient and scalable software to hardware binding using rowhammer. In: International Conference on Detection of Intrusions and Malware, and Vulnerability Assessment, pp. 416–438. Springer (2024). https://doi.org/10.1007/978-3-031-64171-8_22
8. Metz, C.: Aaa protocols: authentication, authorization, and accounting for the internet. IEEE Internet Comput. **3**(6), 75–79 (2002)
9. Naccache, D., M'Raihi, D.: Cryptographic smart cards. IEEE Micro **16**(3), 14–24 (1996)
10. Nashwan, S.: Aaa-wsn: anonymous access authentication scheme for wireless sensor networks in big data environment. Egyptian Inform. J. **22**(1), 15–26 (2021)

11. Sommerhalder, M.: Hardware security module. Trends in Data Protection and Encryption Technologie, pp. 83–87 (2023)
12. Tang, W., Zhang, K., Ren, J., Zhang, Y., Shen, X.: Flexible and efficient authenticated key agreement scheme for bans based on physiological features. IEEE Trans. Mob. Comput. **18**(4), 845–856 (2018)
13. Yao, S., Guan, J., Wu, Y., Xu, K., Xu, M.: Toward secure and lightweight access authentication in sagins. IEEE Wirel. Commun. **27**(6), 75–81 (2020). https://doi.org/10.1109/MWC.001.2000132
14. Zhang, J., Lin, Y., Lyu, Y., Qu, G.: A puf-fsm binding scheme for fpga ip protection and pay-per-device licensing. IEEE Trans. Inf. Forensics Secur. **10**(6), 1137–1150 (2015)
15. Zheng, D., Jing, C., Guo, R., Gao, S., Wang, L.: A traceable blockchain-based access authentication system with privacy preservation in vanets. IEEE Access **7**, 117716–117726 (2019). https://doi.org/10.1109/ACCESS.2019.2936575

A Data Storage and Playback System for Crowdsourced Cyber-Physical Integration Scenarios

Xin Wu[1,2,4], Zhenyu Li[1,2,4(✉)], Yong Ding[1,2,3,4], Ruwen Zhao[1,2,4], and Changsong Yang[1,2,4]

[1] School of Computer Science and Information Security, Guilin University of Electronic Technology, Guilin 541004, China
wx@mails.guet.edu.cn, {zhaoruwen,csyang,lizhenyu}@guet.edu.cn
[2] Guangxi Academy of Artificial Intelligence, Nanning 530028, China
[3] Lion Rock Labs of Cyberspace Security, Institute of Cyberspace Technology, HKCT Institute of Higher Education, Hong Kong, China
[4] Guangxi Engineering Research Center of Industrial Internet Security and Blockchain, Guilin University of Electronic Technology, Guilin 541004, China

Abstract. With the increasing integration of industrial control systems (ICS) into networked environments, the demand for reliable traffic recording and precise replay has grown substantially. However, existing tools suffer from notable limitations in processing high-frequency small packets, enabling efficient storage and indexing, supporting conditional querying, and ensuring data security. To address these challenges, this paper proposes DPSP-RS, a transit-server-based packet storage and replay system that supports real-time data acquisition, compressed storage, flexible conditional queries, and rate-adjustable replay. The system adopts gRPC communication and Protobuf serialization to enhance data processing efficiency and ensure accurate query execution. Experimental results show that, compared with mainstream tools, DPSP-RS provides finer traffic controllability, higher query performance, and improved replay accuracy in ICS environments. Specifically, DPSP-RS increases single-threaded write throughput by up to 22.4%, reduces the average replay time to 55 s at 500 Mbps for replaying 1 GB of data, and achieves a maximum storage compression ratio of 45.6%.

Keywords: Packet Replay · Industrial Control Systems · Data Storage Optimization · Binary Serialization · Rate-controlled Playback

1 Introduction

Industrial control systems (ICS) are characterized by frequent, small-sized, and time-sensitive network interactions. These unique communication patterns make efficient traffic recording and replay increasingly important for testing, debugging, security analysis, and post-incident forensics. In practice, existing network packet replay tools such as GoReplay and Tcpreplay are widely used in

W. Meng et al. (Eds.): ASSS 2025, CCIS 2903, pp. 115–129, 2026.
https://doi.org/10.1007/978-3-032-21600-7_8

general-purpose network testing environments. However, these tools are typically designed around raw PCAP files and plain-text logs, and lack native support for efficient compression, structured storage, or multidimensional query mechanisms [1]. As a result, they are difficult to apply directly to industrial scenarios that require fine-grained temporal control, high-fidelity reproduction, and long-term archival under storage constraints.

When replaying traffic in industrial control networks, several challenges arise simultaneously: high-frequency and small-sized packets, strict latency constraints, multi-criteria filtering (e.g., time, IP, port, protocol), rate control, and the need for structured, indexable storage with strong security guarantees [2,3]. Recent studies have analyzed ICS traffic characteristics and attack behaviors from a security perspective [4]. For example, Mesbah et al. deployed honeypot environments such as Conpot to capture malicious traffic targeting Supervisory Control and Data Acquisition (SCADA) protocols (e.g., Modbus and S7comm), and investigated attackers' protocol usage [5], geographical distribution, and attack patterns [6]. These works highlight the diversity and uniqueness of ICS traffic. However, most existing research focuses on detection and behavior analysis, without systematically addressing how to efficiently store captured traffic [7], build structured indexes, or support controllable replay for scenario reproduction [8,9]. This gap limits the ability of operators and researchers to perform repeatable experiments and fine-grained forensic reconstruction over long time spans.

To bridge this gap, this paper proposes DPSP-RS, a data packet storage and replay system tailored for industrial control networks. DPSP-RS is designed around the requirements of ICS security testing and incident analysis: it integrates data acquisition, compressed and encrypted storage, structured indexing, conditional querying, and rate-adjustable replay into a unified, modular framework. Building on this design, we further develop quantitative models to optimize acquisition, storage layout, and hierarchical indexing, and conduct comparative experiments against representative tools. The main contributions of this work are summarized as follows:

- We design and implement DPSP-RS, a modular relay-server–based packet storage and replay system for ICS, which decouples data collection, index-based storage, querying, and replay control via gRPC.
- We build an optimized acquisition and storage pipeline with multi-threaded capture, producer–consumer buffering, batch writes, and binary serialization, and introduce an adaptive buffer-size model and serialization efficiency metric $S_{\text{efficiency}}(X)$ to improve throughput and query latency.
- We design a hierarchical time-partitioned index for large-scale ICS traffic and formulate a hierarchical index access efficiency model $E_{\text{access}}(q)$, with experiments showing higher compression, throughput, and replay fidelity than GoReplay and Tcpreplay.

The remainder of this paper is organized as follows. Section 2 reviews related work on packet replay and industrial control network analysis. Section 3 presents the overall system architecture and core design principles. Section 4 provides experimental results and performance evaluation. Finally, Sect. 5 concludes the paper and outlines future work.

2 Related Work

Packet replay technology is widely used in network security testing, anomaly reproduction, and system performance evaluation [10,11]. Its core idea is to capture production traffic and retransmit it in a controlled environment to reproduce realistic workloads. Existing replay methods can be broadly categorized into three types [12]: *static replay*, which replays packets from PCAP files at a fixed rate and ignores original timing; *timestamp-based replay*, which restores inter-packet intervals to approximate real network loads; and *event-triggered replay*, which activates traffic replay when specific events or conditions are met, and is often used in security simulations and scenario reproduction [13]. These techniques provide the basic foundation for building replay systems but generally target conventional IT networks rather than industrial control environments.

On the tool side, several representative implementations have been widely adopted in practice. GoReplay is an HTTP-oriented traffic replay tool that supports traffic recording, timing-based replay, concurrency control, and rate limiting, but its design is centered on HTTP workloads and does not natively support industrial protocols or flexible, multi-dimensional query operations [14]. Tcpreplay focuses on PCAP-based TCP/UDP traffic testing and provides functionalities such as rate adjustment and multi-interface replay, yet it stores traffic in raw PCAP format and lacks structured storage or remote orchestration capabilities [15]. While these tools work well for general-purpose network testing, they are difficult to adapt to ICS scenarios that require long-term storage, fine-grained time-window extraction, and secure handling of sensitive industrial data [16,17].

Beyond tool-level implementations, some studies have explored algorithmic optimizations to improve replay fidelity and robustness. A notable example is the Maximum Priority Compression Algorithm (MPCA), which compresses large inter-packet gaps to mitigate packet loss and timing distortion during high-bandwidth replay [18]. By prioritizing critical timing intervals, MPCA achieves more stable replay behavior and lower packet loss compared with simple proportional compression schemes [19]. However, such approaches mainly focus on time-compression strategies and typically lack support for multi-dimensional filtering (time, IP, port), structured indexing, flexible rate adjustment, and modular deployment, which limits their applicability to industrial control networks with stringent real-time, controllability, and scalability requirements [20]. In summary, existing replay tools, ICS-related studies, and compression-based methods provide important building blocks but still fall short in terms of multi-protocol adaptation, indexable and secure storage, flexible querying, and precise replay control. These limitations motivate the design of DPSP-RS, which combines modular packet acquisition, optimized storage, hierarchical indexing, and controllable replay specifically for industrial control environments.

3 Proposed Method

This section presents the overall design of DPSP-RS. We first summarize the system requirements derived from industrial control network characteristics, then introduce the system architecture and core modules. Finally, we describe the key optimization techniques for data acquisition, storage, and hierarchical indexing that enable high-throughput, low-latency replay with precise control.

3.1 System Requirements

Considering the unique characteristics of industrial control network environments, DPSP-RS is designed to satisfy the key functional and performance requirements summarized in Table 1.

Table 1. Classification and Description of System Requirements

Category	Requirement Description
Flexibility	Supports filtering target data based on time range and network attributes (e.g., IP address, port), as well as other multi-dimensional criteria.
High Precision	Capable of replaying data packets with millisecond- or even microsecond-level timestamp accuracy.
Replay Control	Allows users to define custom playback speeds (e.g., 0.1×, 2×) or specify fixed sending rates.
Performance	Maintains stable throughput and low latency even under large-scale data volumes.
Structured Storage	Stores data in a searchable and indexable manner to support precise querying and replay.
Scalability	Supports integration with remote control mechanisms such as gRPC to enable distributed scheduling and multi-node replay management.

3.2 System Overview

To meet the above requirements, DPSP-RS adopts a modular architecture consisting of four core components: the Data Collection Module, Data Storage and Indexing Module, Query and Filtering Module, and Packet Replay Module. These components are decoupled and interconnected via the gRPC protocol, which enables flexible deployment across distributed nodes, facilitates horizontal scaling, and simplifies load balancing.

The architecture is designed specifically for industrial control security testing and incident analysis. It supports both offline traffic replay (e.g., for regression testing and forensic analysis) and online threat simulation with anomaly injection, thereby providing a unified framework that can be integrated with ICS intrusion detection systems (ICS-IDS), attack reproduction workflows, and response mechanism evaluation.

3.3 Core Modules

As shown in Fig. 1, the architecture of DPSP-RS can be divided into four layers: Data Collection, Storage and Indexing, Query and Control, and Replay Layer. On top of this layered design, the system is organized into several core modules that cooperate via gRPC-based interfaces, as summarized below.

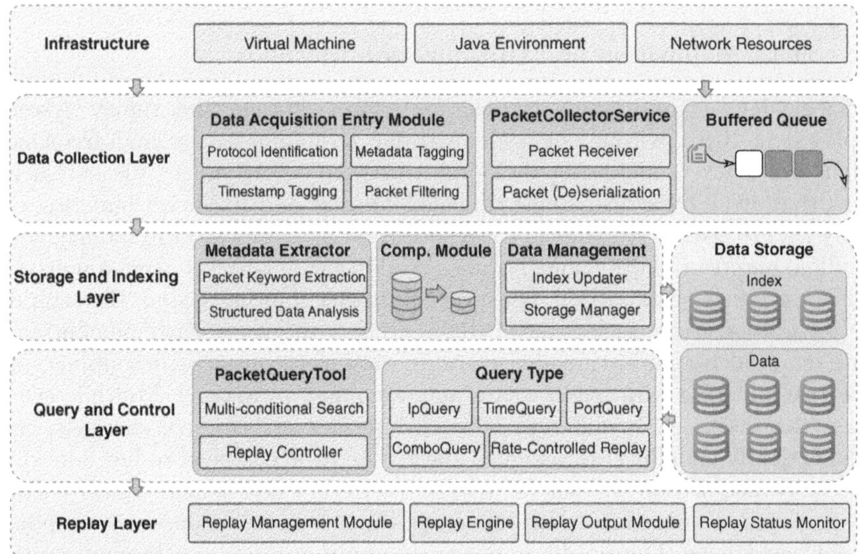

Fig. 1. Overall system architecture.

- **Data Collection Module**: Captures raw packets from network interfaces in real time and generates corresponding metadata (e.g., timestamp, IP, port, protocol) via a `PacketCollectorService` implemented in Java. The module is lightweight and deployable in diverse ICS network topologies, providing high-quality input for downstream processing.
- **Data Storage and Indexing Module**: Stores raw packets and metadata separately. Raw packets are persisted in binary format, whereas metadata are structured and written into index files. A multi-level time-based index is built to accelerate range queries and facilitate event tracing and security analysis.
- **Query and Control Module**: Implemented by `PacketQueryTool`, this module supports multi-dimensional queries based on time, IP, port, protocol, and other attributes. It quickly locates target packet sequences for replay and can be extended to support more complex filtering rules.

- **Packet Replay Module**: The `PacketForwarder` component replays packets at the original rate or a scaled rate (e.g., 2×) according to query results, and supports operations such as start, pause, and rate adjustment. It accurately restores communication processes and is suitable for protocol testing, attack reenactment, and what-if analysis.

The end-to-end processing workflow of these modules is illustrated in Fig. 2. Starting from online packet capture and metadata generation, DPSP-RS performs binary storage and index construction, followed by query-based selection of relevant traffic and controlled replay under configurable timing and rate constraints.

3.4 Data Acquisition and Optimization Methods

Efficient data acquisition is critical for packet storage and replay systems deployed in ICS environments, where traffic is dominated by high-frequency, small-sized packets and strict temporal constraints. Preliminary measurements show that straightforward single-threaded capture and fixed-size buffering can easily lead to packet loss, queue congestion, and increased storage latency when handling bursty or multi-channel traffic. In addition, per-packet synchronous disk writes introduce substantial I/O overhead, further limiting system throughput.

To address these issues, DPSP-RS redesigns the acquisition pipeline with three main ideas: multi-threaded capture, producer–consumer decoupling, and adaptive buffering with batch writes and streaming processing. Multiple acquisition threads listen on different network interfaces or protocol channels, each independently handling its assigned data flow to avoid head-of-line blocking. Internally, acquisition threads act as producers that continuously push packets into a shared queue, while backend storage threads serve as consumers responsible for persistence. This producer–consumer model enables asynchronous writing and improves overall throughput.

To achieve load-aware balancing across processing units, we introduce a dynamic concurrent connection allocation model:

$$\lambda_i(t) = \frac{C_i(t) \cdot \mu_i}{\sum_{j=1}^{n} C_j(t) \cdot \mu_j} \cdot \lambda_{\text{total}}(t) \tag{1}$$

where $\lambda_i(t)$ denotes the request rate assigned to the ith processing unit at time t, $\lambda_{\text{total}}(t)$ is the total system request rate at time t, $C_i(t)$ represents the current load state or capacity weight of the ith unit, and μ_i is its maximum processing capability. This formulation distributes traffic proportionally to the effective capacity of each unit, leading to more balanced resource utilization and stable performance under varying load.

To further enhance write performance and responsiveness, we adopt a batch-write strategy and streaming processing in the data writing phase. Captured packets are first buffered in memory; once the buffer reaches a predefined threshold, packets are flushed to disk in batches. This significantly reduces the overhead

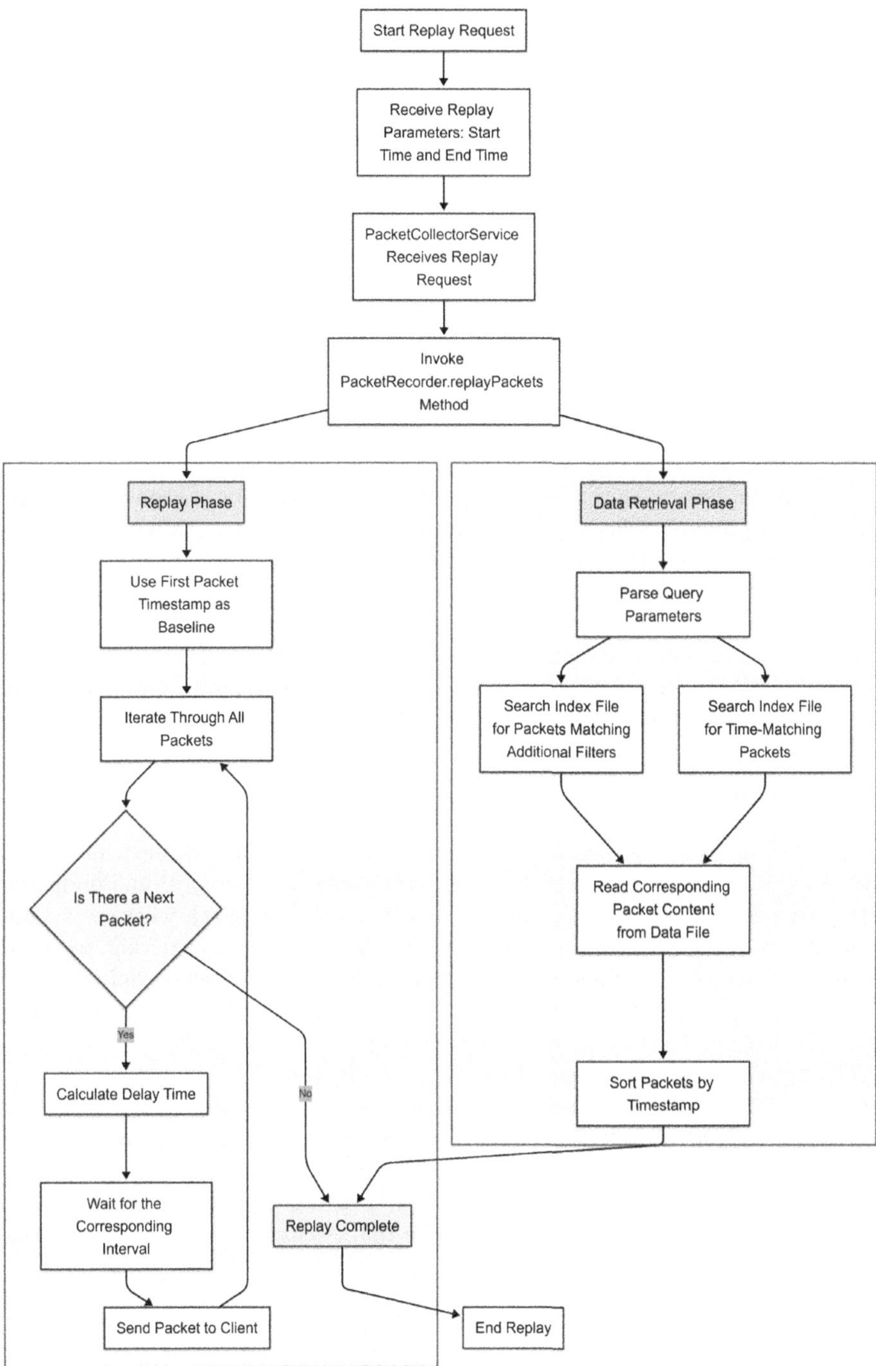

Fig. 2. Flowchart of the proposed traffic replay method.

of frequent disk I/O. At the same time, packets can immediately enter the parsing and indexing pipeline, where metadata extraction and index updates are performed asynchronously, eliminating the need to wait for buffer accumulation and improving end-to-end latency.

In high-concurrency scenarios, fixed buffer sizes may either waste memory or fail to prevent packet loss. Therefore, we design an adaptive buffer-size model that adjusts buffer capacity according to current load, request rate, and queue length:

$$B_{\text{opt}}(t) = B_{\text{base}} \cdot \left(1 + \alpha \cdot \log\left(1 + \frac{\lambda_{\text{current}}(t)}{\lambda_{\text{baseline}}}\right)\right) \cdot \beta^{Q(t)} \tag{2}$$

where $B_{\text{opt}}(t)$ is the optimal buffer size at time t, B_{base} is the base buffer size (default 1 MB), $\lambda_{\text{current}}(t)$ is the current request rate, $\lambda_{\text{baseline}}$ is a baseline request rate, α is the buffer growth factor controlling sensitivity to traffic changes, β is the queue-length impact factor (typically $\beta > 1$), and $Q(t)$ is the normalized queue length (0–1) reflecting queuing pressure.

The model has two key components. First, a logarithmic response to request rate prevents uncontrolled buffer expansion during sudden traffic bursts. Second, an exponential term on $Q(t)$ amplifies the impact of sustained queuing pressure, prompting the system to enlarge the buffer proactively under bottlenecks and thereby reducing packet loss or blocking. Together with batch writing and streaming processing, this adaptive mechanism allows DPSP-RS to automatically balance resource usage and throughput, while maintaining stable performance under varying workloads.

3.5 Data Storage

In the storage layer, the organization of metadata is crucial for query and replay efficiency. ICS workloads frequently require lookups on temporal and endpoint-related fields (e.g., timestamp, source/destination IP and port), whereas payload contents are accessed less often. A naive, flat serialization layout that treats all fields equally leads to unnecessary deserialization overhead when only a subset of metadata is required and forces scanning over variable-length segments during query evaluation.

To better match real query behavior, we analyze the structure and access patterns of `PacketMetadata` and design an optimized serialization scheme that prioritizes high-frequency, fixed-length fields. By reordering fields and incorporating field-level access priorities, DPSP-RS reduces decoding cost, improves memory locality, and minimizes redundant disk reads during time-range and attribute-based searches. To formally guide this design, we define a serialization efficiency index $S_{\text{efficiency}}(X)$:

$$S_{\text{efficiency}}(X) = \frac{\sum_{i=1}^{k} \phi_i \cdot (|X_i| \cdot \log_2(\text{freq}(X_i)))}{\sum_{i=1}^{k} |X_i|} \tag{3}$$

where $S_{\text{efficiency}}(X)$ denotes the serialization efficiency metric for packet X, X_i is the ith field, $|X_i|$ is its size in bytes, $\text{freq}(X_i)$ is its access frequency in queries, ϕ_i is the position-priority factor, and k is the total number of fields.

Moreover, Table 2 maps `PacketMetadata` fields to the symbols in the model.

Table 2. Mapping Between `PacketMetadata` Fields and Formula Symbols

Symbol	Field Name	Description
X_1	`netId`	4 bytes; unique identifier of network interface or node
X_2	`timestamp`	8 bytes; precise capture time of the packet
X_3	`originalSrcIp`	4 bytes; source IP address before relay
X_4	`originalSrcPort`	4 bytes; source port number
X_5	`destIp`	4 bytes; destination IP address
X_6	`destPort`	4 bytes; destination port number
X_7	`packetData`	Variable length; payload preceded by a 4-byte size field
X_8	`statusFlags`	4 bytes; packet status and control flags
X_9	`id`	4 bytes; global packet sequence identifier

From typical analysis tasks, timestamp and IP addresses (`originalSrcIp`, `destIp`) have the highest access frequencies, followed by ports (`original SrcPort`, `destPort`), whereas `id` and `statusFlags` are accessed less often. Accordingly, high-frequency fields are placed at the beginning of the serialization stream; the variable-length `packetData` is placed in the middle; and low-frequency fields appear near the end. Priority coefficients ϕ_i are set according to analytical importance, e.g., $\phi_{\text{timestamp}} = 1.5$ (highest), $\phi_{\text{IP address}} = 1.2$, and $\phi_{\text{other fields}} = 1$.

This layout provides three benefits: (i) key fields can be retrieved without reading the entire record, (ii) parsing time is reduced by arranging fields in descending order of access frequency, and (iii) fixed- and variable-length fields are cleanly separated, simplifying parsing logic. Based on the $S_{\text{efficiency}}(X)$ metric, DPSP-RS further adopts an adaptive serialization optimization algorithm that continuously monitors $\text{freq}(X_i)$ and dynamically adjusts field ordering and ϕ_i. Experimental results indicate that this strategy reduces query response time by 27.4% on average.

For confidentiality, stored traffic is additionally protected by a hierarchical key management scheme. Data Keys are used for encrypting and decrypting stored traffic, while a Master Key encrypts and manages these Data Keys. This design allows secure rotation of the Master Key without re-encrypting the entire dataset, improving both security and operational efficiency.

3.6 Hierarchical Index Access Efficiency Model

In large-scale packet storage systems, index design is a key determinant of query performance, particularly for time-range queries that dominate ICS analysis. Traditional flat index structures maintain a single-level list of offsets or timestamps; as data volumes grow, a single query may require scanning large portions of the index or performing many disk seeks, leading to high and unpredictable latency.

To address this, DPSP-RS employs a hierarchical time-partitioned index that organizes metadata at multiple granularities (e.g., hour, minute, second), significantly reducing the search space for each query. To analyze and tune the performance of this structure under different workloads, we introduce a hierarchical index access efficiency model:

$$E_{\text{access}}(q) = \sum_{l=1}^{L} p_l(q) \cdot \left[c_{\text{disk}} + \sum_{i=1}^{N_l} P_i(q) \cdot \left(T_{\text{seek}} + \frac{S_i}{R_{\text{transfer}}} \right) \right] \tag{4}$$

where $E_{\text{access}}(q)$ is the expected access time for query q, $p_l(q)$ is the probability that q must access index layer l, c_{disk} is the fixed per-access overhead, N_l is the number of index blocks in layer l, $P_i(q)$ is the probability that q accesses block i, T_{seek} is average seek time, S_i is the size of block i, R_{transfer} is the data transfer rate, and L is the total number of index layers.

In this context, hierarchical indexing ($L > 1$) is implemented as:

- **First-level index**: partitioned by hour, each entry covering a one-hour time range.
- **Second-level index**: partitioned by minute within an hour.
- **Third-level index**: partitioned by second, pointing directly to packet locations.

The model explicitly captures multi-layer access probabilities ($p_l(q)$ and $P_i(q)$) and the two-stage I/O cost (fixed overhead plus seek and transfer). This makes it possible to reason about how changes in index layout, block size, or data distribution impact the expected query cost. Compared with simplified models that consider only a single index layer, this formulation more accurately reflects real query paths in hierarchical structures.

Using this model, DPSP-RS can jointly tune logical index structure (e.g., time partitioning granularity, block size) and physical parameters (e.g., prefetch size) to minimize $E_{\text{access}}(q)$ under given workload characteristics. Experimental results show that, compared with flat index architectures, the hierarchical design guided by this model reduces average query latency by 27–35% and increases throughput by about 22% for large time-range queries. When combined with multi-threaded index segmentation, the system further shortens response time under high concurrency and long time windows, significantly improving end-to-end query efficiency.

4 Evaluation

4.1 Development Environment

To evaluate the functionality and performance of the proposed Data Packet Storage and Replay System (DPSP-RS), we implemented and tested the system in the following environment.

DPSP-RS runs on Ubuntu 22.04.5 LTS, using Java 23.0.1 as the primary development language and runtime platform, with IntelliJ IDEA 2024.2.4 as the integrated development environment. The hardware platform is a server equipped with an Intel(R) Xeon(R) Gold 6248 @ 2.50 GHz processor, providing strong concurrency handling and computing capabilities. This setup ensures stable system operation and reproducible performance measurements.

4.2 Experimental Results

We compare DPSP-RS with two widely used replay tools, GoReplay and Tcpreplay, along three core dimensions: (i) compression efficiency, (ii) effective throughput, and (iii) replay time and reliability. To avoid exposing sensitive production traffic, the industrial control protocol used in our experiments is specially designed for the testbed and emulates typical ICS communication patterns. The generated traffic features small packet sizes, strict timing requirements, and periodic exchanges, closely resembling real ICS workloads while eliminating the risks associated with using real industrial deployments. Under these conditions, DPSP-RS consistently outperforms the baseline tools in all three evaluation aspects.

Compression Performance. Figure 3 shows the compression and throughput results under different data volumes. DPSP-RS employs binary serialization combined with Zstd compression and achieves up to a 45% reduction in data size

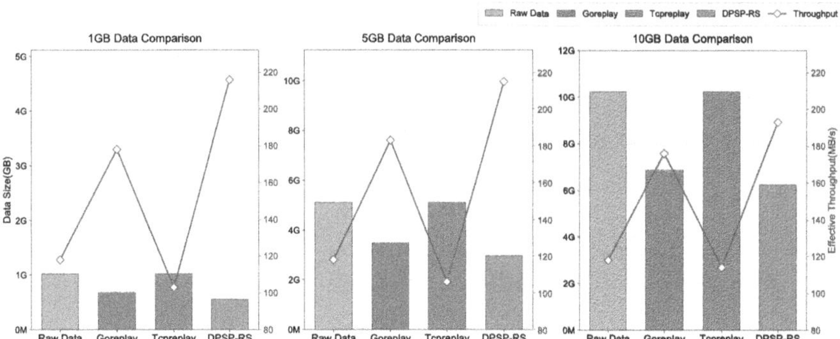

Fig. 3. Compression and throughput comparison across varying data volumes.

compared with raw data. The compression ratio improves further as the dataset grows, since larger datasets contain more repetitive structural patterns that benefit from binary encoding and dictionary-based compression. GoReplay provides limited compression support but remains less efficient than DPSP-RS, while Tcpreplay does not perform compression and stores traffic at its original size. Compared with text-based logs used by GoReplay and raw PCAP files relied upon by Tcpreplay, DPSP-RS offers a better trade-off between storage space and data interpretability, making it particularly suitable for resource-constrained environments and long-term traffic archiving.

Throughput Performance. Throughput was evaluated under three network bandwidth settings: 100 Mbps, 500 Mbps, and 1000 Mbps. As illustrated in Fig. 4, DPSP-RS consistently outperforms GoReplay and Tcpreplay across all bandwidths. At 1000 Mbps, DPSP-RS achieves stable single-threaded write throughput of 189–213 MB/s, benefiting from sequential writes and buffered batch operations. This corresponds to approximately a 22.4% improvement over GoReplay and more than a twofold improvement over Tcpreplay. These results indicate that DPSP-RS can efficiently sustain high-frequency multi-channel ingestion typical of industrial control networks and remains robust under high-concurrency workloads.

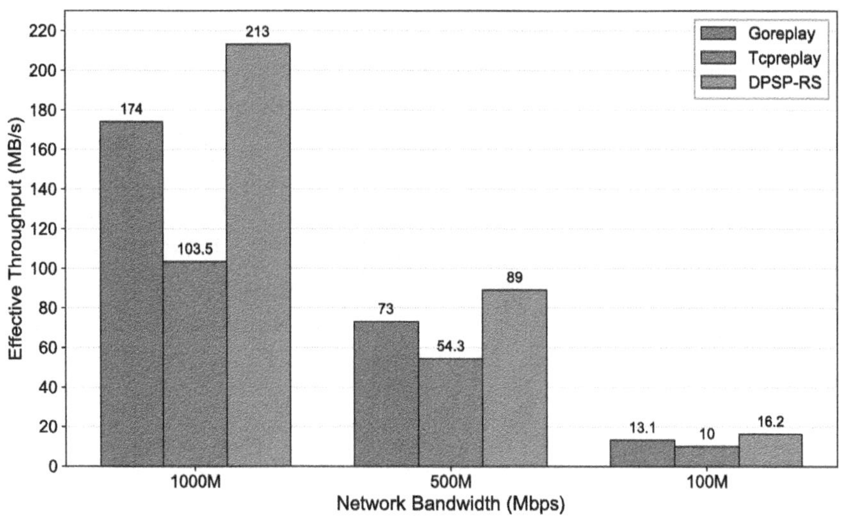

Fig. 4. Comparison of throughput under different bandwidths.

Replay Performance and Reliability. Replay efficiency was evaluated using ten rounds of experiments. As shown in Fig. 5, under a 500 Mbps network with

1 GB of data, DPSP-RS achieves an average replay time of approximately 55 s, outperforming GoReplay (78 s on average) and Tcpreplay (57 s on average). Moreover, DPSP-RS exhibits smaller variance in replay time, reflecting higher stability and determinism. Its timestamp-driven replay mechanism effectively meets the latency and fidelity requirements of ICS scenarios. The average response delay before sending the first packet is less than 20 ms, which is beneficial for interactive testing and attack simulation. During replay, DPSP-RS supports flexible rate control from 0.1× to 100× while keeping CPU utilization within an acceptable range.

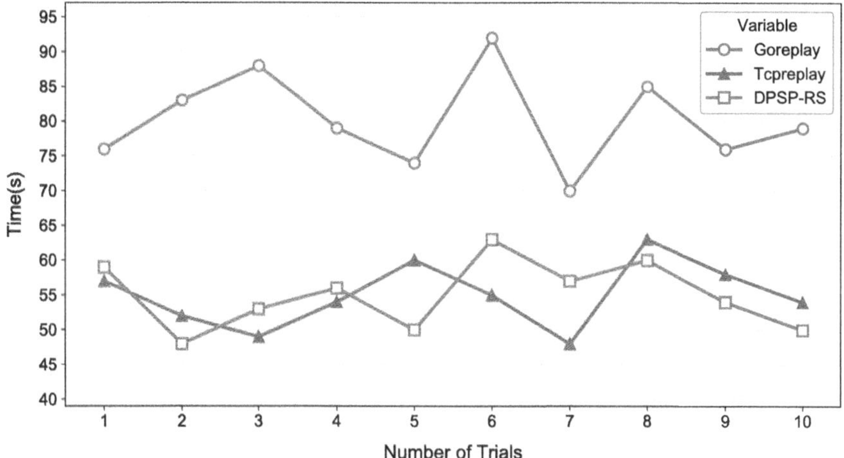

Fig. 5. Comparison of combined storage and replay time.

To assess replay reliability, we further measured packet loss rates under a 500 Mbps environment with 1 GB of replayed traffic. DPSP-RS achieves an average packet loss rate of only 0.027% with low variance (0.014%). In comparison, Tcpreplay exhibits a packet loss rate of 0.040%, and GoReplay 0.109%, both with higher fluctuations. These results show that DPSP-RS can maintain reliable packet delivery even under high replay rates, which is crucial for faithfully reproducing industrial control traffic. In addition, the distribution of packet arrival times remains close to that of the original trace, indicating that the temporal characteristics of ICS traffic are well preserved during replay.

5 Conclusion

This paper presented the design and implementation of DPSP-RS, a data packet storage and replay system tailored for industrial control networks. The system adopts a modular relay-server architecture and leverages gRPC-based inter-module communication to decouple data collection, index-based storage, conditional filtering, and flexible-speed replay. By integrating binary serialization,

Zstd-based compression, and a hierarchical time-partitioned index, DPSP-RS achieves a single-threaded write throughput of 189–213 MB/s and a maximum compression ratio of 45.6%. Experimental comparisons with GoReplay and Tcpreplay demonstrate that DPSP-RS offers more precise replay control, richer conditional query capabilities, and higher compression efficiency. Under a 1000 Mbps network environment, its replay throughput reaches 213 MB/s, significantly exceeding GoReplay (174 MB/s) and Tcpreplay (103 MB/s), while achieving an average replay time of about 55 s and maintaining a lower packet loss rate, thus providing reliable and high-fidelity traffic reproduction for ICS testing and security analysis.

Future work will focus on further enhancing concurrency, adaptability, and real-time performance. First, we plan to introduce thread-pool–based concurrency models and fine-grained scheduling strategies to better exploit multi-core hardware, thereby improving system stability and throughput under high-frequency traffic. Second, we will investigate hybrid compression schemes that combine Zstd with lightweight algorithms such as Snappy or LZ4, aiming to achieve a more flexible balance between compression ratio and end-to-end latency in replay and query operations. In addition, we will explore adapting the hierarchical index and timestamp-driven replay mechanisms to broader traffic types (e.g., web traffic, mixed TCP flows, encrypted traffic) and integrating DPSP-RS more tightly with industrial intrusion detection, forensic analysis, and intelligent operations and maintenance platforms, so as to further expand its applicability in practical industrial environments.

Acknowledgments. This article is supported by the National Key R&D Program of China (2023YFB3107300), the Guangxi Natural Science Foundation (2025GXNSFGA069004), the National Natural Science Foundation of China (62562021,62372067).

References

1. Yang, X.Y., Chi, Y.P., Wang, Z.Q.: Research on SDN network traffic measurement technology based on multi-layer sketch. Inf. Secur. Res. **10**(9), 840–848 (2024). (in Chinese)
2. Li, H., Cui, Z., Shen, X.: A survey of anomaly analysis and detection methods for network traffic characteristics. Inf. Netw. Secur. **25**(2), 194–214 (2025). (in Chinese)
3. Machaka, V., Lorenzo, F.S., Arrizabalaga, S., et al.: Comparative analysis of the standalone and hybrid SDN solutions for early detection of network channel attacks in industrial control systems: a WWTP case study. Internet Things **28**, 101413 (2024)
4. Swileh, N.M., Zhang, S.: Unseen attack detection in software-defined networking using a BERT-based large language model. AI **6**(7), 154 (2025). https://doi.org/10.3390/ai6070154
5. Qin, X., Doss, R., Jiang, F., et al.: Securing ICS networks: SDN-based automated traffic control and MTD defensive framework against DDoS attacks. Comput. Commun. **241**, 108252 (2025). https://doi.org/10.1016/j.comcom.2025.108252

6. Mesbah, S., Abdo, P., Cruz, T., Rosa, L., Simões, P.: Analysis of ICS and SCADA systems attacks using honeypots. Future Internet **15**(7), 241 (2023)
7. Lu, M.Y.: Optimization design of computer network security storage system based on data processing technology. Wirel. Internet Technol. **22**(6), 117–120 (2025). (in Chinese)
8. Ren, Y.: Research on Network Intrusion Detection Algorithms for Industrial Control Systems. Master's thesis, Sichuan University, Chengdu, China (2024). (in Chinese)
9. Wang, T., Xu, Y., Tang, Z.: Toward fast network intrusion detection for web services: partial-flow feature extraction and dataset construction. Int. J. Web Inf. Syst. **21**(1), 77–95 (2025)
10. Koumar, J., Hynek, K., Pešek, J., et al.: NetTiSA: extended IP flow with time-series features for universal bandwidth-constrained high-speed network traffic classification. Comput. Netw. **240**, 110147 (2024)
11. Li, T., Yang, Z., Li, W., et al.: Malicious encrypted traffic detection method based on multi-granularity representation under data imbalance conditions. Knowl.-Based Syst. **316**, 113320 (2025)
12. Cheng, M., Chen, Y., Zhang, D.: A traffic normalization location attention network for cyber attack detection in industrial cyber-physical systems. Ad Hoc Netw. **178**, 103965 (2025). https://doi.org/10.1016/j.adhoc.2025.103965
13. Ghosh, S.: Network traffic analysis based on cybersecurity intrusion detection through an effective automated separate guided attention federated graph neural network. Appl. Soft Comput. **169**, 112603 (2025). https://doi.org/10.1016/j.asoc.2024.112603
14. Huang, X., Wang, X., Liu, Y., Xue, Q.: A distributed traffic replay framework for network emulation. Information **14**(59) (2023). https://doi.org/10.3390/info14020059
15. Liu, M., et al.: Enhanced detection of obfuscated https tunnel traffic using heterogeneous information network. Comput. Netw. **257**, 110975 (2025). https://doi.org/10.1016/j.comnet.2024.110975
16. Tang, M.: Application of data compression technology in communication. Wirel. Internet Technol. **19**(16), 115–117 (2022). (in Chinese)
17. Abdulameer, D.A., Hassan, Z.M.: Improvement of lossless text compression methods using a hybrid method by the integration of RLE, LZW and Huffman coding algorithms. Int. J. Softw. Eng. Appl. **15**(5), 17–27 (2024)
18. Wang, S., Bai, J., Wang, B., et al.: Accelerated traffic replay method based on time compression. J. Netw. Inf. Secur. **7**(5), 178–188 (2021). (in Chinese)
19. Idrees, K.S., Azar, J., Couturier, R., et al.: SZ4IoT: an adaptive lightweight lossy compression algorithm for diverse IoT devices and data types. J. Supercomput. **81**(2), 392 (2025)
20. Farahi, R.: A comprehensive overview of load balancing methods in software-defined networks. Discov. Internet Things **5**(1), 6 (2025)

BCFW: A Blockchain Consensus Firewall for Validator Intrusion Detection and Auditable Response

Zheng Zhu and Wenjuan Li(✉)

Department of Mathematics and Information Technology, The Education University of Hong Kong, Hong Kong, China
lwenjuan@eduhk.hk

Abstract. Validator nodes in blockchain networks face network-layer threats in which traditional enterprise firewalls do not adequately address. In this work, we introduce BCFW, a Blockchain Consensus Firewall that bridges flow-based intrusion detection with on-chain governance for Proof-of-Authority (PoA) deployment. At its core, an FT-Transformer processes the 41 KDD Cup 99 features as tokens, using self-attention to model cross-feature interactions and outputting multi-class predictions with calibrated confidence. Class imbalance is mitigated through log-smoothed weighting and label smoothing. Upon threat detection, an orchestration layer may submit proposed mitigation measures to a multisignature contract. Validators then conduct an on-chain vote, and approved responses—such as rate limiting, isolation, or access-control updates—are automatically executed with complete audit trails. On the KDD Cup 99 benchmark, BCFW achieves 99.95% accuracy and 0.9182 macro-F1 across five attack categories. Our results show that coupling neural detection with blockchain-native governance yields an auditable, collectively controlled defense pipeline for validator infrastructure.

Keywords: Network intrusion detection · Blockchain security · Tabular Transformer · PoA consensus · On-chain governance

1 Introduction

1.1 Background and Motivation

Blockchain platforms, originating from Nakamoto's peer-to-peer cash system [39] and generalized by Ethereum [54], rely on validator nodes that run on commodity infrastructure, expose RPC and P2P interfaces, and operate in adversarial networks. Attackers can target consensus and application layers through selfish mining, reordering, DoS, and contract abuse [8,11,43,45]. In cyber-physical deployments such as smart grids and IoT [13,36,38], compromised validators or gateways create safety and financial risks, while illicit behaviors propagate across on-chain and off-chain interactions [30,51,53,55]. Defenses therefore need to couple transaction analytics with network- and host-layer visibility.

W. Meng et al. (Eds.): ASSS 2025, CCIS 2903, pp. 130–145, 2026.
https://doi.org/10.1007/978-3-032-21600-7_9

Classical network intrusion detection systems (NIDSs) evolved from audit-rule engines [10] and signature systems such as Snort and Bro [44] to flow-based anomaly detection [19] and machine learning [2]. Deep models extend this line with RNNs [56], feed-forward IoT detectors [14], attention-based architectures [28,52], and robustness techniques including dropout [49] and batch normalization [15]. Recent surveys highlight graph and hybrid designs and the need to address class imbalance [3,40,47] using strategies such as focal-style reweighting [24].

However, most existing NIDSs are designed and evaluated in generic enterprise settings. They do not directly account for the operational roles, governance constraints, and consensus assumptions of blockchain validator nodes. This gap motivates a domain-tailored framework that couples flow-based intrusion detection with blockchain-native mitigation, while remaining compatible with widely used benchmark datasets such as KDD Cup 99.

1.2 Problem Statement

Despite decades of progress, three challenges remain for validator protection. (i) Signature systems tuned for enterprise gateways lack visibility into validator-specific behaviors [5,44]. (ii) Public benchmarks only approximate real traffic; KDD Cup 99 [1,50] remains useful, but exhibits redundancy and imbalance, and the domain shift to validator workloads persists [42]. (iii) Deep IDS models [28,56] often optimize accuracy but not auditable automated response; imbalance mitigation still depends on reweighting strategies [24] rather than operational calibration. In PoA settings [9], the asymmetric costs of false positives/negatives [13,45] make the calibration and governance coupling critical.

In this work, we address these challenges by designing a flow-based intrusion detection model tailored to the statistical properties of KDD Cup 99, and integrating it into a blockchain-native consensus firewall that operates over a PoA-based devnet. Our goal is not to claim that KDD99 perfectly reflects validator traffic, but rather to use it as a well-understood testbed for developing and validating a deployable detection-and-response pipeline.

1.3 Our Contributions

To bridge the gap between intrusion detection and blockchain governance, we introduce BCFW (Blockchain Consensus Firewall), a framework that couples an AI-based NIDS with on-chain, multi-signature mitigation logic. Validators in a DevLeChain-based PoA network [9] expose flow statistics to an off-chain analysis platform, where traffic is preprocessed and fed into a Transformer-inspired intrusion detection model. In this paper, we instantiate the detector as *FT-Transformer*, a compact flow-based Transformer model that leverages ideas from modern deep NIDS [28,56] while remaining lightweight enough for the deployment of the validator.

BCFW organizes its components into three planes: (i) a data plane that collects flows from validator and gateway nodes; (ii) an analysis plane that applies the FT-Transformer to KDD-derived features with calibrated confidence; and (iii) a control plane that encodes mitigation policies as on-chain transactions. When the detector raises an alert, the orchestration service proposes responses (e.g., firewall updates, RPC throttling) to a multi-signature contract [29] on a PoA ledger [9], balancing rapid mitigation with collective oversight.

The overall system architecture is illustrated in Fig. 1. Flow records originating from validator nodes are forwarded to the off-chain analysis platform, where they are transformed into model-ready feature vectors. The FT-Transformer outputs per-flow predictions and associated confidence scores, which are used to construct governance proposals on-chain. Once a sufficient number of validators approve a proposal, the blockchain records an auditable decision and triggers the corresponding response, such as updating access control lists or notifying operators through the web frontend.

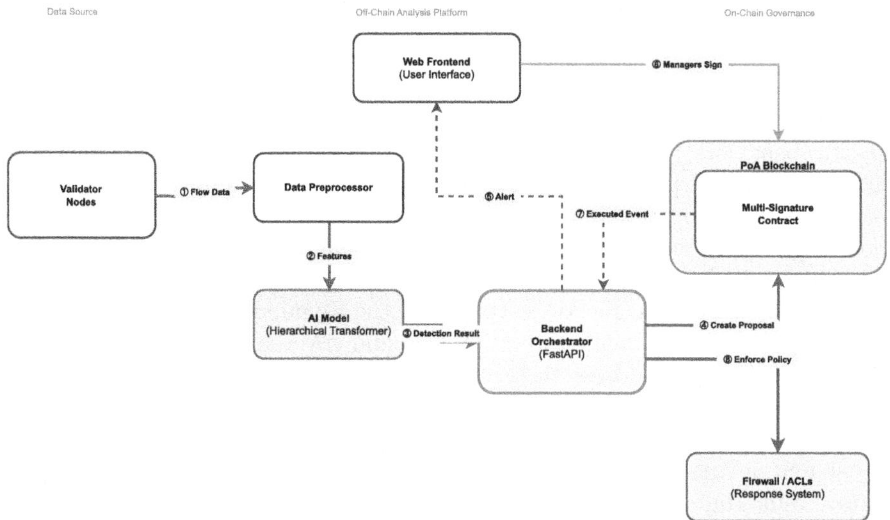

Fig. 1. BCFW system architecture.

Our contributions can be summarized as follows:

1. **Validator-centric threat modeling.** We connect classical NIDS foundations [19] with blockchain attack vectors [13] to derive objectives tailored to PoA validators.
2. **FT-Transformer on KDD Cup 99.** We adapt tabular Transformers [28,52] to KDD Cup 99 [1], addressing redundancy and imbalance with calibrated reweighting.
3. **On-chain, auditable mitigation.** We integrate the detector with a PoA multisignature pipeline [9,29] that turns alerts into verifiable responses, aligning detection accuracy with governance accountability.

The remainder of this paper is organized as follows. Section 2 reviews related work on NIDS and blockchain security. Section 3 presents the system architecture and governance loop. Section 4 details the FT-Transformer model and training. Section 5 reports experimental results on KDD Cup 99 and calibration analysis. Section 6 covers on-chain governance, and Sect. 7 concludes with limitations and future work.

2 Related Work

2.1 Network Intrusion Detection Systems

Early NIDS evolved from audit-rule engines [10] and signature systems such as Snort and Bro [5,44] to flow-based anomaly detection [19]. Classical ML (SVMs, RFs [12,37]) and deep models (RNNs [56], feed-forward IoT detectors [14], Transformers [28,52]) improved accuracy, aided by regularization (dropout, batch norm) and imbalance-aware losses such as focal weighting [24]. Datasets from KDD 99 to CIC-IDS 2017 [46] expose redundancy and skew, motivating models that cope with rare classes rather than only maximizing overall accuracy. In the literature, there are numerous studies on improving the performance of NIDSs such as blockchain [7,21,23,32], trust management [22,26,27,35], and traffic filtration [31,33,34].

2.2 AI for Blockchain Infrastructure Security

AI for blockchain security has centered on on-chain analytics: graph-based learning for illicit transactions [53] and phishing [55], economic structure analysis [30], and honeypot detection [51]. Broader surveys on smart grids and IoT [13,38] show blockchain nodes embedded in heterogeneous environments constrained by resources. Recent blockchain-native defenses for firmware dispatch [4] and rule-sharing firewalls [6] underline the value of auditable automation. Yet, off-chain intrusion detection for validators remains sparse; validators expose consensus and management surfaces [45] that traditional enterprise firewalls do not model.

2.3 On-Chain Governance and Automated Response

Permissioned chains employ governance and threat-modeling discipline [48]. PoA networks replace probabilistic mining with identity-based validators [9], while Schnorr-style multisignatures reduce verification overhead and enforce collective control [29]. Governance failures such as frontrunning [8] illustrate the need to couple detection with enforceable policies; existing frameworks rarely ingest network-layer signals for infrastructure response.

Table 1. A comparison among recent NIDS models and our work

Work	Model	Features	Limitations
Nawaz et al. [40]	LSTM + SMOTE	Multi-class intrusion detection using oversampling and sequence learning	Focuses on imbalance only; no consideration of blockchain validator traffic
Kim and Yoon [18]	CNN + Attention	Ensemble of text CNN and attention layers for packet-level threat classification	Operates at packet level; does not model validator flow behavior
Sharma et al. [47]	Hybrid DL	Evaluation of hybrid models (CapsNet, BiLSTM) across modern IDS benchmarks	Optimizes detection accuracy only; lacks automated response considerations
Manocchio et al. [28]	FlowTransformer	Transformer-based framework for flow-level intrusion detection	Generic IDS framework; not integrated with PoA consensus mechanisms
This work	**FT-Transformer**	Tailored to validator traffic and integrated with a PoA-based consensus firewall	Bridges intrusion detection and auditable on-chain response

2.4 Summary and Research Gap

In summary, NIDS research spans signatures to attention-based models, yet benchmarks such as KDD 99 and CIC-IDS 2017 [46] diverge from validator workloads and remain imbalanced [1,41,50]. Blockchain security has focused on on-chain analytics and governance, but few systems integrate flow-based detection with enforceable policies. We bridge this gap by combining a KDD-grounded Transformer detector with PoA multisignature governance to deliver auditable, validator-oriented mitigation.

Table 1 provides a comparison among recent NIDS models and our work.

3 System Architecture

3.1 Design Goals and Constraints

As shown in Fig. 1, our architecture has three goals: (i) low-latency detection and response at validator nodes, (ii) end-to-end auditability for post-incident reconstruction, and (iii) modular components that can evolve without destabilizing consensus-facing workloads. Given validator exposure across networking and governance interfaces [45], the system must tolerate bandwidth limits, hardware heterogeneity, and asymmetric costs of false positives versus false negatives.

3.2 Data Path and Preprocessing

Using KDD Cup 99 as the benchmark [1], raw labels are mapped to five superclasses: Benign, DoS, Probe, R2L, and U2R, while retaining the 41 original fea-

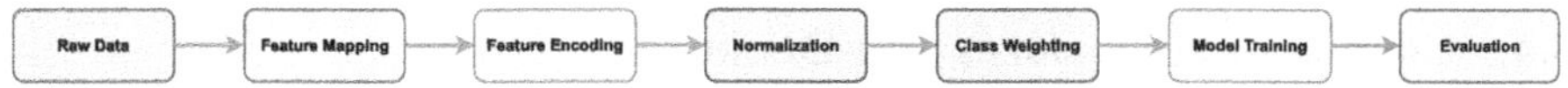

Fig. 2. Unified preprocessing for KDD Cup 99 flows

tures. Protocol and flag fields are label-encoded; service adopts a top-k strategy (top 30, remaining grouped as *other*) to bound embedding size. Numerical features are standardized using statistics fitted on the training split and applied to the test split to keep inference aligned with training distribution. Class imbalance is handled by log-smoothed class weights combined with cross-entropy loss and label smoothing, with a cosine learning-rate schedule to stabilize minority-class gradients. Traffic collected from validators or replay traces is funneled through this shared preprocessing pipeline before reaching the FT-Transformer detector; detailed model settings are discussed in later sections. The end-to-end preprocessing flow is summarized in Fig. 2.

3.3 Detection-to-Governance Loop

The closed loop in Fig. 3 connects detection to governance. The detector emits multi-class predictions with confidence; the orchestration service decides whether to log, alert, or generate a mitigation proposal. Proposals are submitted to a PoA network [9] via a multisignature contract [29]; once the quorum is met, remediation (rate limiting, temporary isolation, access-control updates) is executed and recorded on-chain. This aligns traffic detection with auditable on-chain control so validators can collectively authorize disruptive actions.

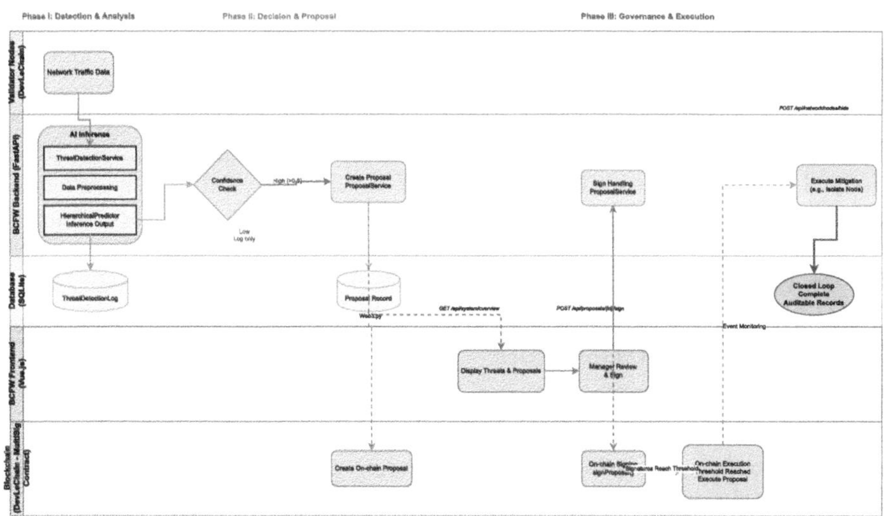

Fig. 3. BCFW governance loop from traffic ingestion to on-chain multisig execution.

3.4 Component Interfaces and Deployment Notes

The monitoring portal consolidates alerts, proposals, and incentive statuses for role-based review and approval. The orchestration layer handles traffic ingestion, preprocessing, detector triggering, and governance decision-making, while its logging and metrics endpoints support operational and auditing requirements. The detection module is decoupled through a feature adapter and inference service, enabling model updates without affecting other system components. The on-chain governance layer monitors proposal lifecycles, validates multisignature approvals, and triggers execution callbacks, while feeding results back to the backend to ensure state consistency. Deployments support independent component scaling, seamless switching between live and historical data sources, and adjustable governance thresholds via environment profiles–all designed to minimize validator impact.

4 Our Model

4.1 Model Overview

We employ a feature-token Transformer for flow-level intrusion detection. The design follows the tabular Transformer principles [28,52]: each feature becomes a token in a shared latent space, self-attention captures cross-feature dependencies, and a classification token aggregates evidence for final prediction. This choice avoids heavy sequence modeling while retaining flexibility over heterogeneous categorical and numerical fields in KDD Cup 99.

4.2 Feature Encoding

As mentioned, the 41 KDD features [1] are partitioned into numerical and categorical fields. Each numerical column is projected independently through a Linear$(1, d_{\text{model}})$ layer, producing one token per column. Categorical fields (protocol, flag) are label-encoded; *service* uses a top-k vocabulary (top 30, others grouped as *other*) to bound embedding size. Each categorical field is embedded into d_{model}. A learnable [CLS] token is prepended, yielding a sequence of length $1 + |\mathcal{F}_{\text{num}}| + |\mathcal{F}_{\text{cat}}|$. The tokenizer thus outputs a matrix $X \in \mathbb{R}^{T \times d_{\text{model}}}$ where T is the token count.

4.3 Transformer Architecture

The encoder stacks 3 TransformerEncoder layers (4 heads, $d_{\text{model}} = 128$, $d_{\text{ff}} = 256$, GELU activation, dropout 0.2, norm-first). Self-attention operates over the token sequence to model interactions across numeric and categorical dimensions. The classifier consumes the transformed [CLS] token via LayerNorm $\rightarrow$ ReLU $\rightarrow$ Linear to produce logits over five classes (Benign, DoS, Probe, R2L, U2R), matching the dataset's super-class mapping. This lightweight stack balances capacity and latency for validator-side or backend deployment; the overall architecture is shown in Fig. 4.

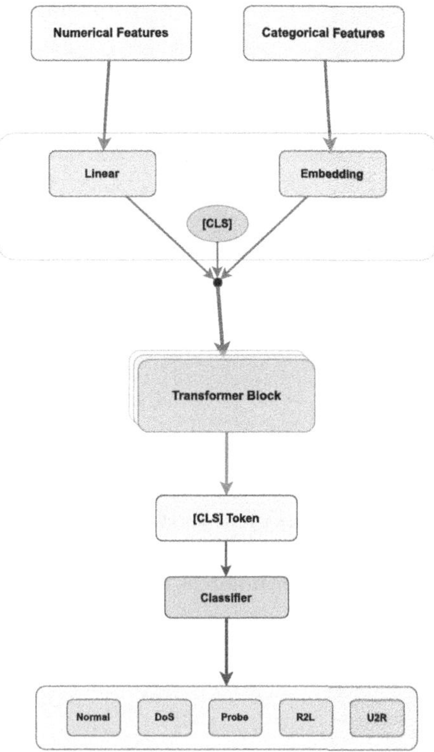

Fig. 4. FT-Transformer Model

4.4 Training and Optimization

Data items are split 80/20 with stratification on the five classes. Numerical features are standardized using statistics fitted on the training split and applied to the test split to align inference and training distributions. Class imbalance is handled by balanced class weights, smoothed via $w'_c = \log(1+w_c)/\mathrm{mean}(\log(1+w_c))$ and fed to a cross-entropy loss with label smoothing ($\epsilon = 0.05$). The loss is

$$\mathcal{L} = -\sum_c w'_c\, y_c \log p_c,$$

where y_c is the smoothed target and p_c the predicted probability. Optimization uses AdamW [25] with learning rate 1e−4, weight decay 1e−4, cosine schedule with warmup, batch size 512 (train) / 1024 (test), 20 epochs, and gradient clipping at 1.0 to stabilize minority-class updates.

4.5 Inference and Governance Coupling

During inference, softmax probabilities from the [CLS] head provide both class decisions and confidence scores. These scores feed the orchestration layer to

Table 2. FT-Transformer hyperparameters

Embedding dimension d_{model}	128
FFN dimension d_{ff}	256
Encoder layers / heads	3 / 4
Dropout	0.2
Batch size (train / test)	512 / 1024
Epochs	20
Learning rate / weight decay	1e−4 / 1e−4
Loss	Cross-entropy, label smoothing 0.05, smoothed class weights
Scheduler	Cosine with warmup
Gradient clipping	1.0

prioritize alerts and to propose mitigations in the multisig workflow (see Sect. 3). Thresholds can be tuned per deployment to trade false positives against response latency without retraining the model.

Table 2 provides the hypermparameters for FT-Transformer.

5 Evaluation

5.1 Experimental Setup

All experiments use the KDD Cup 99 benchmark [1,41,50] with five super-classes (Benign, DoS, Probe, R2L, U2R). We apply the shared preprocessing pipeline (top-30 service encoding, protocol/flag label encoding, train-fit standardization) and retain the 80/20 stratified split described in Sect. 4. The FT-Transformer follows the hyperparameters in Table 2 with smoothed class weights. For comparison, we include a baseline MLP and a CapsNet-BiLSTM reproduction; all models see identical tensors and class mappings.

5.2 Result Analysis

Table 3 reports aggregate metrics. All models achieve near-perfect accuracy and weighted-F1 due to the dominance of Benign and DoS. It is noted that Macro-F1 highlights minority-class performance: the MLP attains 0.9311, the FT-Transformer 0.9182, and the CapsNet baseline trails at 0.7811.

5.3 Per-class Performance

Table 4 details FT-Transformer class-wise metrics. Majority classes (Benign, DoS) exceed 0.99 F1; Probe and R2L sustain >0.93 F1 despite class imbalance. U2R remains challenging with F1 of 0.6667 on only 10 samples, explaining the macro-F1 gap relative to weighted-F1. Figure 5 visualizes per-class comparisons across models.

Table 3. Overall performance on KDD Cup 99 (test split).

Model	Accuracy	Macro-F1	Weighted-F1
CapsNet-BiLSTM	0.9993	0.7811	0.9992
Baseline MLP	0.9994	0.9311	0.9994
FT-Transformer	**0.9995**	**0.9182**	**0.9995**

Table 4. Per-class metrics for FT-Transformer.

Class	Precision	Recall	F1-Score	Support
Benign	0.9991	0.9986	0.9988	19456
Dos	0.9999	1.0000	0.9999	78292
Probe	0.9927	0.9951	0.9939	822
R2l	0.9217	0.9422	0.9319	225
U2r	0.6364	0.7000	0.6667	10

5.4 Training Dynamics and Error Patterns

Training stability is shown in Fig. 6, combining loss and validation macro-F1; curves converge smoothly within the allotted 20 epochs. The confusion matrix in Fig. 7 confirms near-perfect diagonals on majority classes, with residual confusion concentrated on U2R and R2L.

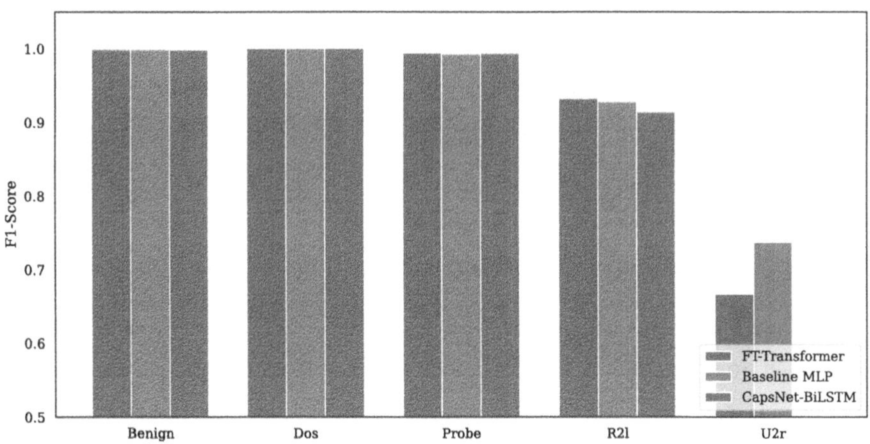

Fig. 5. Per-class performance comparison across models.

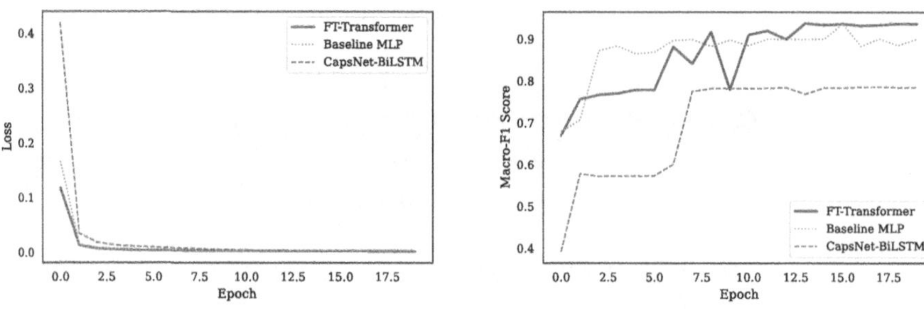

Fig. 6. Training dynamics for FT-Transformer: loss (left) and validation macro-F1 (right).

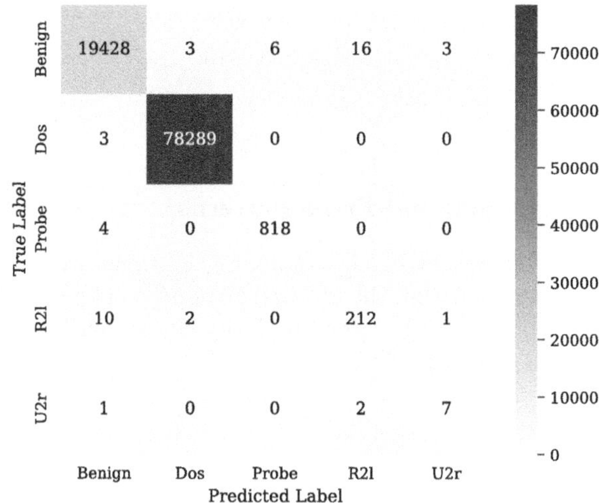

Fig. 7. Confusion matrix on the KDD test split for FT-Transformer.

5.5 Calibration and Threshold Analysis

Precision-Recall curves in Fig. 8 show that minority classes benefit from the FT-Transformer's calibrated outputs. The threshold analysis in the same figure highlights operating points where macro-F1 is stable; these thresholds can inform governance policies when mapping detector scores to multisignature proposals.

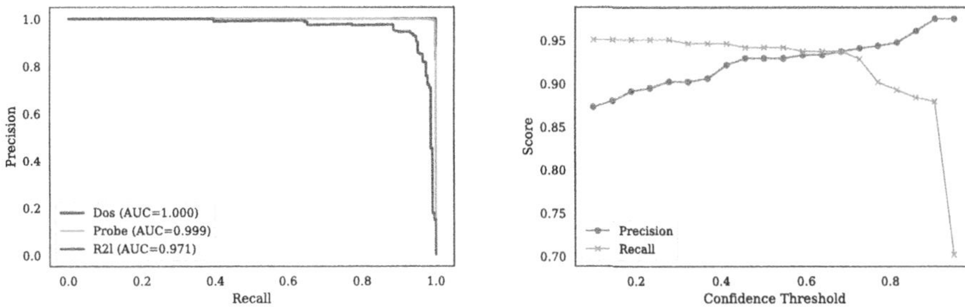

Fig. 8. Calibration and thresholding: Precision-Recall curves (left) and macro-F1 sensitivity to score thresholds (right).

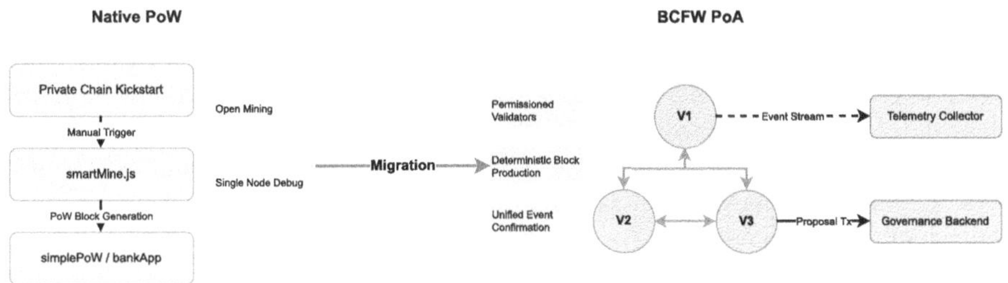

Fig. 9. Consensus migration overview from PoW sandbox to PoA validators.

6 Proof-of-Authority Deployment on DevLechain

6.1 PoW-to-PoA Adaptation

DevLeChain is deployed as a permissioned PoA network to give deterministic block timing, fixed validator identities, and predictable confirmation lags. The original PoW sandbox required miner coordination and tolerated variable block intervals, which would desynchronize telemetry ingestion and governance events. Migrating to PoA aligns detection outputs, proposal submissions, and execution callbacks without depending on mining incentives.

The migration overview is summarized in Fig. 9.

6.2 Multisignature Governance Flow

On the PoA ledger, a multisignature contract [29] enforces quorum-based approvals for security actions. The orchestration backend submits proposals that bundle severity tiers, response templates, and evidence digests; validators vote until the threshold is met or the proposal is vetoed. Contract events mark transitions across submission, voting, approval, execution, and rollback states, providing an auditable trail for every mitigation.

6.3 Integration Challenges and Resolutions

Three integration issues dominated deployment. First, event consistency: backend caches can drift if PoA events reorder; replay windows and checkpoint acknowledgments keep proposal state and on-chain logs aligned. Second, signature coordination: concurrent signers can collide on nonces; a queued signing protocol with deterministic ordering prevents duplicate votes while preserving individual accountability. Third, response mapping: FT-Transformer confidences must translate into controlled actions; a tiered policy table and rollback hooks prevent over- or under-reaction and let operators override decisions when needed.

7 Conclusion

In this work, we presented a validator-focused intrusion detection and governance pipeline grounded in KDD Cup 99. A feature-token Transformer delivers multiclass detection with calibrated confidences, while a PoA-based multisignature workflow turns alerts into auditable, collective mitigation. The unified preprocessing and on-chain evidence trail keeps detection, decisioning, and enforcement reproducible end to end.

We found that modular separation between detection, orchestration, and governance enables staged adoption: offline validation, human-in-the-loop proposal review, and gradually automated execution for high-confidence tiers. Deterministic PoA block timing keeps telemetry, proposals, and signatures time-aligned, which is as critical to operational reliability as model accuracy. Confidence-to-policy mappings and rollback hooks reduce the risk of overreaction and keep human oversight in the loop.

Current evidence derives from benchmark-driven evaluation and PoA-based replay rather than sustained operation on live validator clusters. The governance layer has been exercised with a fixed validator set and static thresholds; larger consortia and bursty incident loads may surface new contention patterns. Policy templates and audit practices still rely on disciplined operational processes beyond the model itself.

In future work, we plan to incorporate richer replay traces and, where feasible, anonymized live traffic to stress-test the detector and governance latency. Adaptive multisignature policies–role and time-aware quorums, dynamic thresholds, and finer-grained response templates—can tighten control during high–risk periods while preserving accountability. Online or adversarial training loops that ingest operator feedback would let the detector absorb emerging attack patterns without sacrificing reproducibility. Finally, releasing sanitized preprocessing and replay artifacts would ease external reproduction and comparative studies. Some new datasets (e.g., automotive IDS [16,17,20]) can be considered as well.

References

1. KDD Cup 1999 Data (1999). http://kdd.ics.uci.edu/databases/kddcup99/kddcup99.html. Accessed Nov 2025
2. Ahmad, Z., Shahid Khan, A., Wai Shiang, C., Abdullah, J., Ahmad, F.: Network intrusion detection system: a systematic study of machine learning and deep learning approaches. Trans. Emerging Telecommun. Technol. **32**(1), e4150 (2021)
3. Bilot, T., El Madhoun, N., Al Agha, K., Zouaoui, A.: Graph neural networks for intrusion detection: a survey. IEEE Access **11**, 49114–49139 (2023)
4. Biró, V., Chiu, W.Y., Meng, W.: Securing IoT firmware dispatch systems with blockchain. In: 2023 IEEE International Conference on Blockchain (Blockchain), pp. 229–238. IEEE (2023)
5. Bro, P.V.: A system for detecting network intruders in real-time. In: Proceedings 7th USENIX Security Symposium (1998)
6. Chiu, W.Y., Meng, W.: BlockFW–towards blockchain-based rule-sharing firewall. arXiv preprint arXiv:2303.13073 (2023)
7. Chiu, W., Meng, W., Ge, C.: NoSneaky: a blockchain-based execution integrity protection scheme in industry 4.0. IEEE Trans. Ind. Inf. **19**(7), 7957–7965 (2023)
8. Daian, P., et al.: Flash boys 2.0: frontrunning, transaction reordering, and consensus instability in decentralized exchanges. arXiv preprint arXiv:1904.05234 (2019)
9. De Angelis, S., et al.: PBFT vs proof-of-authority: applying the cap theorem to permissioned blockchain. In: CEUR Workshop Proceedings, vol. 2058. CEUR-WS (2018)
10. Denning, D.E.: An intrusion-detection model. IEEE Trans. Softw. Eng. **2**, 222–232 (1987)
11. Eyal, I., Sirer, E.G.: Majority is not enough: bitcoin mining is vulnerable. Commun. ACM **61**(7), 95–102 (2018)
12. Farnaaz, N., Jabbar, M.: Random forest modeling for network intrusion detection system. Procedia Comput. Sci. **89**, 213–217 (2016)
13. Ferrag, M.A., Shu, L.: The performance evaluation of blockchain-based security and privacy systems for the internet of things: a tutorial. IEEE Internet Things J. **8**(24), 17236–17260 (2021)
14. Ge, M., Fu, X., Syed, N., Baig, Z., Teo, G., Robles-Kelly, A.: Deep learning-based intrusion detection for IoT networks. In: 2019 IEEE 24th Pacific Rim International Symposium on Dependable Computing (PRDC), pp. 256–265 (2019). https://doi.org/10.1109/PRDC47002.2019.00056
15. Ioffe, S., Szegedy, C.: Batch normalization: accelerating deep network training by reducing internal covariate shift. In: International Conference on Machine Learning, pp. 448–456. PMLR (2015)
16. Kidmose, B., Kidmose, A.B., Meng, W.: Can-Sleuth: sleuthing out the capabilities, limitations, and performance impacts of automotive intrusion detection datasets. Int. J. Inf. Sec. **24**(4), 193 (2025)
17. Kidmose, B., Meng, W.: can-sleuth: investigating and evaluating automotive intrusion detection datasets. In: Li, S., Coopamootoo, K.P.L., Sirivianos, M. (eds.) European Interdisciplinary Cybersecurity Conference, EICC 2024, Xanthi, Greece, 5–6 June 2024, pp. 19–28. ACM (2024)
18. Kim, H., Yoon, Y.: An ensemble of text convolutional neural networks and multihead attention layers for classifying threats in network packets. Electronics **12**(20), 4253 (2023)

19. Lakhina, A., Crovella, M., Diot, C.: Characterization of network-wide anomalies in traffic flows. In: Proceedings of the 4th ACM SIGCOMM Conference on Internet Measurement, pp. 201–206 (2004)
20. Lampe, B., Meng, W.: can-train-and-test: a curated CAN dataset for automotive intrusion detection. Comput. Secur. **140**, 103777 (2024)
21. Li, W., Meng, W., Yeh, K., Cha, S.: Trusting computing as a service for blockchain applications. IEEE Internet Things J. **10**(13), 11326–11342 (2023)
22. Li, W., Meng, W.: BCTrustFrame: enhancing trust management via blockchain and IPFS in 6G era. IEEE Netw. **36**(4), 120–125 (2022)
23. Li, W., Wang, Y., Meng, W., Li, J., Su, C.: BlockCSDN: towards blockchain-based collaborative intrusion detection in software defined networking. IEICE Trans. Inf. Syst. **105-D**(2), 272–279 (2022)
24. Lin, T.Y., Goyal, P., Girshick, R., He, K., Dollár, P.: Focal loss for dense object detection. In: Proceedings of the IEEE International Conference on Computer Vision, pp. 2980–2988 (2017)
25. Loshchilov, I., Hutter, F.: Decoupled weight decay regularization. arXiv preprint arXiv:1711.05101 (2017)
26. Ma, Z., Liu, L., Meng, W.: DCONST: detection of multiple-mix-attack malicious nodes using consensus-based trust in IoT networks. In: Liu, J.K., Cui, H. (eds.) Information Security and Privacy - 25th Australasian Conference, ACISP 2020, Perth, WA, Australia, 30 November–2 December 2020, Proceedings. LNCS, vol. 12248, pp. 247–267. Springer (2020)
27. Ma, Z., Liu, L., Meng, W.: Towards multiple-mix-attack detection via consensus-based trust management in IoT networks. Comput. Secur. **96**, 101898 (2020)
28. Manocchio, L.D., Layeghy, S., Lo, W.W., Kulatilleke, G.K., Sarhan, M., Portmann, M.: FlowTransformer: a transformer framework for flow-based network intrusion detection systems. Expert Syst. Appl. **241**, 122564 (2024)
29. Maxwell, G., Poelstra, A., Seurin, Y., Wuille, P.: Simple Schnorr multi-signatures with applications to bitcoin. Des. Codes Crypt. **87**(9), 2139–2164 (2019)
30. Meiklejohn, S., et al.: A fistful of bitcoins: characterizing payments among men with no names. In: Proceedings of the 2013 Conference on Internet Measurement Conference, pp. 127–140 (2013)
31. Meng, W.: Intrusion detection in the era of IoT: building trust via traffic filtering and sampling. Computer **51**(7), 36–43 (2018)
32. Meng, W., Li, W., Calugar, A.N.: BANN-TMGuard: toward touch-movement-based screen unlock patterns via blockchain-enabled artificial neural networks on IoT devices. IEEE Internet Things J. **12**(2), 1856–1866 (2025)
33. Meng, W., Li, W., Kwok, L.: EFM: enhancing the performance of signature-based network intrusion detection systems using enhanced filter mechanism. Comput. Secur. **43**, 189–204 (2014)
34. Meng, W., Li, W., Kwok, L.F.: Towards effective trust-based packet filtering in collaborative network environments. IEEE Trans. Netw. Serv. Manag. **14**(1), 233–245 (2017)
35. Meng, W., Li, W., Zhu, L.: Enhancing medical smartphone networks via blockchain-based trust management against insider attacks. IEEE Trans. Eng. Manag. **67**(4), 1377–1386 (2020)
36. Moreno Escobar, J.J., Morales Matamoros, O., Tejeida Padilla, R., Lina Reyes, I., Quintana Espinosa, H.: A comprehensive review on smart grids: challenges and opportunities. Sensors **21**(21), 6978 (2021)

37. Mukkamala, S., Janoski, G., Sung, A.: Intrusion detection using neural networks and support vector machines. In: Proceedings of the 2002 International Joint Conference on Neural Networks, IJCNN 2002 (Cat. No. 02CH37290), vol. 2, pp. 1702–1707. IEEE (2002)
38. Musleh, A.S., Yao, G., Muyeen, S.: Blockchain applications in smart grid-review and frameworks. IEEE Access **7**, 86746–86757 (2019)
39. Nakamoto, S., Bit, B., et al.: Bitcoin: a peer-to-peer electronic cash system 2008(2007)
40. Nawaz, M.W., Munawar, R., Mehmood, A., Rahman, M.M.U., Abbasi, Q.H.: Multi-class network intrusion detection with class imbalance via LSTM & SMOTE. arXiv preprint arXiv:2310.01850 (2023)
41. Özgür, A., Erdem, H.: A review of KDD99 dataset usage in intrusion detection and machine learning between 2010 and 2015 (2016)
42. Pan, S.J., Yang, Q.: A survey on transfer learning. IEEE Trans. Knowl. Data Eng. **22**(10), 1345–1359 (2009)
43. Qian, P., Liu, Z., He, Q., Huang, B., Tian, D., Wang, X.: Smart contract vulnerability detection technique: a survey. arXiv preprint arXiv:2209.05872 (2022)
44. Roesch, M., et al.: Snort: lightweight intrusion detection for networks. In: Lisa, vol. 99, pp. 229–238 (1999)
45. Saad, M., et al.: Exploring the attack surface of blockchain: a systematic overview. arXiv preprint arXiv:1904.03487 (2019)
46. Sharafaldin, I., Lashkari, A.H., Ghorbani, A.A., et al.: Toward generating a new intrusion detection dataset and intrusion traffic characterization. In: ICISSp, vol. 1, pp. 108–116 (2018)
47. Sharma, V., Kumar, M.: Improving intrusion detection with hybrid deep learning models: a study on CIC-IDS2017, UNSW-NB15, and KDD CUP 99. J. Inf. Syst. Eng. Manag. **10** (2025)
48. Shostack, A.: Threat Modeling: Designing for Security. Wiley (2014)
49. Srivastava, N., Hinton, G., Krizhevsky, A., Sutskever, I., Salakhutdinov, R.: Dropout: a simple way to prevent neural networks from overfitting. J. Mach. Learn. Res. **15**(1), 1929–1958 (2014)
50. Tavallaee, M., Bagheri, E., Lu, W., Ghorbani, A.A.: A detailed analysis of the KDD cup 99 data set. In: 2009 IEEE Symposium on Computational Intelligence for Security and Defense Applications, pp. 1–6. IEEE (2009)
51. Torres, C.F., Steichen, M., et al.: The art of the scam: demystifying honeypots in Ethereum smart contracts. In: 28th USENIX Security Symposium (USENIX Security 19), pp. 1591–1607 (2019)
52. Vaswani, A., et al.: Attention is all you need. In: Advances in Neural Information Processing Systems, vol. 30 (2017)
53. Weber, M., et al.: Anti-money laundering in bitcoin: experimenting with graph convolutional networks for financial forensics. arXiv preprint arXiv:1908.02591 (2019)
54. Wood, G., et al.: Ethereum: a secure decentralised generalised transaction ledger. Ethereum Project Yellow Paper **151**(2014), 1–32 (2014)
55. Xia, Y., Liu, J., Wu, J.: Phishing detection on ethereum via attributed ego-graph embedding. IEEE Trans. Circuits Syst. II Express Briefs **69**(5), 2538–2542 (2022)
56. Yin, C., Zhu, Y., Fei, J., He, X.: A deep learning approach for intrusion detection using recurrent neural networks. IEEE Access **5**, 21954–21961 (2017)

An Embedded-Assisted Secret Inspection Scheme in Untrusted Host Environments

Haolin Xu[1,3], Kai Li[2], Tiansi Li[2], Hongyi Liu[1,3], and Mengxia Ren[1](✉)

[1] School of Cyberspace Science and Technology, Beijing Institute of Technology, Beijing 100032, China
mengxiaren@hotmail.com

[2] Great Wall Navigation Technology Co., Ltd., Beijing 100032, China

[3] Shandong Key Laboratory of Energy Industry Internet Big Data Technology, Jinan 250003, Shandong, China

Abstract. To address the privacy leakage risks and the challenges posed by untrusted host environments in sensitive keyword retrieval within confidential settings, this paper proposes an embedded confidential computing scheme based on the USB Gadget driver framework. Utilizing a NanoPi R5S development board to construct a physically isolated confidential computing environment, the scheme employs a customized USB Mass Storage Gadget driver to facilitate interaction with the host. This architecture effectively migrates retrieval computation tasks from the high-risk user host to a trusted embedded device, ensuring that data decryption and matching are performed exclusively within the isolated environment. In terms of security mechanisms, a three-way handshake protocol based on the SM4 algorithm and timestamps is designed to achieve mutual authentication between the USB Key and the embedded device, providing robustness against replay attacks. Furthermore, the scheme integrates the SM9 algorithm for end-to-end key exchange, guaranteeing the confidentiality of data transmission. Security analysis and experimental results demonstrate that the proposed scheme effectively defends against threats such as Man-in-the-Middle (MitM) attacks while maintaining system overhead within an acceptable range, thereby providing a secure and efficient solution for classified data inspection.

Keywords: Confidential Computing · Physical Isolation · USB Gadget · Secure Data Inspection

1 Introduction

As data security becomes increasingly paramount, sensitive keyword retrieval within confidential environments faces significant challenges in balancing efficiency with security. Traditional manual inspection is inefficient and entails the risk of data exposure to human inspectors. Conversely, while networked detection schemes improve efficiency, they are ill-suited for physically isolated scenarios and are vulnerable to Man-in-the-Middle (MitM) attacks. Crucially, user

W. Meng et al. (Eds.): ASSS 2025, CCIS 2903, pp. 146–163, 2026.
https://doi.org/10.1007/978-3-032-21600-7_10

terminals often operate in an "untrusted state." Due to latent malware, even Searchable Encryption (SE) techniques cannot fully mitigate memory data leakage. Furthermore, the prohibitive cost of Hardware Security Modules (HSM) limits their widespread deployment.

To address these conflicts, this paper proposes an embedded confidential computing scheme based on the USB Gadget driver framework. Utilizing the NanoPi R5S development board to establish a physically isolated computing environment, the proposed solution migrates data retrieval tasks from the untrusted host to a controllable embedded device. The main contributions of this paper are as follows:

Construction of a Confidential Computing Architecture: By customizing the USB Mass Storage Gadget driver, we achieve physical and system-level isolation between the computing environment and the host environment. This ensures that plaintext data is processed exclusively within the isolated device, thereby circumventing security risks associated with the host.

Design of a Robust Identity Authentication Protocol: To mitigate device spoofing and replay attacks, we design a three-way handshake mutual authentication protocol based on random number and the SM4 algorithm [10], ensuring that only authorized devices can access the system.

Implementation of Full-Process Ciphertext Operations: By combining the SM9 and SM4 algorithms to implement end-to-end encrypted transmission and key exchange, we ensure that data remains in ciphertext form throughout the transmission link and within the untrusted host. This effectively achieves "data invisibility" regarding human inspectors.

2 Related Work

2.1 Sensitive Data Inspection and Retrieval Techniques

In confidential environments, sensitive keyword retrieval constitutes a core component of compliance inspection. Current solutions can be broadly categorized into three types: manual on-site inspection, networked remote detection, and cryptographic retrieval.

Manual and Networked Solutions: Traditional manual inspection relies on trusted personnel operating directly on physically isolated (air-gapped) hosts. While this approach eliminates the need for network connectivity, it suffers from low efficiency. Furthermore, plaintext data is fully exposed to the inspection personnel, creating significant risks regarding privacy leakage and social engineering attacks. Conversely, while networked detection schemes improve efficiency, they necessitate breaching physical isolation boundaries, thereby rendering the system highly vulnerable to Man-in-the-Middle (MitM) attacks or endpoint infiltration [15].

Cryptographic Solutions: Searchable Encryption (SSE) techniques allow for keyword retrieval over ciphertext [2]. However, existing SSE schemes incur high computational overhead and are predominantly designed for cloud storage scenarios. Consequently, they are difficult to apply directly to physically isolated terminals with limited computational resources or completely offline status [9].

Hardware Solutions: Although Hardware Security Modules (HSM) provide high-level key management and computing environments [16,19], their prohibitive deployment costs and closed architectures limit widespread adoption on general-purpose office terminals. In contrast, the scheme proposed in this paper seeks a balance between software-based encryption and expensive HSM hardware, achieving physically isolated retrieval capabilities through low-cost embedded devices.

2.2 Confidential Computing and Isolated Environments

Confidential Computing aims to protect the confidentiality and integrity of "Data-in-Use," [12] addressing the limitations of traditional encryption technologies that primarily protect Data-at-Rest and Data-in-Transit. Instruction Set-based TEE: Mainstream confidential computing technologies (e.g., Intel SGX, ARM Trust Zone) primarily rely on CPU instruction sets to construct Trusted Execution Environments (TEEs), partitioning an encrypted region within shared hardware memory. However, such solutions remain susceptible to side-channel attacks and are heavily dependent on specific processor hardware support.

Physically Isolated Environments: Unlike instruction set-based TEEs, constructing a physically isolated computing environment involves completely shielding the process from the host operating system via independent hardware [4]. The computing environment constructed in this paper, based on the NanoPi R5S development board, falls under the category of device-level confidential computing in a broad sense. By migrating computation tasks to independent embedded hardware, this approach utilizes physical separation to evade potential malware threats latent in the user Host OS, ensuring that data is decrypted and processed exclusively within the memory of the controlled, isolated device.

2.3 Application of USB Gadget Driver Architecture

The USB Gadget framework is a driver subsystem within the Linux kernel designed to implement USB device functions, allowing Linux devices to emulate various types of USB peripherals (e.g., Ethernet adapters, Mass Storage Devices).

Traditional Applications: In conventional use cases, the Mass Storage Gadget (MSG) driver is typically employed to map the storage space of an embedded device as a USB flash drive or CD-ROM on the host, facilitating convenient data transfer.

Security Applications: Recent research has begun exploring the utilization of Gadget drivers to establish security boundaries. For instance, customized g_hub_msg drivers have been used to precisely parse USB device topology and control read/write permissions. Building upon this foundation, this paper further customizes the Gadget driver. Beyond merely facilitating file communication between the host and the embedded device, the customized driver functions as a logical firewall. By controlling data flow at the USB protocol layer and integrating with upper-layer encryption protocols, it constructs a secure transmission channel between the host and the confidential computing environment.

3 System Model and Proposed Scheme

This chapter first elucidates the overall architecture and entity composition of the system. Subsequently, a threat model is established to define security assumptions and attack boundaries. Finally, the initialization process and the confidential retrieval mechanism of the proposed scheme are detailed. The key terms and corresponding descriptions are listed in Table 1.

Table 1. Key Terms and Descriptions

Term	Descriptions
K_{sm4}	Pre-shared SM4 symmetric key for the system
pk	Public key of the SM9
sk	Private key of the SM9
S_{master}	Random master session seed generated by the user host (256-bit)
C_{seed}	Ciphertext of the master seed encrypted using the SM9 public key
K_i	SM4 encryption key for the i-th file derived from the master seed
R_A, R_B	Random numbers used in the challenge-response protocol
C_{auth}	Response ciphertext generated during the identity authentication process
C_{file_i}	Ciphertext of the i-th file content
$\mathrm{KDF}(\cdot)$	Key Derivation Function (KDF) based on the SM3 hash algorithm
$\mathrm{E}_k(\cdot)$	SM4 encryption operation using key k
$\mathrm{E}_{pk}(\cdot)$	SM9 encryption operation using public key pk
$\mathrm{D}_{sk}(\cdot)$	SM9 decryption operation using private key sk
$\|$	Concatenation operator

3.1 System Architecture

The confidential inspection scheme proposed in this paper aims to construct a trusted sensitive keyword retrieval environment via physical isolation and cryptographic techniques. As illustrated in Fig. 1, the system comprises the following five core entities:

- Management Terminal: Operated by the security administrator, this terminal is responsible for generating retrieval keywords and system keys, and for performing the initial configuration of the USB Key and the embedded device. The Management Terminal serves as the root of trust for the entire system.

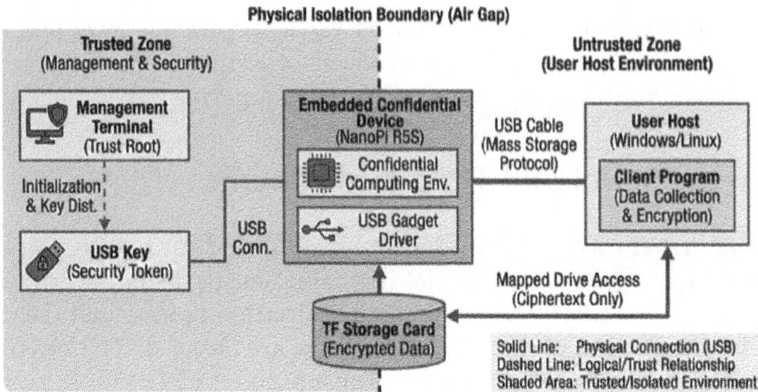

Fig. 1. System Architecture of the Embedded Confidential Retrieval Scheme

- USB Key (Security Token): An authentication device equipped with hardware secure storage. It is used to store the encrypted sensitive keyword database and the private key for identity authentication. The USB Key releases the decrypted keyword data to the embedded device only after a successful mutual identity authentication.
- Embedded Confidential Device: A physically isolated computing node built upon the NanoPi R5S development board. Running a customized Linux system and USB Gadget driver, this device handles authentication interactions with the USB Key, receives and decrypts client-side data, and executes keyword matching tasks within isolated memory.
- TF Storage (Transfer Medium): Acting as an intermediary medium for data transmission, the TF card is mapped to both the embedded device and the user host. It stores only encrypted ciphertext data and public key information, containing no plaintext sensitive information.
- User Host: The target terminal to be inspected (typically a Windows host). The user host runs a lightweight collection program responsible for scanning local files and performing real-time encrypted transmission. This environment is considered untrusted.

3.2 Threat Model

To provide a rigorous analysis of the scheme's security, this paper defines the following threat model and security assumptions:

Attacker Capabilities: We assume the attacker has the capability to control the User Host operating system and eavesdrop on I/O communication channels. Specifically, the attacker can: (1) execute malware (e.g., keyloggers, memory scanners) on the User Host; [8] (2) intercept or tamper with USB communication packets between the User Host and the embedded device, as well as between the embedded device and the USB Key [14]; and (3) physically steal the TF storage card during non-inspection periods.

Trust Boundaries: The Management Terminal and the USB Key are considered fully trusted; the attacker cannot breach the hardware protection of the USB Key to extract internal private keys. The Embedded Device is regarded as a Trusted Execution Environment (TEE) post-initialization. It is assumed that the physical memory and runtime environment of the embedded device have not been physically tampered with, and the attacker cannot compromise the running embedded system via physical interfaces (e.g., serial debugging).

Security Goals: The system must ensure:

Confidentiality: Retrieval keywords and user document contents remain invisible during transmission, storage, and within the User Host memory, being decrypted only within the isolated memory of the embedded device.

Integrity and Authentication: Prevention of unauthorized devices from spoofing the USB Key to access the system, and prevention of replay attacks.

3.3 Scheme Initialization Process

Before distribution to inspection personnel, the system must be initialized by the Management Terminal to establish a basis of trust. The process is illustrated in Fig. 2.

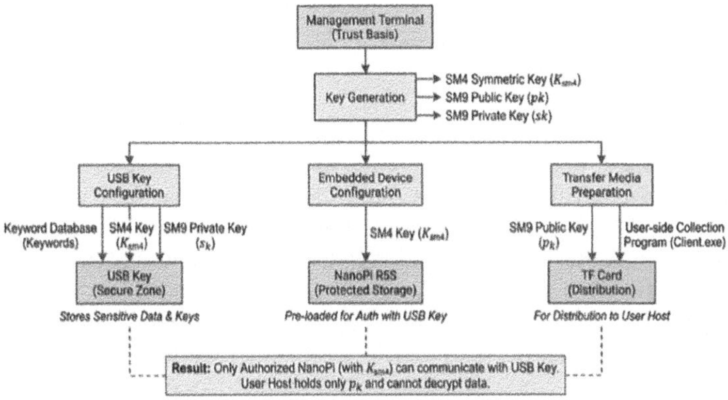

Fig. 2. System Initialization and Distribution Process

1. Key Generation: The Management Terminal generates a global system key $K_{sm4}$and a pair of SM9 asymmetric keys (pk/sk).
2. USB Key Configuration: The Management Terminal writes the keyword database (Keywords) into the secure zone of the USB Key, along with K_{sm4} and sk.
3. Embedded Device Configuration: The Management Terminal pre-loads K_{sm4} into the protected storage area of the NanoPi R5S development board for subsequent identity authentication with the USB Key.

4. Transfer Media Preparation: The SM9 public key pk and the user-side collection program (Client.exe) are stored on the TF card, ready for distribution.

This process ensures that only authorized embedded devices pre-loaded with the identical K_{sm4} can communicate with the USB Key, while the User Host holds only the public key and cannot decrypt data.

3.4 Inspection Workflow

Upon deployment at the inspection site, the operator inserts the USB Key into the embedded device and establishes a connection to the User Host via a USB interface. Leveraging an improved pipeline architecture, the system executes the following core procedures:

1) Mutual Device Challenge-Response Authentication: The embedded device and the USB Key execute a nonce-based challenge-response protocol utilizing a pre-provisioned shared key K_{sm4}. Both entities exchange random challenges and verify the corresponding responses, achieving mutual identity authentication without reliance on system clock synchronization. Upon successful authentication, the USB Key stands ready to process key decryption requests.
2) Master Session Seed Negotiation and KDF Derivation [3]: Upon initialization, the client-side program generates a unique master session seed,S_{master}.
   Seed Protection: The S_{master} is encrypted using the SM9 public key stored on the TF card. The resulting ciphertext header, C_{seed}, is written to the TF card.
   Key Derivation: For each file to be inspected, the client utilizes the $SM3-KDF$ algorithm to derive a distinct file encryption key, K_i, based on S_{master} and file metadata (e.g., filename and size).
3) Pipelined Encrypted Transmission: The client adopts a double-buffering pipeline mechanism to concurrently execute file reading, SM4 encryption, and USB transmission. All file contents are encrypted using the derived K_i and the resulting ciphertext stream is written directly to the storage area mapped by the TF card.
4) Isolated Decryption and Matching: The embedded device reads C_{seed} and requests the USB Key to decrypt it using the internal private key sk to retrieve S_master, which is then transmitted back to the embedded device. Subsequently, the embedded device regenerates the specific key K_i for each file within the isolated memory via $SM3 - KDF$, decrypts the file stream, and executes keyword matching [11].

4 Key Technologies and System Implementation

This chapter details the key technical implementations for constructing the confidential computing environment. It primarily covers the customization and deployment of the USB Gadget driver [5] utilizing the NanoPi R5S development board, followed by the specific implementation workflow of the secure communication protocol based on Chinese National Standard (SM) algorithms [7].

4.1 Construction of Confidential Environment Based on USB Gadget

To migrate the retrieval environment from an untrusted host to a physically isolated embedded device, this study utilizes the Linux kernel's USB Gadget driver framework. By emulating the NanoPi R5S development board as a generic USB Mass Storage Device, a physical data channel is established between the host and the computing environment [18].

Hardware Interface Mode Configuration. The NanoPi R5S is based on the RK3568 SoC, featuring a USB controller that supports the On-The-Go (OTG) specification, allowing switching between Host mode and Peripheral mode. By default, the PHY driver configures the USB port as Host. To enable the user host to recognize the development board as a peripheral, the Device Tree configuration requires modification.

Specifically, in the kernel PHY driver logic, the node named $phy - fe8a0000.usb2 - phy1$ is targeted, and its $dr_{m}ode$ parameter is forcibly changed from the default host to peripheral. Upon system boot, the $rockchip_{u}sb2phy_{s}et_{m}ode$ function reads this configuration and initializes the relevant Gadget drivers, enabling the board to respond to host enumeration requests as a USB slave device.

Driver Customization and Kernel Compilation. This paper adopts and improves the $g_{h}ub_{m}sg$ driver, a Mass Storage Gadget (MSG) driver based on the Composite Framework. To adapt to the confidential retrieval scenario and enhance lightweight characteristics, the driver source code was streamlined by removing unnecessary read-only locking functions and adding support for USB Hub topology.

Prior to deployment, specific parameters in the Linux kernel configuration file (.config) must be set to ensure correct compilation of storage and Gadget functions. Key configurations are as follows:

```
CONFIG_USB_UAS=y
CONFIG_USB_STORAGE=y
CONFIG_USB_GADGET=y
CONFIG_USB_MASS_STORAGE=m
```

Listing 1.1. Congfiguration information

Storage Device Mapping and Loading. After kernel compilation, the driver exists as a kernel module. Upon system startup, the modprobe command is used to dynamically load the $g_{h}ub_{m}sg$ module, mapping the TF storage card inserted in the development board as a USB Mass Storage logical unit. The specific loading instruction is:

$$\mathrm{modprobeg\_hub\_msgfile} = /\mathrm{dev}/\mathrm{mmcblk1p1removable} = 1$$

Here, the file parameter points to the device file path of the TF card in the Linux system (e.g., /dev/mmcblk1p1), and removable=1 indicates that the device supports hot-swapping. Through this mechanism, the user host can access encrypted data on the TF card directly via standard USB read/write operations without installing any proprietary drivers on the host side, thereby achieving a cross-platform physical data channel.

4.2 Design and Implementation of Secure Communication Protocol

To ensure the confidentiality and integrity of data within the transmission channel and storage media, this paper designs a security protocol system based on SM algorithms. The system employs the SM4 block cipher algorithm (128-bit key length) for data encryption and the SM9 identity-based asymmetric algorithm for key exchange [13].

Nonce-Based Challenge-Response Authentication Protocol. To mitigate potential system clock desynchronization issues in embedded devices following power cycling and to eliminate dependencies on absolute timestamps, this scheme incorporates a Nonce-Based Challenge-Response Authentication Protocol. This protocol effectively defends against replay attacks and ensures the real-time liveness of communicating parties.

The protocol workflow is as follows:

1) Authentication Initiation and Challenge: The development board generates a high-entropy random number R_A as the "challenge" and transmits it in plaintext to the USB Key:

$$Msg_1 : R_A$$

2) Response and Counter-Challenge: Upon receiving R_A, the USB Key generates its own random number R_B. Using the pre-shared key K_{sm4}, it performs SM4 encryption on both nonces to construct the response ciphertext C_{auth}. This step simultaneously proves the USB Key's possession of K_{sm4} (response to R_A) and initiates a new challenge (R_B):

$$Msg_2 : C_{auth} = E_{K_{sm4}}(R_A, R_B)$$

3) Authentication Confirmation: The development board decrypts C_{auth} and verifies whether the decrypted R_A matches the one sent in Step 1. A match confirms the legitimacy of the USB Key. Subsequently, the board encrypts R_B using K_{sm4} and transmits it to the USB Key to respond to the counter-challenge:

$$Msg_3 : C_{confirm} = E_{K_{sm4}}(R_B)$$

The USB Key decrypts and verifies the consistency of R_B, completing the mutual authentication.

KDF-Based Pipelined Encryption and Key Exchange. [17] To alleviate the performance bottleneck caused by frequent invocations of the SM9 asymmetric algorithm in scenarios involving massive small files, this paper introduces a Key Derivation Function (KDF) mechanism combined with pipeline technology to optimize transmission efficiency. The specific process is illustrated in Fig. 3.

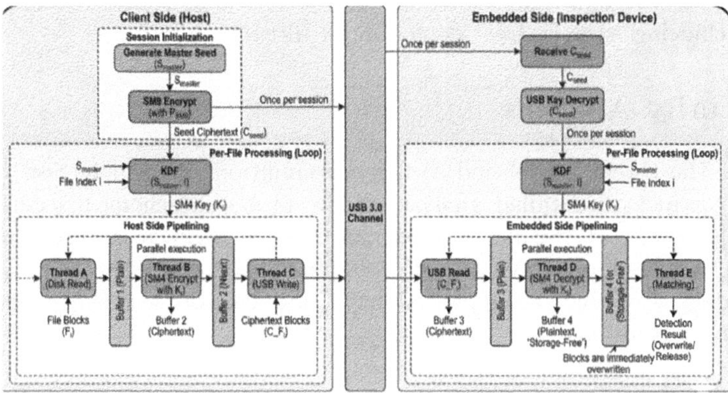

Fig. 3. Optimized Secure Transmission with KDF & Pipelining

1) One-Time Master Seed Negotiation: During the session initialization phase, the client program generates a 256-bit random master seed S_{master}. It encrypts this seed using the SM9 public key pk to generate the seed ciphertext C_{seed}:

$$C_{seed} = E_{pk}(S_{master})$$

This operation is executed only once per inspection session, significantly reducing the computational overhead of asymmetric encryption.

2) Sub-Key Derivation and Encryption:
For the i-th file to be inspected $File_i$, the client utilizes the SM3 hash algorithm as a KDF to derive a unique SM4 key K_i for that file:

$$K_i = SM3 - KDF(S_{master}||Filename_i||Index_i)$$

Subsequently, K_i is used to perform SM4 encryption on the file to obtain C_{file_i}.

3) Double-Buffering Pipelined Transmission: To maximize USB 3.0 bus utilization, the system establishes a Producer-Consumer model on both the client and embedded sides.

Host Side: Thread A is responsible for pre-reading file blocks from the disk, Thread B executes SM4 encryption, and Thread C writes ciphertext blocks to USB storage. These three stages execute asynchronously in parallel, masking I/O latency.
Embedded Side: Upon receiving C_{seed} and retrieving S_master via USB Key decryption, decryption and matching threads are initiated. Decrypted plaintext blocks are immediately overwritten and released after streaming matching, achieving "storage-free" detection for ultra-large files.

5 Security Analysis

Based on the threat model and security assumptions defined in Sect. 3.2, this chapter conducts a detailed analysis of the proposed scheme's security. The analysis focuses on the resilience of communication channels against attacks, the effectiveness of endpoint environment isolation, and demonstrates the advantages of the proposed scheme in confidential inspection scenarios through a comparison with existing solutions.

5.1 Communication Channel Security Analysis

Anti-Replay Attack. In the authentication phase, an adversary may attempt to intercept historical authentication packets (e.g. C_{auth}) and execute a replay attack. The proposed scheme utilizes a random nonce challenge mechanism to effectively thwart this attack vector.

In every authentication session, the development board generates a fresh random challenge nonce, R_A.

- Attack Scenario: Assume an adversary replays an old response packet $Msg_2' = E_{K_{sm4}}(R_A', R_B')$.
- Defense Mechanism: Upon decryption, the development board compares the retrieved nonce R_A' against the locally generated R_A of the current session. Due to the high-entropy randomness of R_A, the probability of a collision is negligible ($\text{Prob}(R_A' = R_A < 2^{-128})$).
- Conclusion: As long as the adversary cannot predict the generated nonce, any replayed historical ciphertext will fail validation. Furthermore, this mechanism operates independently of the device's system time, eliminating security policy failures caused by RTC clock resets or desynchronization.

Key Hierarchy Security and Isolation. Regarding the improved key derivation mechanism, the scheme guarantees security through the following dimensions:

- Master Seed Security: The master seed S_{master} is protected via SM9 public key encryption. Without possession of the USB Key (which houses the internal private key sk), an adversary cannot recover the seed from the ciphertext C_{seed}.

- Sub-Key Isolation: Relying on the one-way property and avalanche effect of the SM3-KDF, even if an attacker compromises a specific file key K_i via side-channel means, they cannot reverse-engineer the master seed S_{master}. Consequently, the decryption of other files $(K_j, j \neq i)$ remains impossible, ensuring granular security.
- Isolation Domain Protection: Although S_{master} must eventually be recovered within the embedded device's memory for sub-key derivation, the physical isolation and volatile nature of the embedded memory ensure that the seed is cleared immediately upon power loss or session termination. This effectively mitigates Cold Boot Attacks and ensures that sensitive key material does not persist in the environment.

5.2 Endpoint and Physical Security Analysis

The core advantage of this scheme lies in the construction of a physically isolated computing environment. Unlike traditional TEEs (e.g., Intel SGX) that share CPU hardware, the NanoPi R5S development board provides board-level physical isolation.

- Execution Environment Isolation: The retrieval and matching logic runs on the embedded Linux system, which is physically separated from the User Host's Windows system. Malware on the host cannot cross the boundary of the USB Mass Storage Protocol to control the CPU or memory of the embedded device.
- Data Visibility Control: The sensitive keyword database is always stored in the secure zone of the USB Key or the isolated memory of the embedded device. Similarly, retrieval result logs are stored in encrypted form. Inspection personnel can only view the final status of "compliance or violation" without direct access to file contents, effectively mitigating the risk of data leakage via social engineering.

5.3 Security Scheme Comparison

While traditional manual inspection maintains physical isolation, its primary security vulnerability lies in the "human factor." Inspectors necessitate direct access to plaintext files to adjudicate compliance. This process is not only inefficient but also fails to eliminate social engineering risks associated with subjective data theft or passive leakage.

By introducing a confidential computing environment, the proposed scheme effectively excludes the "human element" from the data processing loop. The retrieval and matching logic executes automatically within the isolated memory of the embedded device. Inspectors are limited to receiving final Boolean results (Compliance/Violation), thereby achieving the paradigm of "Data Availability without Visibility."

Networked solutions require classified terminals to connect to a dedicated inspection network, which fundamentally breaches the physical isolation boundary. This renders the system highly susceptible to Man-in-the-Middle (MitM) attacks such as ARP spoofing and DNS hijacking. Furthermore, open network ports serve as potential pivot points for Advanced Persistent Threats (APT).

In contrast, the proposed scheme utilizes the USB Gadget driver to strictly confine communication within the physical link of the local USB bus, without activating any network protocol stacks. Integrating the improved Nonce-Based Challenge-Response Protocol, the scheme completely eliminates dependency on the system clock. Consequently, attackers are precluded from forging identities via replaying historical packets or tampering with timestamps. This results in a superior level of channel security compared to inspection tools based on general-purpose network protocols.

6 Performance Evaluation

This chapter presents a systematic experimental evaluation of the enhanced confidential retrieval scheme. The experiments are designed to quantify the performance metrics of the newly integrated KDF key derivation mechanism and pipeline architecture during end-to-end ciphertext retrieval tasks. Furthermore, the evaluation seeks to validate the adaptability and feasibility of the proposed solution within resource-constrained embedded environments.

6.1 Experimental Setup and Configuration

We established a test environment comprising a high-performance User Host and an embedded computing node to evaluate the proposed scheme. The detailed hardware specifications are listed in Table 2. In terms of software implementation, the system integrates SM3-KDF-based key management logic and an asynchronous transmission mechanism utilizing a double-buffering strategy.

Table 2. Hardware Specifications of Experimental Devices

Device Role	Hardware Component	Specifications
User Host	CPU	Intel Core i9-13900HX (13th Gen)
	RAM	64GB DDR5
	Interface	USB 3.0 (SuperSpeed)
Embedded Device	SoC	Rockchip RK3568
	RAM	4GB LPDDR4
	Storage	Class 10 TF Card

The test dataset comprises 100 Microsoft Office documents of varying sizes, with individual file sizes ranging from 100KB to 10MB. This dataset was utilized to evaluate the system's handshake latency and throughput under batch file processing scenarios.

6.2 Protocol Efficiency and Key Negotiation Overhead Analysis

Focusing on the optimized key management mechanism, this section compares the time overhead of the "Traditional Per-File SM9 Negotiation" against the "Proposed KDF Derivation Mechanism."

Traditional Scheme: Involves generating a random key for each individual file and executing one SM9 encryption (on the Host) and one decryption (on the USB Key) operation per file.

Proposed Scheme: Executes the SM9 exchange exclusively for the Master Seed (once per session), while all subsequent file keys are derived via SM3-KDF.

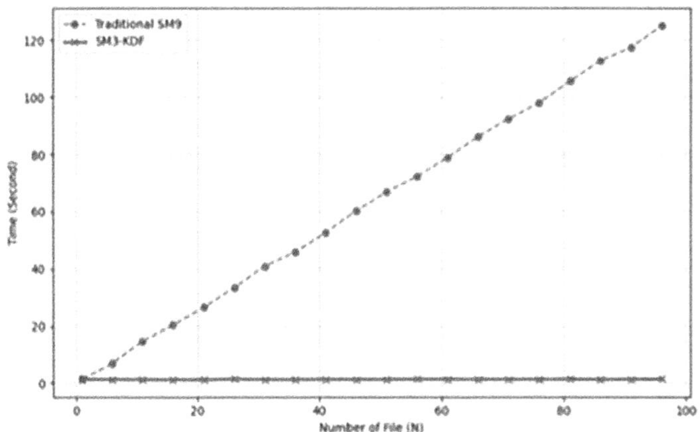

Fig. 4. Comparison of Key Negotiation Latency vs. Number of Files

Experimental data (see Fig. 4) indicates that as the number of inspected files increases, the key negotiation latency of the traditional scheme exhibits linear growth ($O(N)$). [20] Specifically, processing 100 files consumes approximately 124.7 s dedicated to asymmetric encryption/decryption interactions.In contrast, the KDF mechanism adopted in this paper amortizes the computationally expensive SM9 operations over the entire session. Regardless of the number of files processed, the core negotiation latency remains constant at approximately 1.21 s ($O(1)$). This improvement effectively eliminates the computational bottleneck of the USB Key, equipping the scheme with superior scalability for scenarios involving the inspection of massive quantities of small files.

6.3 Embedded Resource Consumption Evaluation

To validate the stability of the streaming processing mechanism within resource-constrained environments, we monitored the resource utilization profiles of the NanoPi R5S during the decryption and retrieval operations.The CPU and memory utilization are illustrated in Fig. 5.

- Memory Footprint: Attributed to the chunking mechanism, system memory usage remained stable at approximately 700 MB (occupying only 17% of total memory), regardless of whether the processed file size was 1 MB or 10 MB. Crucially, no linear growth in memory consumption relative to file size was observed. This demonstrates the scheme's capability to robustly process ultra-large files without triggering Out-of-Memory exceptions.
- CPU Load: Consequently, single-core CPU utilization was sustained at a high level (exceeding 90%), indicating that the available computational resources were effectively and fully utilized for the cryptographic workload.

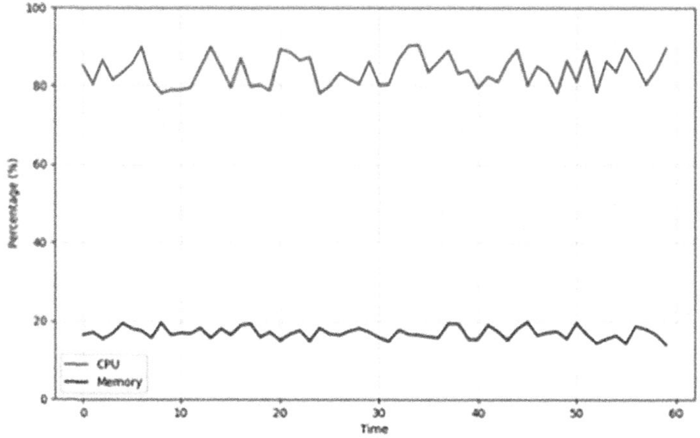

Fig. 5. System Resource Usage Over Time

6.4 Transmission Efficiency Comparison and Overhead Analysis

To quantify the security overhead incurred by the introduction of the confidential computing mechanism and to pinpoint the system's performance bottlenecks, a set of comparative experiments was designed in this section. The experiments aim to determine the theoretical maximum throughput of the physical link (baseline performance) and contrast it with the effective throughput achieved during full-process ciphertext retrieval.

A standard test file with a size of 10 MB was selected for this experiment. The total elapsed time for transmission and processing was recorded under the following two distinct modes:

Baseline Group: In this mode, all encryption, decryption, and keyword matching logic are disabled. The NanoPi R5S operates solely as a standard USB Mass Storage device. The User Host writes the plaintext test file directly to the TF card via the USB 3.0 interface. Data collected from this group reflects the theoretical maximum transmission capability of the USB physical link and the storage medium under the current hardware environment.

Experimental Group: In this mode, the full system logic is enabled, encompassing host-side SM4 encryption, pipelined transmission, embedded-side SM4 decryption, and keyword matching. Data from this group reflects the system's actual processing capability within realistic high-security application scenarios.

Ten repeated tests were conducted for each of the two modes. The specific test results are illustrated in Fig. 6, and the average values are summarized in Table 3.

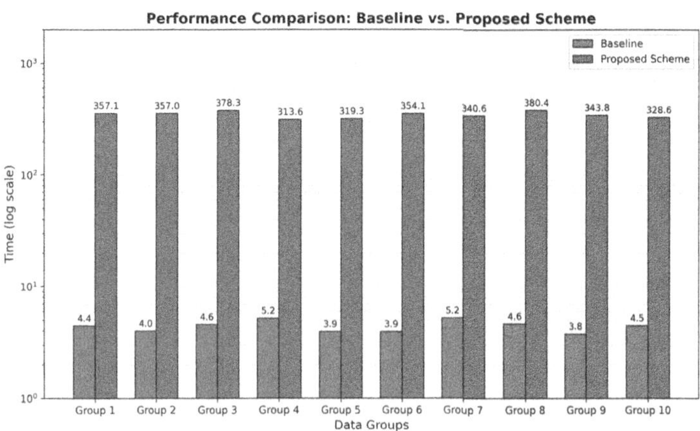

Fig. 6. Performance Comparison: Baseline vs. Proposed Scheme (Log Scale)

The results exhibit an orders-of-magnitude performance gap. The slight fluctuation in the Baseline Group is attributed to USB bus arbitration. Conversely, the significant variance in the Proposed Scheme highlights the sensitivity of intensive cryptography to CPU scheduling and Python Garbage Collection. This confirms that the system is compute-bound rather than I/O-bound.

Table 3. Performance Comparison between Baseline and Proposed Scheme

Test Mode	Data Size	Time Cost	Throughput
Baseline	10 MB	4.1 s	2.43 MB/s
Proposed	10 MB	370.82 s	27.61 KB/s

7 Conclusion and Future Work

This paper presents a physically isolated confidential computing scheme using USB Gadget drivers, achieving "data invisibility" via a KDF-based protocol and

Nonce authentication [1]. Experimental results validate its robust resistance to replay attacks and efficiency in key negotiation ($O(1)$), despite a performance trade-off due to the current Python implementation. Future work will address this compute-bound bottleneck by migrating core modules to C++ with ARM hardware [6] acceleration and integrating Searchable Symmetric Encryption (SSE) to further enhance both security and throughput.

Acknwoledgements. This work was supported by the State Grid Shandong Electric Power Company Technology Project (Project Name: Research on Full-Chain Intelligent Analysis Technology for Power Big Data, ERP Code:52062625000F).

References

1. Bhati, A.S., Dufka, A., Andreeva, E., Roy, A., Preneel, B.: Skye: an expanding prf based fast kdf and its applications. In: Proceedings of the 19th ACM Asia Conference on Computer and Communications Security, pp. 1082–1098 (2024)
2. Bossuat, A., Bost, R., Fouque, P.A., Minaud, B., Reichle, M.: Sse and ssd: page-efficient searchable symmetric encryption. In: Annual International Cryptology Conference, pp. 157–184. Springer (2021)
3. Chen, L., Chen, L.: Recommendation for key derivation using pseudorandom functions. US Department of Commerce, National Institute of Standards and Technology (2024)
4. Chen, T., Tan, Y.a., Li, W., Ci, Z., Shi, N.: Toward secure program execution in multi-tenant cloud fpga environments: T. chen et al. J. Supercomput. **81**(8), 871 (2025)
5. Corbet, J., Rubini, A., Kroah-Hartman, G.: Linux Device Drivers. "O'Reilly Media, Inc." (2005)
6. Dall, C., Nieh, J.: Kvm/arm: the design and implementation of the linux arm hypervisor. Acm Sigplan Notices **49**(4), 333–348 (2014)
7. Guri, M.: Air-viber: Exfiltrating data from air-gapped computers via covert surface vibrations. arXiv preprint arXiv:2004.06195 (2020)
8. Guri, M.: Exfiltrating data from air-gapped computers via vibrations. Futur. Gener. Comput. Syst. **122**, 69–81 (2021)
9. He, D., Ma, M., Zeadally, S., Kumar, N., Liang, K.: Certificateless public key authenticated encryption with keyword search for industrial internet of things. IEEE Trans. Industr. Inf. **14**(8), 3618–3627 (2017)
10. ISO, I.: Iec18033-3: 2010/amd1: 2021information technology-security techniques-encryption algorithms-part3: blockciphers-amendment1: Sm4 (2021)
11. Krawczyk, H.: Cryptographic extraction and key derivation: the hkdf scheme. In: Annual Cryptology Conference. pp. 631–648. Springer (2010)
12. Li, X., et al.: Design and verification of the arm confidential compute architecture. In: 16th USENIX Symposium on Operating Systems Design and Implementation (OSDI 22), pp. 465–484 (2022)
13. Liu, X., Huang, X., Cheng, Z., Wu, W.: Fault-tolerant identity-based encryption from sm9. Sci. China Inf. Sci. **67**(2), 122101 (2024)
14. Nohl, K., Kri, S., Lell, J.: Badusb — on accessories that turn evil (2014)
15. Tan, Y.A., Zhang, X., Sharif, K., Liang, C., Zhang, Q., Li, Y.: Covert timing channels for iot over mobile networks. IEEE Wirel. Commun. **25**(6), 38–44 (2019)

16. Wolf, M., Gendrullis, T.: Design, implementation, and evaluation of a vehicular hardware security module. In: International Conference on Information Security and Cryptology, pp. 302–318. Springer (2011)
17. Zhang, Q., Zhang, Q., Ma, Z., Tan, Y.: An authenticated asymmetric group key agreement for imbalanced mobile networks. Chin. J. Electron. **23**(4), 827–835 (2014)
18. Zhang, X., et al.: Cryptographic key protection against frost for mobile devices. Cluster Comput. **20**(3), 2393–2402 (2017)
19. Zhang, Z., Xue, J., Baker, T., Chen, T., Tan, Y.A., Li, Y.: Cover: enhancing virtualization obfuscation through dynamic scheduling using flash controller-based secure module. Comput. Secur. **146**, 104038 (2024)
20. Zheng, J., Tan, Y.A., Zhang, Q., Zhang, X., Zhu, L., Zhang, Q.: Cross-cluster asymmetric group key agreement for wireless sensor networks. Sci. Chin. Inf. Sci. **61**(4), 048103 (2018)

Author Index

W. Meng et al. (Eds.): ASSS 2025, CCIS 2903, p. 165, 2026.
https://doi.org/10.1007/978-3-032-21600-7

The manufacturer's authorised representative in the EU is Springer Nature Customer Service Centre GmbH, Europaplatz 3, 69115 Heidelberg, Germany. If you have any concerns regarding our products, please contact ProductSafety@springernature.com

Printed and bound by CPI Group (UK) Ltd, Croydon, CR0 4YY
07/07/2026
02160928-0005